Radio's Legacy in Popular Culture

Radio's Legacy in Popular Culture

The Sounds of British Broadcasting over the Decades

Martin Cooper

BLOOMSBURY ACADEMIC
NEW YORK • LONDON • OXFORD • NEW DELHI • SYDNEY

BLOOMSBURY ACADEMIC
Bloomsbury Publishing Inc
1385 Broadway, New York, NY 10018, USA
50 Bedford Square, London, WC1B 3DP, UK
29 Earlsfort Terrace, Dublin 2, Ireland

BLOOMSBURY, BLOOMSBURY ACADEMIC and the Diana logo are trademarks of
Bloomsbury Publishing Plc

First published in the United States of America 2022
Paperback edition published in 2023

Copyright © Martin Cooper, 2022

Cover design: Eleanor Rose
Cover image © Martin Cooper, 2022

All rights reserved. No part of this publication may be reproduced or transmitted in any form or by any means, electronic or mechanical, including photocopying, recording, or any information storage or retrieval system, without prior permission in writing from the publishers.

Bloomsbury Publishing Inc does not have any control over, or responsibility for, any third-party websites referred to or in this book. All internet addresses given in this book were correct at the time of going to press. The author and publisher regret any inconvenience caused if addresses have changed or sites have ceased to exist, but can accept no responsibility for any such changes.

A catalog record for this book is available from the Library of Congress.

ISBN: HB: 978-1-5013-6044-2
PB: 978-1-5013-8823-1
ePDF: 978-1-5013-6042-8
eBook: 978-1-5013-6043-5

Typeset by Deanta Global Publishing Services, Chennai, India

To find out more about our authors and books visit www.bloomsbury.com and sign up for our newsletters.

And as he thus spake for himself, Festus said with a loud voice, Paul, thou art beside thyself; much learning doth make thee mad.
Acts 26.24
Scripture quotation from The Authorized (King James) Version. Rights in the Authorized Version in the United Kingdom are vested in the Crown. Reproduced by permission of the Crown's patentee, Cambridge University Press.

Contents

List of figures — viii

1. Constructing a radio culture: The years up to 1922 — 1
2. Broadcasting on air, 1922 to 1935 — 17
3. Developing ways of listening: Class and distinction, 1935 to 1938 — 39
4. The home front: Modernism, war and its aftermath, 1938 to 1949 — 61
5. The new Elizabethans and new questions, 1950 to 1968 — 85
6. Britain and the fascination with American radio nostalgia, 1969 to 1979 — 109
7. Video killed the radio star: Satire, politics and international listening, 1979 to 1984 — 127
8. Hang the DJ: Critiquing the present, remembering the past, 1984 to 1993 — 147
9. Death and psychology: Radio, genocide and loneliness, 1993 to 2006 — 167
10. Listening back and looking forward: Nostalgia and new technology, 2006 to 2022 — 187

Afterword — 209

References — 211
Index — 241

Figures

1 Van Morrison sings about listening to the radio. *The Last Waltz* (1978), Dir. Martin Scorsese, USA: United Artists/MGM — 2
2 Val Gielgud, the BBC's director of drama, as Julian Caird, a fictionalized version of himself. *Death at Broadcasting House* (1934), Dir. Reginald Denham, UK: Phoenix Films — 26
3 Will Hay as Lord William Garlon, the reclusive director general of the NBG radio station. *Radio Parade of 1935* (1934), Dir. Arthur B. Woods, UK: British International Pictures — 51
4 Peggy Brown (Vera Lynn, right) tries to impress BBC secretary Miss Bohne (Betty Jardine, left) with her newly pressed 78-rpm demo disc. *We'll Meet Again* (1943), Dir. Phil Brandon, UK: Columbia Pictures — 77
5 Hugh Allen (Edward Underdown, left) reads the *Merrill* story as his lover Alycia Roach (Valerie Hobson, far right, out of focus) looks on from behind the control room glass. *The Voice of Merrill* (1952), Dir. John Gilling, UK: Tempean Film — 91
6 Investigators track a land-based pirate radio station. A communications expert (Richard Pescud, left) and detective chief inspector Alan Craven (George Sewell, right). *Special Branch* (1974), UK: Thames TV — 124
7 Robert B (David Beames) sits on the seafront at Weston-super-Mare and tries to tune a transistor radio. *Radio On* (1979), Dir. Chris Petit, UK/Germany: The British Film Institute/Road Movies Filmproduktion — 141
8 Denis Lawson as a flamboyant commercial radio DJ. *The Kit Curran Radio Show* (1984), UK: ITV/Thames TV — 150
9 DJ Max (Charles Bwanika, left) introduces Honoré Butera (Oris Erhuero, right), who begins one of his 'historical reviews' on RTLM. *Sometimes in April* (2005), Dir. Raoul Peck, Rwanda/France/USA: HBO Films — 177

10	*Babel* (2001–6), Cildo Meireles, born 1948; metallic structure, radio sets; (h) 450 centimetres (w) 260 centimetres; Tate. © Cildo Meireles; Photo © Tate	188
11	Mr Bernard Bentley as the 'creative producer' at the new radio station in Sunflower Valley. 'Radio Bob' (2008), *Bob the Builder, Project: Build It*, UK: CBeebies/HiT Entertainment	207

1

Constructing a radio culture

The years up to 1922

It is 25 November 1976, Thanksgiving Day in San Francisco. A man from Belfast walks onto the stage at the Winterland Ballroom. He seems to be wearing a rhinestone-studded brushed-cotton purple two-piece consisting of a shapeless jacket and matching tight trousers, underpinned by a green T-shirt which is just a little too small. He looks somewhat tired and is heavy around the jowls. He glances nervously at the musicians. Taking a breath, he begins to mumble something about a caravan being on its way and some merry gypsies playing and listening to their radio set. Van Morrison is singing his signature show-stopping tune 'Caravan' for a movie directed by Martin Scorsese. It is a song that celebrates freedom, young love and the joy of listening to the wireless. Morrison calls on us, like an evangelical preacher, to turn up the volume of our transistor radio. He is quickly into his stride, unwinding the microphone from its stand (Figure 1) and urging us to understand that the radio has deep spiritual connections. Soon he is closing his eyes and feeling the emotion of the song; guitarist Robbie Robertson lets out a huge grin as he and The Band play along to Morrison's call-and-response. This, they are saying, is what the soul of radio listening is all about. It is referred to again in Chapter 6, and this book sets out to document moments such as this. It explores the intersections between the sounds of the radio, and how they have been portrayed in literature, film, poetry and music. The assumption is this: to evoke the experience of listening to the radio, we can reasonably examine the words, music and pictures of artists, writers and directors – to hear and see what they have had to say about the subject. Radio has fascinated audiences for the past 100 years: it has sustained listeners through the Second World War; entertained baby boomers who danced in their bedrooms to the sounds of Radio Luxembourg and Radio Caroline; and

Figure 1 Van Morrison sings about listening to the radio. *The Last Waltz* (1978), Dir. Martin Scorsese, USA: United Artists/MGM.

it has intrigued new generations finding ways to use sound for online listening and podcasting.

Radio features in creative works such as Douglas Adams's *Hitchhiker's Guide to the Galaxy* (which has been a radio series, a TV show, a movie and a five-part trilogy of books) where, before his adventures, the hero Arthur Dent had worked for the BBC. Other examples include the movie *Radio On*, which featured a radio DJ looking for his brother's killers, J. B. Morton's 'Beachcomber' column in the *Daily Express*, which poked fun at the BBC, and Alice Oseman's teen novel *Radio Silence*, which featured podcasting. There are tracks by Shakespears [sic] Sister, The Clash, Reba McEntire, George Harrison, Elvis Costello and Barry Manilow. There is also an episode of *The Simpsons* in which Bart wins an elephant in a radio competition. Each is a work of fiction that says something relatable and understandable about radio.

Writing a radio history

What follows is an account of how radio has appeared in literary and popular culture over the decades and an exploration of the enduring cultural fascination with the wireless – particularly in Britain. Around 300 novels, movies, songs, poems, works of art and TV shows are included in this book. As a body of creative work, they represent a consistent output of responses during the first 100 years of radio broadcasting, and it seems clear that artists felt they had something to say publicly about the medium during this long period. These works are treated as primary sources for evidence of attitudes towards radio; interpretations of what radio is and what it meant to the creator of the media form in question. They were chosen after sustained research in bibliographies, discographies and film and television programme databases, and I would welcome suggestions for examples to include in future editions of this book.

My approach is similar to that of Wolfgang Schivelbusch, who in 1979 examined nineteenth-century railway history by looking at sources such as fiction, travel writing and art to investigate how such a technology was assimilated into society.[1] This way of considering cultural practices surrounding a specific technology also informed my 2011 study of the railway industry and rail preservation in Brazil by using movies, TV *novelas*, songs and novels.[2] In a similar manner, music historians are developing ways to move beyond writing histories *of* popular music and instead to think about how to use music *as* history itself to create new narratives.[3] This is a technique I employ here when I seek evidence from the songs about radio across the decades. In the realm of media practice, Sarah Lonsdale has discussed the portrayal of journalists in British fiction – a profession linked to radio broadcasting from its early years. Indeed, there is a growing body of work which investigates media history through its representation in fictional forms.[4] Hence, this present book takes the cultural products made by radio listeners who also happen to be professional writers, musicians and moviemakers, and attempts to create a narrative of radio history from the early years of the twentieth century onwards.

---

[1] Wolfgang Schivelbusch ([1979] 1986), *The Railway Journey: The Industrialization of Time and Space in the 19th Century*, Berkeley, CA: The University of California Press.
[2] Martin Cooper (2011), *Brazilian Railway Culture*, Newcastle upon Tyne: Cambridge Scholars Publishing.
[3] Paul Long and Nicholas Gebhardt (2019), 'Listening Again to Popular Music as History', *Popular Music History*, 12 (2): 147–51.
[4] Sarah Lonsdale (2016), *The Journalist in British Fiction & Film: Guarding the Guardians from 1900 to the Present*, London: Bloomsbury. See also: Brian McNair (2010), *Journalists in Film: Heroes and Villains*, Edinburgh: Edinburgh University Press; Barbara Korte (2009), *Represented Reporters: Images of War Correspondents in Memoirs and Fiction*, Bielefeld: transcript-Verlag; Matthew C. Ehrlich and Joe Saltzman (2015), *Heroes and Scoundrels: The Image of the Journalist in Popular Culture*, Chicago: University of Illinois Press.

How to read, watch and listen across the decades

There are two ways of thinking from the arena of French public intellectuals which are useful here. Firstly, Jacques Rancière has suggested that fiction can be a window to reality. This means that novels, for example, can offer some form of explanation, description and analysis of our daily worlds. He argues that each piece of fiction, by being somehow grounded in a reality by its author, can – after Aristotle's *Poetics* – go beyond a basic historical narrative.

Hence, 'the construction of a fictional plot [. . .] says how things *can* happen, how they happen as a consequence of their own possibility, where history only tells us how they arrive one after the other, in their empirical succession'.[5] The historian David Lowenthal took a similar position when he said about novels, 'all fiction is partly true to the past'.[6] This way of thinking about such works means that they can be used to explore the world around us. Rancière uses the example of *Madame Bovary*, a novel in the realist vein by Gustave Flaubert that explored the moral problems faced by French provinciality, and he argues that because the story is laid out with recognizable emotions and events, it acts as a window onto that real world itself.[7] However, not all fiction is realist: and Rancière uses the example of crime fiction in which, even if it employs a narrative that suggests things are not what they seem, the plots themselves are grounded in a rationality which is recognizable as relating in some way to the real.[8] Such thinking allows me to take the creative works that follow here and use them to examine how radio was represented by, reasonably, assuming that their fictions indeed bear a strong relationship to perceived reality.

Further to this is the notion that when we read (or in our case, listen) we are ourselves creating a new meaning in a text. This brings together the links between language, reality and meaning and reflects ideas from previous generations of thinkers such as Jacques Derrida and Ferdinand de Saussure. Garry Potter summarized his own approach to this critical realism by saying, 'The act of reading is an act of creation. Or, to express the same thought more precisely, it is an act of production.'[9] However, I argue that this is not always instantaneous; it

---

[5] Jacques Rancière ([2017] 2020), *The Edges of Fiction*, trans. Steve Corcoran, Cambridge: Polity, p. 129. Emphasis in original.
[6] David Lowenthal (2015), *The Past is a Foreign Country - Revisited*, Cambridge: Cambridge University Press, p. 373.
[7] Rancière, *The Edges of Fiction*, pp. 13–15.
[8] Rancière, *The Edges of Fiction*, p. 83.
[9] Garry Potter (2001), 'Truth in Fiction, Science and Criticism', in José Lopez and Garry Potter, eds, *After Postmodernism: An Introduction to Critical Realism*, London: The Athlone Press, p. 190.

can sometimes be a whilst before a reading is turned into a creation and the act of 'production' is realized. In fact, the strongest example of how British writers and musicians pondered long and hard before responding to what they heard on the radio is to be found in the 1970s and is described in Chapter 6.

A second way of thinking about the mechanics of such responses therefore follows a heuristic developed by Michel de Certeau, who calls audiences 'users' as opposed to (in our case) listeners. He says our responses to culture are often fleeting, 'struggles against oblivion'.[10] In his examples, he includes talking, reading, moving about, shopping and cookery, and to this list I add here listening to the radio.[11] I argue that this is because a listener makes their own interpretation of what they hear. To continue with de Certeau's logic, 'He [the reader/listener] insinuates into another person's text the ruses of pleasure and appropriation: he poaches on it, is transported into it, pluralizes himself in it', and as this happens, 'A different world (the reader's) slips into the author's place'.[12] In other words, the act (here) of listening to the radio makes the programme, the show, the friendliness of the DJ or the music and news reports offered to the listener their own. Following de Certeau, the radio broadcasters are producers making 'strategies'; and the listeners ('consumers') are responding with 'tactics'.[13] To extend this point, this means that a small minority of listeners are responding with a tactic that involves making something fresh and public: perhaps a movie, or a novel, or a song or even another radio show. Each one has been prompted by listening to the radio; it has been a response (a 'tactic'), which has been published and in turn has become a 'strategy' to be reconsumed by audiences. These latter items are the cultural products examined in this book.

One example illustrates this: the authorly responses to the *Shipping Forecast* on BBC Radio 4. At the time of writing, it is broadcast four times each day on either or both the long wave and FM frequencies of the station. It is a service to seafarers in the British coastal waters and, in de Certeau's wording, is a 'strategy' to give information to a section of the audience, but it has inspired many others (mostly non-mariners) to offer their reactions. There is a miscellany published by BBC Books and edited by Nic Compton – a writer with sailing experience – who describes the forecast as, 'Utilitarian poetry, both in the beauty of its pared-

---

[10] Michel de Certeau (1984), *The Practice of Everyday Life*, trans. Steven Rendall, Berkeley, CA: University of California Press, p. xvi
[11] de Certeau, *The Practice of Everyday Life*, p. xix.
[12] de Certeau, *The Practice of Everyday Life*, p. xxi.
[13] de Certeau, *The Practice of Everyday Life*, pp. 35–7.

back language and in its unique rhythms'.[14] Others who have found inspiration in this broadcast include poets such as Seamus Heaney, Carole Ann Duffy and Sean Street, as well as musicians ranging from Jethro Tull, Tears for Fears, The Prodigy, Radiohead and Blur.[15] Books have been produced too, including a humorous travelogue by Charlie Connelly (2004) and a volume mixing history and memoir by a former newsreader and announcer Peter Jefferson (2011).[16]

The field of 'fan writing' could, in some respects, be regarded as analogous. The academic Henry Jenkins uses de Certeau's ideas and examines fan culture of the late 1980s and early 1990s, mostly amateur writing and artworks. What is useful, Jenkins suggests, is that de Certeau does not specify where meaning resides – either with the reader or the author, or even with an academic. Instead of worrying about the location, he calls on us to consider the essence of the reaction (the 'poaching') itself. That in turn allows for reinterpretations of the original media products. In the case of fandom it could be alternative storylines; in our case of radio listening, it can be a reinterpretation of what has been heard on the airwaves.[17] Hence, it is plausible to think of the responses I analyse in the chapters that follow as reinterpretations and critiques of radio listening; that they have been produced by professional writers and musicians makes them less of a subculture and more of a series of transformative texts that extend the meaning and understanding of the medium of radio. They are portrayals of the everyday action of listening to the radio: of paying attention to the programmes, the discussions, the documentaries, the dramas, the daily shows and the DJs. Joe Moran observes that ethnographers and sociologists have a habit of making the ordinary into something extraordinary: 'In cultural studies, the banal is usually turned into something else, made interesting and significant by acts of subaltern resistance or semiotic reinvention.'[18] Radio listening, in its early years, was an extraordinary activity. One hundred years later it has now become so commonplace as to be almost unnoticed, yet it remains a significant practice. So, the films, music, poetry and novels – described in the pages which follow – each captures part of the experience of listening to the radio. Each one tells of

---

[14] Nic Compton (2016), *The Shipping Forecast*, London: BBC Books, p. 4.
[15] David Hendy (2007), *Life on Air: A History of Radio Four*, Oxford: Oxford University Press, pp. 383–4. Compton, *The Shipping Forecast*, pp. 16–17.
[16] Charlie Connelly (2004), *Attention All Shipping: A Journey Round the Shipping Forecast*, London: Little, Brown; Peter Jefferson (2011), *And Now the Shipping Forecast: A Tide of History Around our Shores*, Cambridge: UIT Cambridge.
[17] Henry Jenkins (1992), *Textual Poachers: Television Fans and Participatory Culture*, London: Routledge, pp. 33–4.
[18] Joe Moran (2005), *Reading the Everyday*, Abingdon, Oxfordshire: Routledge, p. 12.

the way individuals paid attention to radio programmes and reacted to them. It recalls work carried out by Adalaide Morris, who edited a collection of essays which reflected on how a number of authors, from James Joyce (discussed in Chapter 4) to Samuel Beckett, John Cage and Caribbean dub poets, integrated sound into their written work, and how they reflected the aurality of noises around them into their fictions and poetry.[19] Such investigations suggest it was not only radio broadcasting which inspired creatives, but the very presence of noise and sound in their environments.[20]

A number of academics have studied aspects of radio listening as featured in other media forms. Paul Young looked at silent movies and the early talkies and found that at times the cinema could add a face to the invisible radio voices.[21] Todd Avery examined interwar writers who used radio as a creative outlet: many poets, critics and journalists had spotted an opportunity to appear on the radio. For example, T. S. Eliot and Virginia Woolf (I discuss Woolf in Chapter 3) each wrote programme scripts and appeared on-air at the BBC.[22] Other authors who spotted an opportunity in the new medium included Vita Sackville-West, W. H. Auden (discussed in Chapters 2, 3 and 4), George Orwell (Chapter 3) and J. B. Priestley (Chapter 3). These writers generated a complex range of responses to the radio and the manner in which it could create audiences and publicize ideas. Elsewhere, Emily Bloom looked specifically at work for radio by Irish writers W. B. Yeats, Louis MacNeice (I include MacNeice here in Chapters 3 and 4), Elizabeth Bowen and Samuel Beckett.[23] Daniel Morse considered how E. M. Forster's broadcasts on the BBC's Empire Service in the 1940s spoke about the subjects of colonization and end of empire.[24] Keith Williams, who examined fiction and non-fiction writing of the Left in the 1930s and 1940s, observed that a two-way process of narrative styles quickly emerged as authors who worked

---

[19] Adalaide Morris, ed. (1997), *Sound States: Innovative Poetics and Acoustical Technologies*, Chapel Hill, NC: University of North Carolina Press.

[20] I concentrate, for the most part, in this book on British radio. For discussions about 'the auditory environment' in North American and Australian contexts, see Joy Damousi (2007), '"The Filthy American Twang": Elocution, the Advent of American "Talkies", and Australian Cultural Identity', *American Historical Review*, 112 (2): 394–416. Justin St Clair (2013), *Sound and Aural Media in Postmodern Literature*, New York: Routledge, has a chapter on radio in novels by Don DeLillo, Thomas Pynchon and other American postmodernists.

[21] Paul Young (2006), *The Cinema Dreams its Rivals: Media Fantasy Films from Radio to the Internet*, Minneapolis, MI: University of Minnesota Press.

[22] Todd Avery (2006), *Radio Modernism: Literature, Ethics, and the BBC, 1922–1938*, Aldershot, Hampshire: Ashgate, pp. 28–31, 138.

[23] Emily Bloom (2016), *The Wireless Past: Anglo-Irish Writers and the BBC, 1931–1968*, Oxford: Oxford University Press.

[24] Daniel Morse (2011), 'Only Connecting?: E. M. Forster, Empire Broadcasting and the Ethics of Distance', *Journal of Modern Literature*, Indiana University Press, 34 (3): 87–105.

in radio (and film) used these self-same film and radio techniques in their writings.[25] Jeffrey Richards compared cinema and the radio in the United States and Britain between 1920 and 1950 and made the useful general point that radio drama in America had a symbiosis with Hollywood, whilst in Britain – with Val Gielgud (brother of the actor John) as the BBC's director of drama – there was a closer relationship with the West End theatre.[26]

Institutional histories of the BBC between 1922 and 1987 have been written separately by Asa Briggs and by Jean Seaton.[27] Commercial radio of the interwar years is discussed by Seán Street, and Tony Stoller has traced Independent Local Radio (ILR) from the 1970s to the beginning of the new century.[28] And, as Asa Briggs pointed out, cultural histories are also important.[29] Hence this present volume attempts to address this aspect of the history of radio broadcasting and listening over the past 100 years and, in doing so, goes a little way to address Paddy Scannell and David Cardiff's lament that 'The fleeting, unrecorded character of early radio seems obstinately to resist the possibility of historical reclamation'.[30] My work also expands on existing research that has used the novel as the basis for creating a historical narrative in other media forms. For example, David Trotter (2013) considered how authors such as D. H. Lawrence (here in Chapter 2) included radio, and technology generally, in their stories, and Michael Ryan (2010), who analysed how writers and filmmakers portrayed radio in Germany in the 1920s.[31] My hope is that by reading responses to radio an understanding of what it was like to listen across the century can be built.

---

[25] Keith Williams (1996), *British Writers and the Media, 1930–1945*, Basingstoke, Hampshire: Macmillan.

[26] Jeffrey Richards (2010), *Cinema and Radio in Britain and America, 1920–1960*, Manchester: Manchester University Press.

[27] Asa Briggs (1961–95), *The History of Broadcasting in the United Kingdom*, 5 vols. Oxford: Oxford University Press; Jean Seaton ([2015] 2017), '*Pinkoes and Traitors*': *The BBC and the Nation, 1974–1987*, 2nd edn, London: Profile.

[28] Seán Street (2006), *Crossing the Ether: Pre-War Public Service Radio and Commercial Competition in the UK*, Eastleigh, Hampshire: John Libbey; Tony Stoller (2010), *Sounds of Your Life: The History of Independent Radio in the UK*, New Barnet, Hertfordshire: John Libbey.

[29] Asa Briggs ([1980] 1991), 'Problems and Possibilities in the Writing of Broadcasting History', in Briggs (1991), *The Collected Essays of Asa Briggs: Vol. III, Serious Pursuits: Communications and Education*, Urbana, IL: University of Illinois Press, pp. 114–27.

[30] Paddy Scannell and David Cardiff (1991), *A Social History of British Broadcasting, Volume One: 1922–1939, Serving the Nation*, Oxford: Basil Blackwell, p. xiii.

[31] David Trotter (2013), *Literature in the First Media Age: Britain between the Wars*, Cambridge, MA: Harvard University Press. Michael P. Ryan (2010), 'Radio Fimmel: German Radio in Popular Fiction, Film, and the Urban Novel, 1923–1932', PhD diss., University of Pennsylvania.

An outline of the book

The chapters that follow take a broadly chronological path, allowing a historical narrative to develop across the decades. The divisions are, to some extent, arbitrary, but have been made for three reasons: firstly, in order to reflect historical changes in British society; secondly, to follow developments in radio broadcasting; and lastly, so that some equal distribution of the source material can be achieved across the chapters. Printed literature dominates the early years, film rises to prominence before and after the Second World War, whilst popular music is dominant – along with TV and the movies – in the later years. The works used here are by and large English texts, reflecting the nature of this study which follows the development of British radio. North American examples that have circulated in Britain are included at key moments in the narrative to illustrate the point that foreign techniques and cultures have influenced British radio across the years. Also included are references to a number of examples and experiences from other countries: Brazil, Germany, France and Ireland amongst them. The study of radio's inspiration in other nations and languages is the topic for a future volume.

Chapter 2 charts the first thirteen years of broadcasting in Britain, the creation of the BBC and the emergence of commercial radio stations in Europe which had spotted potential in broadcasting in English to Britain. Writers discussed in their novels how the radio had appeared as a new media form, what exactly it could do and the limits of its permissiveness. It was acknowledged to be a technology that could span distances and bring the sounds of the metropolis into provincial towns and villages. Novelists including Rose Macaulay and D. H. Lawrence found radio to be a mark of both middle- and upper-class domestic alienation, even as it was a status symbol of modernity in the home. Films such as *Death at Broadcasting House* (1934) introduced the public to the Art Deco Modernism of the BBC's new headquarters and demonstrated how the radio studio was a room largely without visual adornment. It was also the first British movie to link criminal behaviour and untimely death to the new medium.

Authorly responses to the act of listening dominate Chapters 3 to 5. New techniques of listening, and a growing understanding of the medium by the audience, are first discussed in Chapter 3, where Winifred Holtby's *South Riding* (1936) provides a contemporary example of the development of ways of tuning in. The novelist was a keen listener and contributor to the BBC, and in her book she used the wireless as a narrative tool to create dramatic interactions between characters. Holtby highlighted solitary and communal listening, how radio could be an aural backdrop to daily life and how a royal broadcast from London could be part of events in a Yorkshire town yet also suggest a dissonance between the capital and the poverty of the north.

Chapter 4 discusses the Second World War and its aftermath, when the BBC became both a public voice of the nation and an imagined community builder. This led to a mix of portrayals in fiction, drama and film: James Joyce grappled with the modernity of long-distance listening; W. H. Auden and Christopher Isherwood prophesied about the coming of war, and Vera Lynn used the medium to lift hearts and minds. This was also a time of experimentation and cross-fertilization of media ideas. After the war ended, Stephen Potter and Joyce Grenfell helped launch the BBC's new station, the Third Programme, with a wry satirical dramatization of the way listeners often failed to pay attention.

In the 1950s, black humour and surreal comedy were mixed with post-war optimism. Chapter 5 charts the changing, darker, image of radio in Britain seen in novels and films in this period. John Wyndham used it as a narrative device in his apocalyptic tale of the Triffids, whilst Evelyn Waugh fictionalized his mental strain of being interviewed on the BBC in *The Ordeal of Gilbert Pinfold* (1957). For Waugh, it was a series of events that added to his developing psychosis and mental breakdown. By the 1960s, the offshore pirate stations had captured both the nation's imagination and the wrath of the Establishment. They featured in pop songs, and on TV and cinema screens, showing them to be lawbreakers involved in stories about smuggling and espionage, and confirming the label 'pirate'.

Chapter 6 considers the 1970s, when ILR – commercial radio carrying advertisements – began in mainland Britain. Influences from the United States came in the form of a first wave of radio nostalgia. George Lucas's *American Graffiti* (1973) appeared to hark back to a simpler, more innocent, time for the post-war generation of radio listeners who were now approaching their late-twenties. It was, in the event, a film that heralded a nostalgic tendency which has lasted until the present day. Meanwhile, the advent of punk and new wave at the end of the 1970s saw The Clash and Elvis Costello regard British music radio, both BBC Radio 1 and the new commercial stations, as stifling creative musical talent.

Chapters 7 and 8 therefore continue to consider critiques of both standards of radio production and DJ presentation styles. This begins in Chapter 7 with an observation that for some artists the DJ was still a friend who was welcomed into the audience's private space.

Charlie Dore, Roxy Music and The Buggles sang about late-night presenters, lost loves and the enduring nostalgia of radio. But other creative producers were concerned about the political differences emerging in this period. The movie *Radio On* (1979) showed a DJ taking a road trip through a bleak post-industrial English landscape, whilst *The Ploughman's Lunch* (1983) portrayed radio journalists as a shallow breed. Chapter 8 highlights the re-emergence of North American influences, particularly the art of DJ presentation with films such as *Good Morning, Vietnam* (1987) and *Talk Radio* (1988). British pop stars, meanwhile, continued their criticism of the medium as songs by Queen and The Smiths both accused radio stations of purveying mindless content. Their message was implicitly underscored by the idea that radio was 'better' in the imagined past, a theme taken up by Van Morrison and Paul Durcan as they sang 'In The Days Before Rock 'n' Roll' (1990). In the last decade before the millennium approached, the focus shifted from the DJs and on-air personalities back to the listeners themselves.

Chapter 9 considers the effect radio can have if used for evil, as in the case of the genocide in Rwanda in 1994 and how it came to be fictionalized on film. At the same time, in middle-class North America, movies and TV programmes were showing how radio could bring the intimate into the public sphere. The film *Sleepless in Seattle* (1993) turned a private romance into a spectacle, whilst the sitcom *Frasier* (1993–2004) took viewers behind the scenes to reveal a radio host ridden with snobbery and disdain for his audience.

The final chapter examines a renewed interest in radio through internet and on-demand services. Nostalgia reached its peak in this period too: the films *The Boat That Rocked* (2009) and *The King's Speech* (2010), together with a 2014 episode of the TV series *Downton Abbey*, each looked back at imagined pasts from radio's history. Elsewhere, British television continued to show radio as a place of death and intrigue and offered portraits of stations of variable quality in episodes of *New Tricks* (BBC), *Rebus* (ITV), *Father Brown* (BBC), *Midsomer Murders* (ITV) and *Doc Martin* (ITV). Meanwhile, the institutional inadequacies of the national BBC bureaucracy were satirized in a sitcom *W1A* (BBC), which took its title from the postcode of Broadcasting House in London.

This book shows that radio critiques by other media forms have changed and matured over the decades: from initial observations and speculations about the way audiences listened, to the manner in which radio output was either an aural backdrop, a propaganda tool or a force for social cohesion. However, three significant tendencies have persisted across the decades. Firstly, a tendency to invoke the nostalgic feeling of listening to the radio; secondly by linking the medium to negative stories of murder, spying and corruption; and thirdly the use of satire and ridicule by comedy scriptwriters when mentioning radio production and radio listening. Through the years, these reactions have continued to be refined as artists have called radio to account for being either mindless entertainment, restrictive in its output, or purely driven by profit without artistic merit. Judging by the number of books, films and TV programmes, this has been an enduring cultural fascination across the decades.

Pre-history: Before the days of the BBC

The beginnings of radio had a somewhat haphazard gestation stretching through the years of the second industrial revolution of the late 1800s until after the First World War. As a result, it can be a frustrating genesis for historians who prefer to describe a neat timeline of clear-cut events.[32] On the other hand, it had its own intrinsic excitement:

> The early history of radio [was] mired in controversy, accusations of intellectual theft and dishonesty, patent infringements, disputed court rulings, spurious science, enormous egos, self-publicity and disputed legacies. It is a history animated by the basest of human instincts, ambition and greed, but also by undisputed genius and the triumph of the human imagination.[33]

Radio telephony, or point-to-point communication, gave way to broadcasts as enthusiasts started playing gramophone records on air instead of using Morse code. For a number of people, the idea of hearing voices out of nowhere, via a wireless receiver, carried with it the notion of a supernatural phenomenon which went against all known human experience at the beginning of the twentieth century. Indeed, there was a widely held view that wireless was somehow a magical spirit-based technology, as the academic Jane Lewty has observed:

> Esoteric fancies of communing with the past and divining the future could be verified by an instrument which seemingly collapsed space to an instant. Moreover, the insularity of the upper middle-classes in London during this

---

[32] Aitor Anduaga (2009), *Wireless and Empire: Geopolitics, Radio Industry, and Ionosphere in the British Empire, 1918-1939,* Oxford: Oxford University Press, p. 56; Alasdair Pinkerton (2019), *Radio: Making Waves in Sound,* London: Reaktion Books p. 154.
[33] Pinkerton, *Radio: Making Waves in Sound,* p. 51.

period of transition – between dying Victoriana and the emerging modern spirit – may have caused wireless to be a whispered phenomenon in literary societies and private clubs before any commercial distinction.[34]

For example, 'Wireless' by Rudyard Kipling (1902) was a short story which had a drug-induced vision at the heart of its narrative. It involved three friends: the narrator, a pharmacist and a young radio enthusiast who used the back room of the shop to set up receiving equipment. After a dose of mind-altering drugs, a heady mixture of Morse code and wireless waves affected the chemist who in a trance-like state started to write the poetry of Keats. Here the science of early radio was presented as a secret guarded only by enthusiasts. On the edge of mysticism, the apothecary's dark arts linked wireless listening to 'receiving messages' from the unknown through 'the ether'. The radio enthusiast said, 'Marvellous, isn't it? And, remember, we're only at the beginning. There's nothing we sha'n't be able to do in ten years. I want to live – my God, how I want to live, and see things happen!'[35] Kipling's short story involved Morse code, not the spoken word. However, in a similar manner in 1926 Agatha Christie linked broadcasting to imagined voices beyond the grave in her short story also called 'Wireless', mentioned in the next chapter. One of the first films to show radio in use was *Caught by Wireless* (1908), an American silent short starring D. W. Griffith in an acting role. He played a policeman tracking a villain on an ocean liner between Ireland and the United States. The criminal was arrested as he stepped ashore, all because a telegram had been sent on ahead to alert the authorities. It prefigured the true story of Dr Crippen by two years. The ship's radio operator was shown in command of the technology and gave the viewing public, 'collective access, purely visual though it [was], to the newest wonder of technological progress'.[36] It also reinforced how radio telegraphy (and afterwards broadcasting) was an immediate medium, like the theatre, because the audience received the message at the time it was made. Cinema, photographs, gramophone records and newsprint did not share this temporal quality of 'now-ness'.[37]

---

[34] Jane Lewty (2002), 'Broadcasting Modernity: Eloquent Listening in the Early Twentieth Century', PhD diss., University of Glasgow, p. 41. For an account of American popular fantasies about radio broadcasting in this era, see chapter 2 of Susan J. Douglas ([1999] 2004), *Listening in: Radio and the American Imagination*, Minneapolis, MN: University of Minnesota Press.
[35] Rudyard Kipling (1902), 'Wireless', *Scribner's Magazine*, XXXII (2): 136.
[36] Young, *The Cinema Dreams its Rivals*, p. 52.
[37] Andrew Crisell (2002), *An Introductory History of British Broadcasting*, 2nd edn, London: Routledge, pp. 4–5.

As wireless telegraphy had an essential military role in the First World War, the trope of it 'finding' criminals and those in danger became a recurring theme in fiction. The British-born writer William Le Queux, who specialized in thriller and espionage novels serialized in magazines and newspapers, was a radio enthusiast who wrote two novels involving radio telegraphy: *Tracked by Wireless* and *The Voice from the Void*, both published in 1922. They concentrated on wireless telegraphy rather than broadcast radio, and each used the narrative trope of the villains being apprehended or foiled by the use of technology. The hero of *Tracked by Wireless* was a male research engineer with the Marconi Company in Chelmsford and London, working on 'a piece of apparatus far too technical to here describe'.[38] Radio was, for Le Queux, a man's world where women, he said, had a 'superficial knowledge' at best; whilst his heroine observed, 'The public speak airily of wireless, yet they little know to what marvellous perfection it is being brought.'[39] In the story it was the timely use of radio communications that brought justice. *Tracked by Wireless* drew to a close with a foretaste of broadcasting and the Sunday afternoon orchestral concert from The Hague, in the Netherlands, 'to which all wireless men [sic] in England listen so eagerly'. It reflected on the modernity of being able to listen remotely to such an artistic event 'in any part of the house'.[40] Without realizing or fully articulating it, Le Queux was documenting how wireless was bringing the public sphere into the private: a dialectic tension that academics and critics have returned to over the decades.[41] Such a shift was happening across Europe. Michael Ryan, who considered how early German cinema depicted radio, observed:

> Especially cities witnessed a swell of interest in pulp fiction, jazz, spectator sports, high fashion, and film. But the advent of public broadcast was different, for it ushered in [a] crucial shift: true the urban centers were fast becoming the hubs of a new sensory culture but now, with radio, so was the home. This fundamental change in how the public accessed art and information amazed German, British, and American audiences.[42]

---

[38] William Le Queux ([1922] 2019), *Tracked by Wireless*, Fairford, Gloucestershire: Echo Library, p. 15.
[39] Le Queux, *Tracked by Wireless*, p. 145 and 128. For a discussion of broadcast technology and gender, see Justine Lloyd (2020), *Gender and Media in the Broadcast Age: Women's Radio Programming at the BBC, CBC, and ABC*, New York: Bloomsbury Academic, pp. 31–4; and Shaun Moores (2000), *Media and Everyday Life in Modern Society*, Edinburgh: Edinburgh University Press, pp. 46–7.
[40] Le Queux, *Tracked by Wireless*, p. 141. Regular musical concerts had been broadcast from The Hague since 1919. Some had been sponsored by the *Daily Mail*, again aware of the publicity value. See Street, *Crossing the Ether*, pp. 40–2.
[41] See, for example, Simon Dawes (2017), *British Broadcasting and the Public-Private Dichotomy: Neoliberalism, Citizenship and the Public Sphere*, Cham, Switzerland: Palgrave Macmillan, pp. 22–4.
[42] Ryan, 'Radio Fimmel', pp. 7–8.

William Le Queux's other novel that year, *The Voice from the Void: The Great Wireless Mystery*, had a plot which presented wireless as a tool both for criminals and for detectives of crime, with good eventually winning out over evil. Meanwhile listening to broadcasts was quickly coming of age. The hero enthusiastically listened to an evening concert from London: 'A certain prima donna of world-wide fame was singing a selection from *Il Trovatore*, and into the room the singer's voice came perfectly.'[43] However, Le Queux again made clear that the technology was a male domain because, he said, women refused to put headphones over their heads as it would disturb their hair. In his view, this meant they were not fully engaged with the technology.[44]

Birth of the BBC

Tuesday the 14th of November 1922 was the day before a general election – the first since the recent partition of Ireland. Wireless radio engineers from Marconi's company had spent all day preparing the studio and the rooftop transmitter of 2LO in the Strand for the evening broadcast.[45] At six o'clock, Arthur Burrows introduced the station with its call sign and physical location as usual, 'This is 2LO, Marconi House. London calling'. Except this evening the British Broadcasting Company was now on-air.[46] It employed four people on that first day of transmission and had only a low-powered transmitter (100 watts on 350 metres, 857 kilohertz) reaching to the edges of London during daylight with any clarity. Even so, the station already had an estimated total audience of 50,000 licensed listeners, wireless enthusiasts and amateurs, some as far away as northern Scotland, when reception conditions after dark improved.[47] Burrows was a trained journalist and a consummate public relations man, who knew how to turn a good story and promote it to the public. He was the key to the early success of broadcast radio in Britain and became the BBC's first director of programmes. He had already joined forces a number of times with the *Daily*

---

[43] William Le Queux ([1922] 2019), *The Voice from the Void: The Great Wireless Mystery*, CreateSpace/Amazon print-on-demand, p. 41.
[44] Le Queux, *The Voice from the Void*, p. 16.
[45] Arthur Burrows (1924), *The Story of Broadcasting*, London: Cassell, p. 59.
[46] Asa Briggs (1961), *The History of Broadcasting in the United Kingdom, Volume I, The Birth of Broadcasting*, Oxford: Oxford University Press, pp. 20–1.
[47] Briggs (1961), *The History of Broadcasting, Vol I*, p. 12 and p. 75.

Mail in those first years, each organization feeding off the other for publicity.[48] Radio was showing its 'power to enthral and entertain', and the promotional work Burrows carried out ensured women (the *Mail*'s target readership) would be aware of radio's potential and would demand to have a wireless receiver in the home. Radio was quickly making its mark as a medium for the masses.[49] The notion of what audiences deserved to hear from a British radio company, and indeed the very idea of radio as a utility at the service of the public, would subtly change and develop as a new man, John (later Lord) Reith, took charge a couple of weeks later in December 1922.

---

[48] Briggs (1961), *The History of Broadcasting, Vol I*, p. 77. Early press coverage of radio broadcasting tended to emphasize uncritically the technology and the very idea of being able to hear distant voices. See Paul Rixon (2015), 'Radio and Popular Journalism in Britain: Early Radio Critics and Radio Criticism', *Radio Journal: International Studies in Broadcast & Audio Media*, 13 (1–2): 23–36. From the late 1980s onwards, the *Daily Mail* was to become one of the leading critics of the Corporation. See: Patrick Barwise and Peter York (2020), *The War Against the BBC*, London: Penguin, pp. 95–100. See also: Seaton, *'Pinkoes and Traitors'*, pp. 10 and 33.

[49] Pinkerton, *Radio: Making Waves in Sound*, p. 98. See also: Simon Frith (1983), 'The Pleasures of the Hearth: The Making of BBC Light Entertainment', in Formations Editorial Collective, eds, *Formations of Pleasure*, London: Routledge & Kegan Paul, pp. 101–23.

2

Broadcasting on air, 1922 to 1935

Radio: A history of discovery

From the first transmissions of the BBC the very idea of regular broadcasting came into being. Writers, comedians and filmmakers found inspiration in what they heard, and this chapter considers how the range of responses to radio broadcasting during the 1920s and early 1930s highlighted two questions: What is it? And what does it do? Songs and movies explored the very idea of radio itself, and sometimes responded with an exclamation of 'You can't do that!', as if to attempt to limit radio in some way. One way to think about this period in the development of radio is to understand that 'the history of broadcasting was a history of *discovery*', not a history of the implementation of an existing knowledge about how to do it, or even what form the content should take.[1] So, writers were intrigued by the way radio constructed its own sense of geography peculiar to the technology. There were, for example, some authors in this period who had a character sitting in an isolated rural spot in England listening to Paris or Luxembourg, as if to make the point that the wireless was capable of bringing far away voices close to hand and thereby shrink physical space itself. This chapter also offers examples of how the radio became part of the fabric of the home, as novelists included listening as part of their narratives of domesticity, and movies began to show characters in the act of tuning in. Just as important was the ability of cinema to show to listeners what the inside of a radio studio looked like: both demystifying and glamourizing it at the same time.[2]

---

[1] Suzanne Lommers (2012), *Europe – On Air: Interwar Projects for Radio Broadcasting*, Amsterdam: Amsterdam University Press, p. 29 (emphasis in the original).
[2] Jeffrey Richards (2010), *Cinema and Radio in Britain and America, 1920-1960*, Manchester: Manchester University Press, p. 147.

Writers ask what radio can, and cannot, do

Writers as diverse as P. G. Wodehouse and Herman Hesse saw problems ahead with wireless, and each wrote about the limits of this technology even as it was changing from a military communication system and a hobby for demobbed enthusiasts to a mass-broadcast daily media form. The historian Asa Briggs had a fondness for a quote by George (Lord) Riddell, who said in December 1923, 'I do not like the description 'wireless': why describe a thing as a negation?'.[3] The point here was that behind the joke Lord Riddell knew, as the owner of the *News of the World* with a circulation of three million at the time, that his business would not suffer in the short term if his readers put down their newspapers and tuned in to the radio.

Indeed, he expected that his readers would do both. He was one of the few who reckoned radio would find a place alongside existing media such as theatre, concerts and the printed word.[4] But still, there were those writers and performers who enjoyed talking up the negative and satirizing the technology.

One example was the collaboration between the English duo P. G. Wodehouse and George Grossmith Jnr, who worked with the American musician Jerome Kern, to create a stage musical called *The Beauty Prize*, which ran for six months in the autumn and winter of 1923–4 in London's West End. It was a comedy of manners about young couples whom fate had kept apart. In the middle of the show, they were all on an ocean liner bound for the United States lamenting in song that 'You Can't Make Love by Wireless'. One of them had bribed the ship's radio operator to send a bogus telegram in an attempt to get the couples back together. It did not work, and Wodehouse and Grossmith in the song portrayed Morse code and Marconigram messages as a soulless functional communication system. Despite this, all the lovers were finally reconciled and reunited at the end of the show. Meanwhile, broadcast radio to the general population had taken off rapidly. Twelve months after its creation, the BBC had eight transmitters covering much of England, Scotland and Wales; it had moved into studios in Savoy Hill, on a narrow street behind the famous London hotel; employed just short of 200 people and had started publishing the *Radio Times* listings magazine.

---

[3] Asa Briggs (1961), *The History of Broadcasting in the United Kingdom, Volume I, The Birth of Broadcasting*, London: Oxford University Press, p. 15; also quoted in Asa Briggs and Peter Burke (2002), *A Social History of the Media: From Gutenberg to the Internet*, Cambridge: Polity, p. 215.

[4] In the 1920s and 1930s, both newspaper owners and music hall impresarios attempted to restrict what the BBC could broadcast, fearing unwanted competition from the wireless.

In that time the number of licences had increased from 36,000 to more than half a million.[5] Even in 1922 the Company's objectives stated that it was to exist, 'for the creation, establishment and operation . . . of stations as a public utility service to the public'. It was also to provide 'news, information, concerts, lectures, educational matter, speeches, weather reports, theatrical entertainment and any other matter which for the time being may be permitted by or be within the scope or orbit of said Licence [given by His Majesty's Postmaster-General]'.[6] In other words, to 'inform, educate and entertain' were included even in its founding documents. However, sociologist Tom Burns articulated the business objectives of the time more directly: 'The BBC [Company] was founded . . . to transmit broadcasts in the sure hope that this would expand the market for wireless receivers manufactured by the member firms, as well, of course, as providing a market itself for all the apparatus required for transmitters.'[7] Programmes were going out daily, mostly in the evenings. The work for the small team in the winter of 1922 was relentless, and the then director of programmes, Arthur Burrows, mentioned this to John Reith, who joined one month later, on 14 December. Reith left his mark on the culture of the organization from the beginning: 'By the end of 1923 in most people's eyes he *was* the BBC. To many people, including his critics, he has remained the BBC ever since.'[8]

Reith's vision would help to transform the Company into a Corporation, enshrine the concept of public service broadcasting as a form of public utility and give his surname to the embodiment of these values.[9] It was Reith who imprinted his own world view on the day-to-day operation of the early BBC, creating an organization which reportedly frowned upon divorce, demanded respectable behaviour in public from its staff, was paternalistic and regarded Sundays as a day to avoid broadcasting anything which might be thought of as light entertainment of a non-religious nature.[10] As a result, for many years it was not a happy organization to work for.[11] Also, at times, a number of the

---

[5] Mark Pegg (1983), *Broadcasting and Society: 1918–1939*, Beckenham, Kent: Croom Helm, p. 7.
[6] The British Broadcasting Company, Limited (1922), 'Objects of the Company, clause 3', quoted in Briggs (1961), *The History of Broadcasting, Vol I*, p. 127.
[7] Tom Burns (1977), *The BBC: Public Institution and Private World*, London: The Macmillan, p. 7.
[8] Briggs (1961), *The History of Broadcasting, Vol I*, p. 135. Emphasis in original.
[9] Simon Dawes (2017), *British Broadcasting and the Public-Private Dichotomy: Neoliberalism, Citizenship and the Public Sphere*, Cham, Switzerland: Palgrave Macmillan, p. 44.
[10] Reith's biographer said the new director general's first order in 1922 to Arthur Burrows was, 'that we would observe Sundays'. Ian McIntyre (1993), *The Expense of Glory: A Life of John Reith*, London: HarperCollins, p. 117.
[11] Paddy Scannell and David Cardiff (1982), 'Serving the Nation: Public Service Broadcasting Before the War', in Bernard Waites, Tony Bennett and Graham Martin, eds, *Popular Culture: Past and Present - A Reader*, Beckenham, Kent: Croom Helm, p. 171. See also Penelope Fitzgerald ([1980]

programmes were somewhat difficult to listen to, and through the 1930s many listeners were tempted to tune in to commercial competitors that offered consistent entertainment and relaxation such as Radio Normandy (from 1931) and Radio Luxembourg (from 1933).[12] However, the BBC (1922–7) was keen to promote itself in the other new medium of the era: the cinema. An intertitle of a silent Pathé Pictorial newsreel called *London Calling! Behind the Scenes in an 'OB'* (c1925) said, 'And catching every sound, the inoffensive looking but all-powerful microphone'.[13] It was an attempt to create a public perception of the omnipresence of this technology which dealt with the transmission of voices through the unseen. But there were still problems. Early radio reception was sometimes haphazard, and comments of the period were often about the quality of the transmissions instead of the actual programme content.[14] Crystal sets had no powered amplifier and required headphones. As technology developed, valve amplifiers improved the signal reception and drove loudspeakers at home. It was something the industry and the set-makers were aware of: relatively small studio spaces, and the technical limitations both of contemporary microphones and of medium- and long-wave broadcasting, meant that full orchestral arrangements of classical music were often pared down to small chamber ensemble versions, altering significantly the original musical score.[15] In a long letter published in *Music and Letters* in April 1923, H. R. Rivers-Moore admitted to technical problems, particularly in the broadcast of opera and orchestral music.[16] However, his aim was to promote the positive aspects of radio ownership, and he asserted that rather than being a 'new craze of no musical importance', radio was a force to increase cultural capital, and it 'must have a very great bearing on the improvement or otherwise of national musical taste, and in a country with a greater perception of the importance of such things to mankind'.[17]

The daily practice of listening was a different matter and was often fraught. For the German-born writer Herman Hesse, who had in the early 1920s taken up

---

2014), *Human Voices*, London: Fourth Estate. In Chapter 7, I discuss her fictional account of working for the Corporation in the late 1930s and 1940s.

[12] Seán Street (2006), *Crossing the Ether: Pre-War Public Service Radio and Commercial Competition in the UK*, Eastleigh: Hampshire: John Libbey, p. 65; Lommers, *Europe - On Air*, p. 176.

[13] *London Calling! Behind the Scenes in an 'OB'* ([c1925] 2014), UK: Pathé Pictorial, 13 April. Available online: https://youtu.be/vb6bwYqdbD4 (accessed 24 May 2021).

[14] Shaun Moores (2000), *Media and Everyday Life in Modern Society*, Edinburgh: Edinburgh University Press, p. 44.

[15] Lommers, *Europe - On Air*, pp. 266–8.

[16] Rivers-Moore was a member of the May 1922 'conference' on broadcasting between the Post Office and the set manufacturers, mentioned in Briggs (1961), *The History of Broadcasting, Vol I*, p. 410.

[17] H. R. Rivers-Moore (1923), 'The Wireless Transmission of Music', *Music & Letters*, 4 (2): 158.

Swiss nationality, radio was nothing but trouble especially for a lover, like him, of classical music. *Steppenwolf*, published in Germany in 1927 and translated into English in 1929, was a semi-autobiographical novel that dealt with emotional crises and mental trauma. Towards the end of the story, the main character and narrator, Harry, inside the Magic Theatre encountered Mozart who, instead of playing piano, was tuning a radio set which announced:

> 'Munich calling. Concerto Grosso in F major of Handel.'
>
> At once, to my indescribable astonishment and horror, the devilish metal funnel spat out, without more ado, its mixture of bronchial slime and chewed rubber; that noise that possessors of gramophones and radio sets are prevailed upon to call music. And behind the slime and the croaking there was, sure enough, like an old master beneath a layer of dirt, the noble outline of that divine music. I could distinguish the majestic structure and the deep wide breadth and the full broad bowings of the strings.
>
> 'My God,' I cried in horror, 'what are you doing, Mozart? Do you really mean to inflict this mess upon me and yourself, this triumph of our day, the last victorious weapon in the war of extermination against art? Must this be, Mozart?'
>
> How the uncanny man laughed![18]

Hesse was using the historical fact that Mozart adapted some of Handel's scores to suggest that the wireless was 'reworking' in its own awful way this music, and thus gave a damning critique of the quality of wireless transmissions. The character Mozart went on to explain the music coming from the radio and the constituent parts provided by each instrument. But he added that the radio 'strips music of its sensuous beauty', and delivered it to listeners who were not paying attention to the melody and tune:

> And now you hear not only a Handel who, disfigured by radio, is, all the same, in this most ghastly of disguises still divine; you hear as well and you observe, most worthy sir, a most admirable symbol of all life. When you listen to radio you are a witness of the everlasting war between idea and appearance, between time and eternity, between the human and the divine.[19]

What concerned the novelist about the radio was that it was making a poor reproduction of a concert masterpiece and rendering it almost unintelligible. He

---

[18] Herman Hesse ([1929] 1965), *Steppenwolf*, trans. Basil Creighton, Harmondsworth, Middlesex: Penguin, p. 246.
[19] Hesse, *Steppenwolf*, p. 247.

'was not a supporter of mass broadcasting. In fact, Hesse was seemingly horrified by the device'.[20] But more than that, 'In Hesse's view, radio was not simply mass entertainment or a new-age method of education, it was a weapon. And not just classical music was under attack'.[21] Hesse understood that radio propaganda was emerging as a cultural weapon in Weimar Germany and foretold the abuses of broadcasting by the National Socialist (Nazi) party in the 1930s and 1940s. The topic of radio and the build-up to the Second World War will be considered in the next two chapters.

Radio causes trouble: The human side of broadcasting

The British film *Out of the Blue* (1931) provided an example of how moviemakers considered radio to be trivializing culture. The story opened with a scene in a radio studio, and played on the fact that the actors were invisible to their wireless audience. They were seen half-heartedly performing a murder-drama for the microphone whilst variously reading a newspaper and playing cards. The suggestion was that radio was less authentic than cinema because at the movies the audience could both see and hear, and not be fooled. It was not a flattering portrayal, given that broadcasters and technicians, then as today, worked hard to bring their best to air. The impression given was that radio actors did not care much for their craft, just as Hesse for his part thought radio trivialized and stripped classical music of its beauty. *Out of the Blue* was the first major film for the stage and musical star Jessie Matthews (another of her movies with a radio narrative *Head over Heels* (1937) is mentioned in Chapter 3). Here she played the poor daughter of a baronet, and the storyline showed that her romance with a radio star would lead to trouble: offering a choice of either a positive image for audiences who liked danger, or a negative one for those who preferred to live cautious lives. The movie was based on a West End Musical, *Little Tommy Tucker*, which ran only for a short time in 1930. The film, like the stage version, was not a popular success.[22] Incidentally, Matthews's major radio role would not come until 1963, when she took over the title role in the daily weekday serial

---

[20] Michael P. Ryan (2010), 'Radio Fimmel: German Radio in Popular Fiction, Film, and the Urban Novel, 1923–1932', PhD diss., University of Pennsylvania, p. 4. For a discussion of recording and transmission techniques during this period, see Street, *Crossing the Ether*, pp. 115–34.
[21] Ryan, 'Radio Fimmel', p. 5.
[22] Richards, *Cinema and Radio*, p. 165.

Mrs Dale's Diary on the BBC Light Programme – renamed and revamped as *The Dales* shortly before her arrival.

Transgression was a popular motif in the responses to radio during its first decade across Britain. One example was a comedy review number, 'We Can't Let You Broadcast That' (1932), by Norman Long which was itself banned by the BBC when first published. It made fun of the BBC's self-censorship of material in the late 1920s and 1930s, and concern by the Corporation over possible *double entendres*, offensive words, political comments and advertising.[23] Norman Long told at the start of the song how he had been invited by the BBC to appear on-air. However, in the verses that followed he said the Corporation had told him his suggested rendition of the Rudyard Kipling poem 'Boots' could be deemed to be an advertisement for the shop chain Boots the Chemist. In another stanza he explained to producers that a song about drinking was published by Boosey (& Hawkes). They immediately rejected it because they thought it sounded like 'boozy'. These jokes still worked in Britain 100 years later, and they mocked an institution struggling to maintain a chaste tone. This satirizing of the BBC's moral position would continue with comedy work by Clapham and Dwyer in films such as *Radio Parade* (1933, discussed in the following text) and *Sing as You Swing* (1937, Chapter 3).

For all the appearance of being a precisely organized professional outfit managed on military lines, the BBC was lampooned for its human errors and its mistakes.[24] One example of the fine line between high-quality broadcast and mayhem was penned by Norman Hunter, who wrote short stories for young people. His Professor Branestawm tales were written for broadcast on the BBC's *Children's Hour*. They were then collected and first published together in 1933 with illustrations by W. Heath Robinson.[25] The narrative framework of each short story was one of misadventure and misunderstanding as the bumbling professor made mistakes which had unfortunate consequences. In 'The Professor Does a Broadcast', he was invited 'to do a broadcast', giving it a sense of some physical

---

[23] Some of the verses are printed in: Seán Street, ed. (2004), *Radio Waves: Poems Celebrating the Wireless*, London: Enitharmon Press, pp. 36–7.

[24] The BBC began, in the late 1920s, to allow programme makers to satirize themselves. David Cardiff mentioned an occasional radio series, *Airy Nothings* (1928-1931), which included sketches that poked fun at the Corporation's characters on both sides of the microphone. David Cardiff (1988), 'Mass Middlebrow Laughter: The Origins of BBC Comedy', *Media, Culture & Society*, 10 (1): 53.

[25] Norman Hunter's children's stories have been enduringly popular, with the last of the book series published in the early 1980s and subsequent TV adaptations (Thames TV, 1969; BBC, 2014 and 2015). A new radio version of five of his stories were broadcast by the BBC in 2001. None of these featured the 'Professor Does a Broadcast' story.

chore rather than a creative process.[26] The story also provided young readers with an understanding of how radio worked. A friend advised the professor, 'They only let you have so much time to broadcast, I believe. Suppose you hadn't finished and they turned you off for the Children's Hour or something.'[27]

Indeed, Hunter extracted humour from the fact that the absent-minded professor was unable to work out exactly how long his script was, or to be able to talk coherently without digressing. In contrast, speaking to a colleague in the hallway of the radio station an announcer complained, 'He's due to broadcast in a few minutes. The time is now exactly twenty-seven and a half minutes to five', making the joke that on-air speech was a peculiar form of the everyday.[28] The story ended with the professor reading his talk so fast that he had to repeat it in order to fill up the time slot until *Children's Hour* began. Written by an author who had experience of the broadcast industry, it suggested that live radio was full of hazards and problems, often involving people trying – and failing – to keep to time.[29] Decades later, Jimmy Perry – who co-wrote the BBC TV sitcom *Dad's Army* (1968–77) – wrote a four-part nostalgic comedy for Radio 2 about the early years of the BBC, reflecting some of these early mishaps.[30]

That mistakes could happen in live radio made it a human medium for many listeners. This appeal was aided by movies which helped to promote radio personalities by visualizing these unseen voices, even if some of them were portrayed as having deep moral problems.

One film which introduced audiences to the physical concept of the medium was *Death at Broadcasting House* (1934). Indeed, as the title suggested, it linked radio to murder.

Somewhat sensationally it portrayed a killing live on-air, listened to by a potential audience of millions. The story had started life as a novel published in the same year co-written by Val Gielgud, soon to be the BBC's director of drama, and Eric Maschwitz writing under the pen name of Holt Marvell, later the BBC's director of light entertainment. Gielgud said in his memoirs:

---

[26] Norman Hunter ([1933] 1946), *The Incredible Adventures of Professor Branestawm*, Harmondsworth, Middlesex: Penguin, p. 136.
[27] Hunter, *Branestawm*, pp. 137–8.
[28] Hunter, *Branestawm*, p. 142. See: Paddy Scannell (1996), *Radio, Television and Modern Life: A Phenomenological Approach*, Oxford: Blackwell, p. 149.
[29] See, for example: Simon Elmes ([2012] 2013), *Hello Again . . . Nine Decades of Radio Voices*, London: Arrow, p. 33.
[30] *London Calling* (1994), Jimmy Perry, BBC Radio 2, 19–22 September.

As a book it had had a considerable success, and it seemed to our untutored minds that it was from the film point of view 'sure-fire'. Broadcasting House, if only as a new building and rather a box of tricks, was still 'news'. Most people seemed curious to know what went on behind its concrete battlements; seemed eager to enjoy any opportunity of 'seeing the wheels go round'.[31]

The movie was filmed on a small budget, and the radio studio sets were built at the film studios rather than using Broadcasting House itself. They reproduced the Art Deco interiors, gave movie representations of radio technology and showed how the use of multiple studios gave different sonic atmospheres and ambiances to a drama.[32] This story, and the film version, offered a view from the radio professional's perspective of the craft of broadcasting. The book, in order to explain the twists of the plot, included floor plans of the sixth, seventh and eighth floors of Broadcasting House in London which had opened in 1932, together with studio running orders and facilities booking sheets.[33]

The novel began thus: 'Broadcasting House has been called a good many names, and described as a good many things. Names and descriptions have varied from the complimentary to the scurrilous, and almost from the sublime to the ridiculous.'[34] In a similar manner, the film opened with a slow camera tilt down the exterior of Broadcasting House to show off its grandiose Art Deco design, an establishing shot used in numerous movies during this period (see also Chapters 3 and 4). The plot of *Death at Broadcasting House* introduced audiences to the idea that some parts of domestic radio output were recorded, a relatively recent technical innovation in 1934, to be rebroadcast on the BBC Empire Service, a technical detail which allowed the detectives to trick the murderer into thinking the sound of his wristwatch had been recorded. The film carefully explained the importance of waiting for a cue light before talking on-air. However, Val Gielgud's on-screen performance as a producer given to rushing between studios and looking stressed (Figure 2) left the viewer thinking that the act of creating radio drama was unduly complex. In this respect, the characterization resembled Norman Hunter's Professor Branestawm.

Two other films of this era also presented radio broadcasting in the context of illegal activities. Instead of murder, they featured pirate broadcasting and

---

[31] Val Gielgud (1947), *Years of the Locust*, 1947, London: Nicholson & Watson, p. 130. *Death at Broadcasting House* was adapted for BBC Radio 4 by Sue Rodwell in 1996.
[32] Richards, *Cinema and Radio*, pp. 169–71.
[33] The *BBC Yearbook* for 1932, published by the Corporation, had also included detailed floor plans of Broadcasting House.
[34] Val Gielgud and Holt Marvell (1934), *Death at Broadcasting House*, London: Rich & Cowan, p. 1.

Figure 2 Val Gielgud, the BBC's director of drama, as Julian Caird, a fictionalized version of himself. *Death at Broadcasting House* (1934), Dir. Reginald Denham, UK: Phoenix Films.

petty theft. The first, *Big Ben Calling* (1935, also known as *Radio Pirates*), was a musical about a fictional station PBQ based in London and set up by a trio of a café manageress, a shop owner selling wireless sets and a struggling songwriter. Leslie the radio salesman (Leslie French) and the musician (Warren Jenkins as Willie) declared together:

> Leslie: Broadcasting! If the BBC won't plug your songs, we'll start a rival wireless station.
> Willie: And plug my numbers ourselves!
> Leslie: Before you know where you are you'll be the best-known composer in Europe.

It was a comment which reinforced the international reach of radio in the interwar years. *Big Ben Calling* was a movie about joyful transgression; however, the initials PBQ were never explained. They could have denoted 'Please be quiet' or perhaps the vulgar version, 'Pretty bloody quiet', in an ironic reference to the pirate station's transmissions. The trio avoided capture by hiding in coffins, and then whilst giggling and laughing they set up their transmitter on top of Big Ben, a signifier of authority, government, and the BBC which broadcast the chimes.[35] The illegal broadcasters were not caught but knew somehow, never explained, that their transmissions must end. With smiles on their faces, they gave up the idea of pirate radio and decided to settle down in 'proper jobs' instead. Another film which connected crime and broadcasting was *Street Song* (1935). The movie offered an opening shot of a brief glimpse of the front door of Broadcasting House and the rooftop aerials. Tom Tucker (John Garrick), the lead character, was a frustrated singer who tried to get work on the radio.[36] However, he failed in his initial attempt and continued to be involved with a gang of thieves. It was a morality tale that suggested some of the broadcast stars may have had criminal backgrounds before they became famous. Tucker eventually got his break by simply walking unannounced into a studio where the dance band was playing (led by a character called 'Roy Hall' in a close approximation of the actual bandleader Henry Hall). He took up the sheet music and sang live on-air. The band appeared to enjoy the rule-breaking of the scene, judging by their smiles. The movie eventually closed with a happy ending, and a camera tilt up over the full height of Broadcasting House as the musicians reached their final crescendo. These examples of films, songs and a short story poked fun at the medium: showing that radio could be a haunt of befuddled academics, lawbreakers and lazy actors.

The effect was to humanize the medium of radio and to imagine broadcasters as ordinary people doing extraordinary things on a public stage. Such portrayals would come to be repeated and replayed in the decades to come.

How far can it go? Radio's geographic coverage

Audiences were also presented with examples of the everywhere-and-nowhere nature of radio broadcasting. The wireless allowed a voice in London to be heard whispering from a receiver in another city, appearing instantaneously to span vast distances. It gave listeners the sounds from Paris, Limoges, Nice, Luxembourg and Stockholm a place in the living room next to the antimacassar-

---

[35] Moores, *Media and Everyday Life*, p. 55.
[36] Richards, *Cinema and Radio*, p. 163.

covered armchairs and lithographs of Landseer's 'Monarch of the Glen' beloved of genteel lower middle-class homes of returning war veterans and their wives.

Radio was the technology which, for the first time, was able to bring the world into the home and 'was bound up with ideological desires to connect people and places wirelessly, instantaneously and over vast geographical distances'.[37] As a result, after initial flirtations at the turn of the century with the mysticism of the ether (mentioned in the previous chapter), writers were keen to situate radio in the material world.

For example, Margery Allingham highlighted the physical distance between the rural and the metropolitan in her novel *Look to the Lady* (1931).[38] The story was about the attempted theft of a priceless family heirloom, and the solving of a mysterious murder. The hero was the aristocratic Albert Campion, her enduring detective character. Allingham had the radio as part of the backdrop to a deep rural existence, but with a listener using it to search out alternatives to the London-centric BBC:

> A weed-grown brick path led up to the front door which stood open, revealing an old man in a battered felt hat seated on a low wooden chair beside an atrocious loud-speaker which was at this moment murmuring a nasal reproduction of the advertising gramophone music from Radio Paris. The old man cocked an eye at their approach, and rising with evident regret, switched off the instrument.[39]

He was also a solitary listener, connected from France back to rural Suffolk. It may have been a poor-quality transmission he was listening to, but the effect on the reader was to confirm that tuning to a foreign station was preferable to having to deal with the reality of the here and now in front of him. Such a disconnect between the real and the virtual has more recently been at the heart of criticisms of twenty-first-century new media technologies. If nothing else, the villager was an excellently attentive radio listener albeit not to the BBC.[40]

A contrasting setting for radio broadcasts was offered by W. H. Auden, the English-born poet who took up American citizenship after moving to the

---

[37] Alasdair Pinkerton (2019), *Radio: Making Waves in Sound*, London: Reaktion Books, p. 115.
[38] It was published in the United States as *The Gyrth Chalice Mystery*. In Britain, a ninety-minute radio adaptation was produced in 1961 by the BBC as part of the *Saturday Night Theatre* series on the Home Service. A two-part TV version with a screenplay by Alan Plater was broadcast on BBC 2 on 22 and 29 January 1989. Plater's version remained faithful to the novel and mentioned Radio Paris; the radio drama did not.
[39] Margery Allingham ([1931] 1950), *Look to the Lady*, London: Penguin, p. 161.
[40] David Trotter (2013), *Literature in the First Media Age: Britain between the Wars*, Cambridge, MA: Harvard University Press, pp. 327–8, note 34.

United States just before the outbreak of the Second World War. He published the first version of *The Orators: An English Study* in 1932, a complex mixture of poetry and prose that was his 'literary manifesto of the thirties, and it was to govern his verse for the rest of that tempestuous decade'.[41] It was regarded, in all its multifaceted voices and approaches, as a key example of Modernist poetry. Book II of *The Orators* was the 'Journal of an Airman', and the tone of this section was 'introspective and doomed' according to one critic.[42] It read as a series of notes in preparation for a war, battle or armed conflict. Black humour, weak jokes and a sense of death pervaded. What Auden depicted was a fragmented world, full of struggles and uncertainties against which the Airman was trying to codify his universe with sometimes trite but nonetheless insightful definitions and observations. In a section called 'The Airman's Alphabet', Auden presented definitions in his ironic style of the period, including:

> Wireless Sender of signal
> and speaker of sorrow
> and news from nowhere[43]

Auden implied that radio – as both military telephony and a broadcast medium – was in a tension between a system designed to share useful vital information and a method of transmission that bore only bad news. His epigram included a possible passing mention of William Morris's 1890 socialist utopian novel *News from Nowhere*, in which the world had returned to a pre-industrial, peaceful existence. However, Auden's wireless was the real presence of a messy, selfish, here-and-now full of 'sorrow', a theme he continued in his collaborations for theatre discussed in Chapters 3 and 4. For him, it spoke only depressing, negative thoughts of the times: of economic misery in the 1930s and of rising political uncertainty, which reflected the scarred emotions of a generation still aching spiritually from the effects of the First World War. Its aftermath ran deep; indeed, many of those employed in senior positions by the rapidly expanding BBC in the 1920s and 1930s had previously held a military rank of officer class,

---

[41] John R. Boly (1981), 'W. H. Auden's *The Orators*: Portraits of the Artist in the Thirties', *Twentieth Century Literature*, 27 (3): 247.
[42] Boly, 'W. H. Auden's The Orators', p. 247.
[43] W. H. Auden (1932), 'The Orators: An English Study', in W. H. Auden (1986), *The English Auden: Poems, Essays and Dramatic Writings 1927–1939*, ed. Edward Mendelson, London: Faber and Faber, p. 80.

which could go some way to explain the management structure of the Company and the Corporation for the decades which followed. [44]

Elsewhere, radio was busy inventing genres for the new medium, for example how to introduce gramophone records and construct a show based on recorded music. Cinema audiences were in 1933 able to watch Christopher Stone, acknowledged to be the first DJ on the BBC, in the film *Radio Parade* (1933).[45] He sat in what looked like a large living room and gave a movie re-creation of his on-air work in the radio studio by talking about each 78-rpm disc before playing it on his gramophone player. The movie then cut to the artists themselves as they performed their acts. The film acknowledged the difference between the scripted speech of BBC talks and news summaries, and the (mostly) unplanned utterances of music show presenters. Stone became popular not only on the BBC between 1927 and 1934, but also when he went on to work for Radio Luxembourg.[46] Stone's style in the movie might be dismissed as unprofessional by today's DJs, consisting as it did of hesitations, incoherent asides and muttered comments. Even so, his mixture of sloppy informality and what looked like under-rehearsed announcements had plausible links to representations in the 1980s and early 1990s of fictional British DJs such as Kit Curran and Smashie and Nicey, described in Chapter 8. *Radio Parade* featured contemporary radio stars including the double act Clapham and Dwyer, and Flotsam and Jetsam – a male comedy singing duo in the vein of Flanders and Swann, who performed a doleful song about the chimes of Big Ben announcing the end of the day's transmission: 'Big Ben is Calling from London Town'.[47] Others to appear were Elsie and Doris Waters – as Gert and Daisy, also mentioned in the next chapter, and Florence Desmond doing impersonations of contemporary movie stars including a riff on Greta Garbo meeting Gracie Fields. Such acts were already well-known to many who, for the first time, were able to hear these variety artists on their living room wireless sets. The cost of receiving equipment dropped steadily between 1922 and 1935. Hire-purchase deals abounded for such a long-term household investment, and 'radio could provide one of the cheapest retreats for a long winter evening – in terms of cost per hour of entertainment'.[48]

---

[44] Burns, *The BBC*, pp. 21–7. See also David Hendy (2014), 'The Great War and British Broadcasting: Emotional Life in the Creation of the BBC', *New Formations*, 82: 96–7.
[45] The film was also known as *Hello Radio* (1933). Reel one is missing. See Richards, *Cinema and Radio*, p. 162.
[46] Elmes, *Hello Again*, pp. 40–4.
[47] Seán Street (2009), *The A to Z of British Radio*, Lanham, MD: The Scarecrow Press, p. 115.
[48] Pegg, *Broadcasting and Society*, p. 48.

Already by the mid-1930s, stations including Radio Paris, mentioned earlier by Margery Allingham, were broadcasting in English on a regular basis. Likewise, the BBC was audible across much of Europe on long wave during the day and medium wave after dark, whilst in 1932 it started the Empire Service, using short-wave transmissions to reach around the globe.[49] Graham Greene's *England Made Me* (1935) revealed the geographic disjoint of being expatriates and multinationals who were both somewhere and nowhere: just like the radio they listened to. One passage in the novel directly compared BBC programming, and suggested it had a certain predictability of tone not present in other broadcast organizations. The scene was a card game in Stockholm between expats and their Swedish host:

'That's a fine wireless set,' Gullie said. 'Yes?' Krogh said. 'I never play it.'

'Half-past nine,' Anthony said. 'The last news in London.'

Kate turned the pointer. 'A depression advancing from Iceland,' a smooth anonymous voice said and was cut off.

'Good old London.'

'There's Moscow,' Kate said, swinging the pointer; 'there's Hilversum, Berlin, Paris....'

'Aimer à loisir, Aimer et mourir,

Au pays qui te ressemble.'

'The Duke of York, opening the new premises of the Gas Light and Coke...'

The voices went out one by one like candles on a Christmas cake, white, waxen, guttering in the atmospherics over the North Sea, the Baltic, the local storms on the East Prussian plains, rain beating on Tannenburg, autumn lightning over Westminster, a whistle on the ether.

'You can always tell Paris,' Anthony said, 'aimer, aimer, aimer.' 'Your deal, Mr. Farrant,' Hall said.

'But it was a good voice,' Gullie said reverently, 'a good voice.'[50]

Greene's implication here was that the international broadcasters offered geographic and linguistic exoticism through a reading of Charles Baudelaire's poem 'L'invitation au voyage', and while the BBC had, according to Greene,

---

[49] Briggs (1961), *The History of Broadcasting, Vol I*, pp. 322–4, and Briggs (1965), *The History of Broadcasting in the United Kingdom, Volume II, The Golden Age of Wireless*, Oxford: Oxford University Press, p. 370.
[50] Graham Greene ([1935] 1943), *England Made Me: A Novel*, Harmondsworth, Middlesex: Penguin, p. 179.

a smooth anonymous broadcast tone, it was up against some high-quality competition elsewhere on the dial.[51]

Part of the fabric of the home: Domesticity and social class

It was within the home where radio opened up and altered both the sonic and the media landscape. Previously, newspapers gave the news from the outside world, whilst pianos and gramophones provided home entertainment for those who could afford them. But these were each without the live element that radio offered. For such a stimulus, people had to travel outside to public meetings, church services, the pub, dance halls, concerts, sporting fixtures and the theatre. For some writers, the arrival of the radio into the home was wireless' deterministic moment, bringing a permanent change to the domestic environment. For example, the link between ownership, listening and class was observed in the novel *Blindness*, by Henry Green (1926). Another of his books is discussed in the following text, but in *Blindness* the radio was a hoped-for luxury that only gave an illusion of social advancement. It was a symbol of down-at-heel suburbia and all the negative lower-middle-class meanings of 'shabby-genteel'.[52] The stepson had lost his sight in an accident, and those around him faced decisions about how to care for him. One option, to sell their rural home and move nearer to the city, was immediately ruled out: 'To be blind in one of those poky little suburban villas, with a wireless set, and with aeroplanes going overhead, and motor bikes and gramophones. No.'[53] The implication being that even if owning a radio was by the late 1920s an aspiration, the reality was that suburbia brought with it its own sufferings. Radio listening was linked to neighbourhood and class, and the family would rather suffer poverty than a utilitarian soulless modernity. This representation of the hopes of the working class was echoed in some of the writings discussed in the next chapter.

The insertion of radio into daily habits did not happen without comment. Rose Macaulay, in her novel *Crewe Train* (1926), offered a comedy of manners about upper-middle-class society. The narrative featured a tomboyish girl Denham,

---

[51] Keith Williams (1996), *British Writers and the Media, 1930–1945*, Basingstoke, Hampshire: Macmillan, pp. 57, 120, and 141-2. For a discussion of the emergence of the 'BBC announcer', see Lynda Mugglestone (2008), 'Spoken English and the BBC: In the Beginning', *Arbeiten aus Anglistik und Amerikanistik*, 33 (2): 197–215.
[52] Trotter, *Literature in the First Media Age*, p. 171.
[53] Henry Green ([1926] 2001), *Blindness*, Dallas, TX: Dalkey Archive Press, pp. 60-1.

raised by her father in Andorra, who married a man called Arnold and slowly began an unhappy transition into metropolitan London life. In a scene early in their relationship, Macaulay used technology to highlight their character differences:

> Arnold put on a pair of ear-phones, and prepared to listen to Mozart's Sonata in D Major, interpreted by Mr. Norman O'Neill. He did not mind how many things he did at once, such as talking, doing puzzles, and listening to music. Denham seldom listened in; music bored her rather, and speeches more. She asked Arnold, however, to tell her when the weather bulletin came on; that was normally the only part of the programme to which she cared to listen. Arnold tried to make her listen to some of the news and speeches, because he found them funny, and wanted her to laugh at them with him, but it was no use, Denham lacked that kind of sense of humour. Perhaps she lacked every kind; she laughed neither at nor with things, was amused neither by P. G. Wodehouse, Paul Morand, Charles Chaplin, nor sentimental solemnities. In a world uproariously amusing she remained gravely intent on her own business. Arnold had to smile at his jokes by himself when they were alone together. It was a pity.[54]

In short, according to Macaulay the couple were mismatched: women did not have the patience to do technical things.[55] Instead, Denham still maintained an interest in the outdoor life she once knew as a child. The author was also inserting into this passage real names of celebrities in order to fix wireless listening into a contemporary reality of the age. The solitary nature of the characters in this scene was highlighted by the lack of a valve amplifier and a loudspeaker to allow joint listening. Additional headphones ('ear-phones') would have been possible but would have required some replugging of the outputs of the receiver.[56] Macaulay was a prolific writer and critic (see Chapter 4), and regularly contributed to BBC programmes, often as a panellist on shows such as the *Brains Trust*. She understood how the radio was a dubious marker of technological modernity, just as Henry Green had. In her 1928 novel *Keeping Up Appearances*, Macaulay's lead character, an upwardly mobile working-class journalist and writer who hid the fact that she wrote lowbrow women's fiction, considered the financial rewards of her vocation and her first novel: 'If *Summer's Over* and its successors should afford them journeys abroad, feed and clothe their little ones, pay their income tax, their gambling debts, their car and wireless licences [. . .] these words would

[54] Rose Macaulay ([1926] 1938), *Crewe Train*, Harmondsworth, Middlesex: Penguin, p. 101.
[55] See also Paddy Scannell and David Cardiff (1991), *A Social History of British Broadcasting, Volume One: 1922-1939, Serving the Nation*, Oxford: Basil Blackwell, pp. 356–9.
[56] Moores, *Media and Everyday Life*, pp. 45–7.

not have been written in vain.'[57] Here Macaulay had listed a series of consumer items that were desirable to middle-class households, a trend that subsequent commentators have observed in writings of the period: 'New technologies such as the cinema, radio broadcasting, and the gramophone began to re-orientate the daily life of many lower-middle-class households towards leisure and recreation.'[58] Macaulay's novel was published six years after the start of British radio broadcasting, and she had confidently added the technology to her list of items which formed part of aspirational middle-class society as Winifred Holtby and George Orwell were later to do (see Chapter 3).

For the upper classes, wireless technology could be used as a retreat from pain and isolation. In *Lady Chatterley's Lover* (1928), D. H. Lawrence had Sir Clifford, the cuckolded husband of her ladyship, finding solace in this technology which brought the public sphere into his home: 'He preferred the radio, which he had installed at some expense, with a good deal of success at last. He could sometimes get Madrid, or Frankfurt, even there in the uneasy Midlands.'[59] For Sir Clifford, it was the wireless broadcasts which consoled him and made up for a lack of human contact. For Lawrence, it was a recognition of the importance of new technology which represented both connection and dis-connection.[60] The writer fictionalized the act of listening to foreign stations, not just the BBC, emphasizing again that the Corporation did not have a monopoly of the airwaves in the interwar years.[61] In the late 1920s, listening to the wireless was becoming part of life at home, albeit in this example a rather sad retreat from a failing marriage and an attempt to find solace in a new media technology. As if to reflect ahead to three decades of public reaction to *Lady Chatterley*, D. H. Lawrence wryly commented on censorship and moral agency in a poem from 1929 called 'Broadcasting to the G. B. P.' (Great British Public), which consisted of extracts from a number of nursery rhymes, each interrupted with lines such as the following:

Stop that at once!

You'll give the Great British Public a nervous shock![62]

---

[57] Rose Macaulay ([1928] 1986), *Keeping Up Appearances*, London: Methuen, p. 132.
[58] Xiaotian Jin (2014), 'Undoing Shame: Lower-Middle-Class Young Women and Class Dynamics in the Interwar Novels by Rose Macaulay and Elizabeth Bowen', *Women's Studies*, 43 (6): 697.
[59] D. H. Lawrence ([1928] 2010), *Lady Chatterley's Lover*, London: Penguin, p. 108.
[60] Aleksandr Prigozhin (2018), 'Listening in: D. H. Lawrence and the Wireless', *MFS Modern Fiction Studies*, 64 (2): 264–85; Trotter, *Literature in the First Media Age*, p. 115.
[61] See, for example, Street, *Crossing the Ether*.
[62] D. H. Lawrence ([1929] 2004), 'Broadcasting to the G. B. P.', in Seán Street, ed. (2004), *Radio Waves: Poems Celebrating the Wireless*, London: Enitharmon Press, pp. 49–50.

This suggested that Lawrence was aware that radio broadcasting, too, could offend just as easily as it could be a comforter to the solitary. The use of radio by Lawrence's Sir Clifford was similar to a character in Henry Green's 1929 novel, *Living*. Here it was listened to by the overbearing owner of the working-class boarding house, Mr Craigan, on his own. Like Sir Clifford, he found escape from reality:

> Lily Gates was saying half smiling to Jim Dale it gave her creeps Mr Craigan always sitting at home of an evening. He listened to the wireless every night of the week except Mondays. And look what Sunday was, was as much as they could do to get him out to the Lickeys she said. No when you asked he said he would not come, and what for? all the morning listening to preachers in foreign countries, why when you didn't know the language she couldn't see what was in it, and the afternoon and the evening the same, right till he went to his room, she said.[63]

Craigan wanted connection for connection's sake and had become obsessed, like Sir Clifford. Solitary listening, lack of authority and failed leadership were linked together by both Green and Lawrence, each having their characters withdraw from their physical surroundings by tuning into the radio.[64] However, E. M. Forster, a novelist and writer who contributed material to the BBC from the 1920s to the early 1960s, noted in 1928 with some regret that radio and the modern world meant: 'We do not get away from each other as we did.'[65] The wireless had, for him, become unavoidable and everywhere: an irrevocable reality of modernity. It would be a view reflected down the decades by other writers.

Agatha Christie observed the deadly effects of radio listening in her short story 'Wireless' (1926).[66] A nephew plotted to kill his aunt by scaring her to death with strange voices on the radio, in an attempt to inherit her fortune. Christie highlighted the generational differences by describing how the young man enjoyed fiddling with the wireless, whilst the elderly aunt said, 'I do not

---

[63] Henry Green ([1929] 1991), *Living*, London: Harvill/HarperCollins, p. 45.
[64] Trotter, *Literature in the First Media Age*, pp. 203–4; Williams, *British Writers and the Media*, p. 65.
[65] E. M. Forster (1985), *Commonplace Book*, ed. Philip Gardner, Aldershot, Hampshire: Wildwood House, p. 38. See also Debra Rae Cohen, Michael Coyle and Jane Lewty (2009), 'Introduction: Signing On', in Cohen, Coyle and Lewty, eds, *Broadcasting Modernism*, Gainesville, FL: University Press of Florida, p. 5; and Mary Lago (1990), 'E. M. Forster and the BBC', *The Yearbook of English Studies*, 20: 132–51.
[66] Agatha Christie ([1926] 1964), 'Wireless', in Agatha Christie, ed., *The Hound of Death*, Glasgow: Fontana/Collins, pp. 75–88.

know that I care for these new-fangled things.'[67] In her 1931 novel *The Sittaford Mystery*, Christie used radio imagery to describe personality differences between two characters. A young journalist called Enderby told the girl he was in love with to be quiet: 'Will you stop talking, Emily? It's like a talk to Young Men on the Wireless!'[68] The implication here was that the BBC radio talks – which were often fifteen minutes of scripted monologue read by a writer or intellectual personality – were boring, patronizing and difficult to understand, a similar reaction suggested in Norman Hunter's Professor Branestawm story. Emily declined Enderby's proposal of marriage, explaining that she loved another. As the literary historian Alison Light observed about Christie, 'Her stories suggest[ed] an inter-war imagination in which the middle class [were] the modern class, less sentimental, more unbuttoned than their pre-1914 versions.'[69] In *The Sittaford Mystery*, for the heroine – who had just solved the case – to refuse the hand of an eligible bachelor (even if he was a newspaper reporter), and instead marry the one she truly loved, was an example of this exciting new world Christie was documenting.

Finally, one film documentary placed the Corporation visually at the heart of society. *BBC: The Voice of Britain* (1935) was produced by Stuart Legg and John Grierson, the latter a leading and highly influential member of the British documentary film movement of the period.[70] *The Voice of Britain* was one of the most technically accomplished films of its type, with synchronized sound, swift 'counterpoint' editing and cost more than £7,000 to make.[71] If *Death at Broadcasting House* had been the fiction, then *The Voice of Britain* was the face of the new Corporation, visually cementing the BBC in contemporary political, intellectual and cultural life.[72] However, at the time it was not well received by one critic, who said:

---

[67] Christie, 'Wireless', p. 76.

[68] Agatha Christie ([1931] 1965), *The Sittaford Mystery*, London: Pan Books/Collins, p. 202. For a discussion of the early development of 'talk' on the radio, see Scannell and Cardiff, *A Social History of British Broadcasting*, pp. 153–78.

[69] Alison Light (1991), *Forever England: Femininity, Literature and Conservatism Between the Wars*, London: Routledge, p. 86.

[70] Stuart Legg was also the director of the documentary. It was made by the GPO Film Unit, a division of the British General Post Office. The GPO was responsible for collecting the ten shillings radio licence payments from households. The unit's most famous film was the documentary *Night Mail* (1936), set to the poetry of W. H. Auden.

[71] Ros Cranson (2008), 'BBC: The Voice of Britain', in *Addressing the Nation: The GPO Film Unit Collection*, Vol. 1, DVD booklet, London: BFI, pp. 51–2.

[72] Richards, *Cinema and Radio*, pp. 147–9.

A pleasant film from an entertainment point of view, but with no vast profundity of implication and providing us with no special insight into broadcasting or the methods of the B.B.C. The impressionistic sequence of events is at times rather disturbing, as it is difficult to know exactly what is happening or why.[73]

This suggested that there was an unmet desire by audiences to know and to understand the processes involved in radio broadcasting. Even so, the film offered a chance to see some of the names behind the microphone. People such as J. B. Priestley, G. K. Chesterton, H. G. Wells and George Bernard Shaw. It also featured Henry Hall and the BBC Dance Orchestra, but in a nod to their lower-brow status they were shown directly after the more formal BBC Symphony Orchestra. One media commentator later observed, 'Between them [the two orchestras] represented the extreme edges of rarefied and popular culture then projected by the BBC.'[74] One message sent out by *The Voice of Britain* was about the essence and essentiality of time. The link was made between the developing obsession with timekeeping in broadcasting, mentioned by Norman Hunter in his Professor Branestawm story, and the eventual realization of the need to begin and end programmes at the exact 'junction' so that transmitters could be switched cleanly. Such an attention to detail emerged in both live and pre-recorded BBC radio programming and was a storyline in Arthur Askey's 1942 film *Back-Room Boy*, discussed in Chapter 4.

This chapter has provided examples of how writers set about questioning what this new medium was, how radio could be fallible and prone to errors, how it was both everywhere and nowhere and how it quickly became part of life at home – all within the first thirteen years of the BBC being created. In the next chapter, the way audiences listened from the mid-1930s onwards is examined in more detail: how they talked about radio shows, and how they listened both at home and at major public events. Each reflected that radio was now becoming an established medium in British society.

---

[73] 'BBC – The Voice of Britain' (1935) *The Monthly Film Bulletin*, London: British Film Institute, September 1935, 2 (20): 117.
[74] Charlotte Higgins (2015), *This New Noise: The Extraordinary Birth and Troubled Life of the BBC*, London: Guardian Books, p. 39. Henry Hall was the director of the BBC Dance Orchestra from 1932 to 1937. See George Nobbs (1972), *The Wireless Stars*, Norwich, Norfolk: Wensum Books, pp. 43–51. Hall's 1935 film *Music Hath Charms* is mentioned in the next chapter.

3

Developing ways of listening
Class and distinction, 1935 to 1938

Forming listening habits: From the personal to the public

This chapter considers how novelists and filmmakers depicted radio both at home and in public places. Four aspects of radio listening are identified: firstly, the experience of listening attentively alone; secondly, talking about the radio with another person who had not heard the broadcast and so turning 'the radio' into a conversation topic; thirdly, there were authors during this period who pointed out that owning a radio was, as Rose Macaulay had hinted in the previous chapter, both an essential item in the home and an indicator of social advancement or at the very least the aspiration of it. Finally, the radio was used in the 1930s for communal listening, with varying degrees of success, including to a major event such as a royal jubilee.

Reviewing the long twentieth century, the historian David Edgerton said, 'In the rich world the household was to take up technologies of leisure such as the radio, TV and video recorders much faster than washing machines or vacuum cleaners.'[1] This trend had started early. There had been both intrigue and enthusiasm in the late 1920s and early 1930s, as the radio had become part of everyday life. Programmes engaged with listeners across Britain, and the wireless altered daily routines and changed how social values were transmitted and shared.[2] This 'domestication' was not a technologically determined event but was a negotiated process. The wireless had to be 'house-trained' and integrated into

---

[1] David Edgerton (2006), *The Shock of the Old: Technology and Global History Since 1900*, London: Profile, p. 55.
[2] Shaun Moores (2000), *Media and Everyday Life in Modern Society*, Edinburgh: Edinburgh University Press, pp. 42-7. See also Todd Avery (2006), *Radio Modernism: Literature, Ethics, and the BBC, 1922-1938*, Aldershot, Hampshire: Ashgate, p. 6, and Ross McKibbin (1998), *Classes and Cultures: England 1918-1951*, Oxford: Oxford University Press, p. 458.

daily routines and environments.[3] For example, broadcasts by the BBC in the late 1920s expanded to an hour at lunchtime and from half-past-five until half-past-ten in the evening on weekdays. Sundays were limited to two hours of orchestral music in the afternoon, and evening programmes from half-past-eight to half-past-ten. By 1935, this had become continuous broadcasting from ten in the morning until midnight on weekdays, and half-past twelve until eleven at night on Sundays.[4] With his tongue firmly in his cheek, Evelyn Waugh remarked upon radio's immediacy in a scene in *Scoop: A Novel About Journalism* (1938). It was a comedy about the sometimes inept role of foreign correspondents, and it was a story which resonated amongst fellow journalists then, as now.[5] The naïve hero of the story, William Boot, asked his senior editor about the printing presses whilst on a tour of the basement of the newspaper's London headquarters, and added, 'I mean, you have to get it written and printed and corrected and everything all on the same day, otherwise the news would become stale. People would have heard it on the wireless.'[6] The idea of the radio altering the evening routines of reading the newspaper, talking, making music or playing gramophone records was still novel. News summaries began only in the evenings by agreement with the major newspaper proprietors who feared earlier radio bulletins would harm their morning sales. The wireless, as a domesticated media, was now able to offer the public into the private: it was a physical item that sat in the intimacy of the living room and offered the experiences, sounds and opinions from outside: from the political meeting, the dance hall and the church.[7]

Winifred Holtby and the fictionalizing of radio

The novel *South Riding* was set in Yorkshire in northern England in the early 1930s and was published in 1936, shortly after Winifred Holtby died of renal failure at

---

[3] Thomas Berker, Maren Hartmann, Yves Punie and Katie Ward (2006), 'Introduction', in Berker et al., eds, *Domestication of Media and Technology*, Maidenhead, Berkshire: Open University Press, p. 2.

[4] For the early development of BBC schedules and the introduction of listener research, see Paddy Scannell and David Cardiff (1991), *A Social History of British Broadcasting, Volume One: 1922–1939, Serving the Nation*, Oxford: Basil Blackwell, pp. 370–80.

[5] Sarah Lonsdale (2016), *The Journalist in British Fiction & Film: Guarding the Guardians from 1900 to the Present*, London: Bloomsbury, pp. 116–17.

[6] Evelyn Waugh ([1938] 1943), *Scoop: A Novel About Journalism*, Harmondsworth, Middlesex: Penguin, p. 30. See also Chapter 5, where the 1957 Waugh novel *The Ordeal of Gilbert Pinfold* paints a negative picture of BBC radio.

[7] Berker et al., *Domestication of Media*, p. 4.

the age of thirty-seven.[8] In order to give the story a contemporary context, she included mentions of the entertainers Elsie and Doris Waters and the BBC's royal commentator Commander Stephen King-Hall, who brought a touch of reality to her fiction. The novel had a panoramic sweep and documentary feel, with a four-and-a-half-page list of characters printed at the beginning of the book to help the reader.[9] The wireless was important to Holtby herself as well as the characters in her novel: it was there in the home; the sound of light classical music drifted through exterior scenes; and in the public park in the town as loudspeakers carried royal commentary to the crowds. She was fascinated by it both as a listener, a contributor and as a supporter of women in the new media.[10] Holtby herself found work in print journalism and at the BBC, which were male-dominated workplaces.[11] Indeed, Virginia Woolf picked up on the issue of women in the media and the Establishment in her 1938 essay *Three Guineas*: 'If [. . .] we turn on the wireless of the daily press we shall hear what answers the fathers . . . are making to those questions now. "Homes are the real places for women".'[12] As well as regarding radio and print journalism as patriarchal domains, Woolf also thought speaking on the wireless served somehow to destroy the supremacy of the written word. She took part in just three BBC broadcasts.[13]

Solitary listening

Winifred Holtby appreciated that having the wireless switched on and tuned in at home was an important form of engagement, and indeed could be a comfort

---

[8] Lisa Regan (2010), 'Introduction', in Lisa Regan, ed., *Winifred Holtby, 'A Woman in Her Time': Critical Essays*, Newcastle upon Tyne: Cambridge Scholars Publishing, p. 2. A film version of *South Riding* was made in 1938. See Anthony Aldgate and Jeffrey Richards (1999), *Best of British: Cinema and Society from 1930 to the Present*, London: IB Tauris, pp. 39–54. The movie version made no mention of radio listening. The novel was also adapted into two TV dramatizations in 1974 (ITV) and 2011 (BBC), and four BBC radio versions, including plays and readings, in 1949, 1971, 1974 and 1999.
[9] Winifred Holtby ([1936] 1954), *South Riding: An English Landscape*, Glasgow: Fontana, pp. 13–17.
[10] Jane Lewty (2002), 'Broadcasting Modernity: Eloquent Listening in the Early Twentieth Century', PhD diss., University of Glasgow, p. 170; Gill Fildes (2010), 'Winifred Holtby and "The Voice of God": A Writer's View of Radio and Cinema between the Wars', in Lisa Regan, ed., *Winifred Holtby, 'A Woman in Her Time': Critical Essays*, Newcastle upon Tyne: Cambridge Scholars Publishing, p. 89; Kate Murphy (2016), *Behind the Wireless: A History of Early Women at the BBC*, London: Palgrave Macmillan, p. 45.
[11] Murphy, *Behind the Wireless*, p. 117.
[12] Virginia Woolf ([1938] 1966), *Three Guineas*, Orlando, FL: Harcourt Brace, pp. 140–1.
[13] Kate Whitehead (1990), 'Broadcasting Bloomsbury', *The Yearbook of English Studies*, 20: 123. For a discussion of writers including Eliot, Woolf, Pound, Orwell and Beckett, who contributed material to the BBC including talks, scripts and plays, see Debra Rae Cohen, Michael Coyle and Jane Lewty, eds. (2009), *Broadcasting Modernism*, Gainesville, FL: University Press of Florida.

in times of pain, providing an intimacy with public voices from far away. This was also understood by the British politician Stanley Baldwin, who was prime minster three times in the interwar years. He was known for his skill in delivering his radio talks in the form of a 'fireside chat', addressing the listener directly.[14] *Radio Pictorial*, a weekly listings magazine, declared in 1938 that wireless listening was 'the bachelor woman's answer to "loneliness"'.[15] Married women found comfort too. One avid radio listener in *South Riding* was Lily Sawdon, who with her husband Tom ran a local pub where business was doing badly. Eventually Tom began to drink too much, whilst for Lily the pain from her untreated cancer had become unbearable:

> On her good days she would sit and read or listen to the wireless. It was dangerous to sew or move about too much; she might startle to life the sleeping pain. But voices came to her out of the silence, singers and jesters and actors from Broadcasting House. She acquired favourites and enemies. She loved the songs she had known as a girl. [. . .] She found certain comics funny. Mrs Waters' daughters made her laugh, and Lily Morris she found vulgar but a real scream.[16]

For Lily Sawdon, the radio was an escape from poor health and a failing relationship. It was also an engagement with voices and people who, to her, were real and very much part of her life.

Radio's ability to heal was the underlying storyline in a 1937 British film *Command Performance*. In a slightly convoluted plot, Arthur Tracy, a professional singer playing himself, had a fictional mental breakdown and ran away from his heavy schedule. He went to stay, incognito, with a group of gypsies where he fell in love with Susan (Lilli Palmer). Tracy ended up singing a special song on the radio dedicated to Susan's little sister, who lay in her caravan recovering after a serious car accident. At this point, it became a story about solitary listening and the therapeutic power of radio. The girl heard the song, got better and the lovers were reunited. However, in addition, the film showed to cinema audiences what the whole range of listening looked like: the viewer could see other audiences

---

[14] John Ramsden (1978), *A History of the Conservative Party. Vol. 3: The Age of Balfour and Baldwin 1902–1940*, London: Longman, p. 208. See also Simon Elmes ([2012] 2013), *Hello Again . . . Nine Decades of Radio Voices*, London: Arrow, p. 95.

[15] Quoted in Maggie Andrews (2012), *Domesticating the Airwaves: Broadcasting, Domesticity and Femininity*, London: Continuum, p. 15. *Radio Pictorial* ran from January 1934 to September 1939 and gave the schedules for all the European stations broadcasting in English, unlike the *Radio Times*, which only listed BBC radio programmes. See also Justine Lloyd (2020), *Gender and Media in the Broadcast Age: Women's Radio Programming at the BBC, CBC, and ABC*, New York: Bloomsbury, pp. 12 and 19.

[16] Holtby, *South Riding*, p. 313.

including those watching Tracy sing in the theatre, the backstage staff observing in the wings, the worried family next to the wireless in the caravan and the unconscious child who heard the broadcast and miraculously opened her eyes. This cinematic display of listening became a trend in other movies.

The radio could also console the solitary traveller far from home. Louis MacNeice's book *I Crossed the Minch* (1938) was an account of his trip to the Hebrides, a series of Scottish islands he apparently knew very little about. His writing was both self-aware and self-deprecating – yet he recognized that he was the misplaced outsider:

> The next day in Stornoway I rushed to the stationer's to try to buy a copy of the *Listener*.
>
> QUESTION: What did you listen to?
>
> ANSWER: I listened to the voice of London enunciating facts for the masses with a soi-disant impartiality. I heard my late landlord in Birmingham, a professor of economics, discuss the industrial Midlands. I heard an art critic whom I know discuss the portrait of a writer whom I know, painted by a painter whom I know. And the glorious fact dawned on me that really I knew everybody. I knew hardly a soul in the Hebrides, but that's not where *everybody* lives. How lovely to belong to that wider civilisation – how lovely to belong to that clique![17]

MacNeice was born in Belfast in 1907, and was known as a poet and playwright with links, during his days at Oxford, to W. H. Auden and C. Day-Lewis. He worked for the BBC as a radio producer from 1941 until his death in 1963.[18] For MacNeice, the Corporation's reassuringly metropolitan high culture was a comfort on a journey to an unfamiliar place and served to highlight the otherness of the Scottish islanders. The literary historian Keith Williams said, 'MacNeice encapsulated the gross disproportionality between BBC claims to provide a National Service and BBC exclusiveness as it sounded in the regions.'[19] Indeed, figures for the distribution of radio licences across the country between 1931 and 1938 suggested the majority of the BBC audience lived in the Home

---

[17] Louis MacNeice ([1938] 2007), *I Crossed the Minch*, Edinburgh: Polygon, p. 8. Emphasis in original. *The Listener* (1929–1991) was a weekly BBC literary magazine.
[18] Alan Bennett (1990), 'Louis MacNeice', in *Poetry in Motion*, London: Channel 4 Television, pp. 71–84.
[19] Keith Williams (1996), *British Writers and the Media, 1930–1945*, Basingstoke, Hampshire: Macmillan, p. 64.

Counties and the Midlands.[20] Metro-centricity was to be an issue which would dog the Corporation for decades.

Another lonely character in Holtby's *South Riding* was the school matron who dreamt of retirement: a happy alternative to her life at the High School, when 'she would take a little cottage, or rooms with some nice woman; she would have a wireless set, a dog, a subscription to Boots' Library'.[21] Her dreams were borne out of her working conditions at the school where she felt victimized by both her colleagues and the girls. One evening she returned to her lodgings and unhappily discovered that 'Her wireless battery had run down and she had decided to economise by selling the whole thing'.[22] It was as if without radio her life had fallen apart. The matron and the wife of the pub landlord in this novel were chronically lonely women. Radio, according to Holtby, was a form of escapism as well as part of the dream of middle-class comfort. The literary historian Jane Lewty noted, 'The self-contained radio listener in the multitude is a feature of *South Riding*, the individual who may reach a plateau of understanding, not chiefly a solution, but a brief respite from angst.'[23] The wireless in *South Riding* provided a sociability in the midst of the private sphere. The radio was able to bring the sounds of audiences laughing, and members of the public talking, into the home and provide comfort.

Radio as a conversation-starter and as a marker of social class

It was this 'sociability' of radio programmes which encouraged solitary listeners to share their experiences.[24] For Winifred Holtby's characters, talking about the radio was an attempt to reach out from a personal listening space to connect with others. In this, she recognized that wireless listening was a catalyst for conversations in the same way as people talked about movies, music hall acts and newspaper articles with one another. An example in *South Riding* again involved Lily Sawdon:

---

[20] Mark Pegg (1983), *Broadcasting and Society 1918–1939*, Beckenham, Kent: Croom Helm, pp. 10–11; Seán Street (2006), *Crossing the Ether: Pre-War Public Service Radio and Commercial Competition in the UK*, Eastleigh, Hampshire: John Libbey, p. 141.
[21] Holtby, *South Riding*, pp. 270–1. Boots the Chemist ran a private book lending library in its nationwide chain of branches from 1898 to 1966.
[22] Holtby, *South Riding*, p. 323.
[23] Lewty, 'Broadcasting Modernity', p. 238.
[24] Paddy Scannell (1996), *Radio, Television and Modern Life: A Phenomenological Approach*, Oxford: Blackwell, p. 25.

It happened that Lily had had a good day [with her cancer]. She was thinking: Perhaps it's all nonsense; perhaps I shall grow out of it.

She sat darning stockings and listening to the radio.

'Oh, Tom, do stop and listen a bit,' she pleaded, her charming head on one side, her lips parted. 'It's Elsie and Doris Waters. They are a scream.'[25]

The radio programme thus became a way for Lily to attract her husband Tom's attention and engage him in conversation. It elicited in her an excited response to a comedy act, whom if they lacked sophistication certainly made up for it in their broad appeal.[26] Tom's response was unknown; however, Holtby was perhaps describing the reality of mass listening: a world away from the highbrow Reithian values usually ascribed to the BBC in this period – for Lily, this was a moment of pure entertainment, without any edifying information or education. The Waters sisters were the popular radio act Gert and Daisy, who later became regulars for a number of years on the BBC show *Workers' Playtime* (1941–64) on the Home Service, broadcast three times a week from a factory canteen.

Variety shows such as this, as well as musical entertainment, were key broadcast moments for thousands of listeners. In the movie *Music Hath Charms* (1935), the bandleader Henry Hall (also mentioned in the previous chapter) was shown during a 'typical' day rehearsing the BBC Dance Orchestra for a regular broadcast scheduled at a quarter past five each weekday, just before the first news at six o'clock. In an exchange between the bandleader and one of his clarinet players, he discussed their popularity with typical self-deprecating humour: 'Hm! All kinds of people listen to us from the North Pole to the equator. [. . .] I suppose I've got a lot to answer for.' Later Hall asserted that his music cheered millions of people up when they were depressed and lonely. The movie, lacking any solid narrative thread, went on to show band members in a number of vignettes, from the dramatic to the comic. Cinema viewers were able to watch 'listeners' interacting with Hall's radio show by seeing people just like themselves on screen talking to others about it, enjoying the music together, and dancing. This was again an example of contemporary movies showing audiences in the act of listening, and is discussed in a moment, but, first, another popular bandleader, who performed on the BBC and Radio Luxembourg, was Jack Hylton. He and his band were the stars of the film *She Shall Have Music* (1935), about live radio

---

[25] Holtby, *South Riding*, p. 115.
[26] Andrew Crisell (2002), *An Introductory History of British Broadcasting*, 2nd edn, London: Routledge, p. 40.

broadcasts from a cruise ship – foretelling, perhaps, the offshore radio of the 1960s. The overall tone of this, and the Henry Hall movie, bore comparison to pop music movies of the early 1960s which promoted acts such as The Beatles (*A Hard Day's Night*, 1964), Cliff Richard (*Expresso Bongo*, 1959, and others), the Dave Clark Five (*Catch Us If You Can*, 1965) and the Small Faces (*Dateline Diamonds*, 1965); the latter is discussed in Chapter 5.

Winifred Holtby understood that conversation about the radio could also be a social leveller. In one scene from *South Riding*, she combined talk about the radio with a popular neutral topic, the weather, often used by the British as a way of avoiding deep conversation. An exchange took place between the squire, Robert Carne, and his Master of Foxhounds, the latter being a member of the agricultural working class. As they gathered for the start of a local hunt meeting at the village war memorial, the two started chatting. The Master of Foxhounds began the conversation:

> 'Thought it was going to be frost. Said so last night on the damned wireless.'
> 'Never listen to the things,' said Carne. 'Don't believe in 'em.'
> 'You're right. You're dead right.'[27]

Holtby allowed her characters to have an easy disdain for radio in this briefest of exchanges. It may well have been the case that both the Master of Foxhounds and the country squire could indeed have enjoyed listening to various radio programmes, but they were unable to articulate similar pleasures to one another: an example of how *South Riding* was about status rather than just class and how the social construct of their roles forbade making such connections.[28] Another character, a corrupt businessman and politician Alderman Anthony Snaith, dismissed his working-class constituents and their aspirations: 'These tenants in our council houses belong to a new generation – the age of the easy purchase system, of wireless and electricity and Austin Sevens. [...] They *want* libraries and schools and clinics and cheap secondary education.'[29] Such comments harked back to observations by Rose Macaulay, mentioned in the previous chapter.

---

[27] Holtby, *South Riding*, p. 95.
[28] Nattie Liliana Golubov (2002), 'British Women Writers and the Public Sphere between the Wars: Winifred Holtby, Storm Jameson, Naomi Mitchison, and Rebecca West', PhD diss., Queen Mary College, University of London, p. 134.
[29] Holtby, *South Riding*, p. 439. Emphasis in original.

At the movies: People like us listening to the wireless

Films already mentioned, such as *Music Hath Charms* and *Command Performance*, meant that the interwar years were when 'the English began to see themselves and [. . .] their cultural behaviours', at the cinema.[30] They could now listen to themselves on the radio too. The experience of hearing a voice reproduced was a crucial moment; something Holtby had already noticed, 'Like most of her generation and locality, Elsie [the maidservant at Maythorpe Hall] was trilingual. She talked B.B.C. English to her employer, Cinema American to her companions, and Yorkshire dialect to old milkmen like Eli Dickson.'[31] Characters like Elsie could visit the movies and hear 'northern' voices such as George Formby, mentioned later in this chapter, as well as Hollywood stars.[32] J. B. Priestley underlined this point in his book *English Journey* (1934), where he made distinctions between the old rural life, the industrial towns and the emergence of a new society. Everywhere he travelled he saw the impact of popular movies on life, especially through speech and language:

> The third England, I concluded, was the new post-war England, belonging far more to the age itself than to this particular island. America, I supposed, was its real birthplace. This is the England of arterial and by-pass roads, of filling stations and factories that look like exhibition buildings, of giant cinemas and dance halls and cafés, bungalows with tiny garages, cocktail bars, Woolworths, motor-coaches, wireless, hiking, factory girls looking like actresses, greyhound racing and dirt tracks, swimming pools, and everything given away for cigarette coupons.[33]

Aside from the Americanization of culture, he included the wireless as one of the intrusions into what he regarded as traditional society. It was felt by some that BBC English was so far removed from any form of daily speech of the era as to be probably 'based on a rather artificial conception of the English of the upper classes'.[34] The formality of received pronunciation on the radio was mocked in a song by The Western Brothers, 'We're Frightfully BBC' (1935). It also satirized

---

[30] Alison Light (1991), *Forever England: Femininity, Literature and Conservatism Between the Wars*, London: Routledge, p. 215.
[31] Holtby, *South Riding*, p. 35.
[32] McKibbin, *Classes and Cultures*, pp. 511–13.
[33] J. B. Priestley (1934), *English Journey*, London: William Heinemann, p. 401. His somewhat downbeat description of 1930's England bears a resemblance to Chris Petit's visualization in the 1979 movie *Radio On*, discussed in Chapter 7.
[34] John Stevenson (1984), *British Society 1914–1945*, London: Penguin, p. 344.

the Oxbridge metro-centricity of the Corporation, as the comedy duo recounted in exaggerated clipped tones how they had both been expelled (sent down) from their university college for an unspecified misdemeanour.

A barbed comment about radio listening came in John Betjeman's poem 'Slough' (1937), which was well known for its couplet suggesting that the Berkshire town and its inhabitants should be razed to the ground by dropping bombs on it. The poem also took a swipe at the office clerks who lacked any cultural capital. Betjeman said, 'It's not their fault they do not know / The birdsong from the radio', suggesting that intellectually uplifting programmes were wasted on the lower classes.[35] Such a view questioned John Reith's vision to provide public service broadcasting that gave what it was thought listeners needed, rather than what they actually wanted.[36] The reality may well have been that listeners who craved easy-listening entertainment simply tuned to another station when the 'boring' programmes appeared on the BBC.

The cultural capital of radio listening was also referred to by George Orwell, in his novel *Keep the Aspidistra Flying*. The central character, Gordon Comstock, tried to reject the trappings of consumer society – including owning a wireless set – and to fight against any attempts at social advancement:

> That was what it meant to worship the money-god! To settle down, to Make Good, to sell your soul for a villa and an aspidistra! To turn into the typical little bowler-hatted sneak [...] who slips home by the six-fifteen to a supper of cottage pie and stewed tinned pears, half an hour's listening-in to the BBC Symphony Concert, and then perhaps a spot of licit sexual intercourse if his wife 'feels in the mood'! What a fate![37]

Despite his character's criticisms of material culture, Orwell was another author who recognized the aspirational tendencies of society at large in the interwar years. In his non-fiction work *The Road to Wigan Pier*, he reflected on the poverty of parts of Britain, as well as the development of the consumer society and technology since the First World War: 'It is quite likely that fish-and-chips, art-silk stockings, tinned salmon, cut-price chocolate (five two-ounce bars for

---

[35] John Betjeman ([1937] 1983), 'Slough', in *John Betjeman's Collected Poems*, compiled by The Earl of Birkenhead, London: John Murray, pp. 22–4.

[36] See Williams, *British Writers and the Media*, p. 16 and pp. 26–7. Reith re-emphasized his original vision, of a public service that informed, educated and entertained, in his evidence to the parliamentary Ullswater Committee in 1935. See Ian McIntyre (1993), *The Expense of Glory: A Life of John Reith*, London: HarperCollins, p. 216.

[37] George Orwell ([1936] 1962), *Keep the Aspidistra Flying*, Harmondsworth, Middlesex: Penguin, p. 53.

sixpence), the movies, the radio, strong tea, and the Football Pools have between them averted revolution.'[38] Orwell was suggesting that such consumer goods were the cultural emollients, what he called 'the cheap palliatives' for the working class that softened them, pacified them and 'promoted the myth of capitalist progress'.[39] However, radio was more than this and for a class that was for the first time rising above poverty it represented an attainable luxury.[40] Listening was growing exponentially in popularity during the period, and the challenge for Reith and his BBC staff was to respond to the audience(s). The reality, according to Simon Frith, was that during the 1930s BBC radio became a mass medium not of cheap culture, but of the middlebrow: 'Balanced entertainment thus meant not pluralism, numerous different sorts of humour and music, but relaxation, programmes guaranteed soothing ("wholesome") by their exclusion of all excesses. Balance in light music meant, similarly, avoiding both sounds that were too highbrow *and* sounds that were too lowbrow.'[41]

Middlebrow culture in the form of programmes on the wireless had thus arrived in the home of the masses. The left-wing writer Harold Heslop acknowledged this in his 1935 novel *Last Cage Down*, which was about the coal-mining industry where he once worked. One character, Jim Cameron, complained that *Children's Hour* from the BBC was 'fatuous balderdash', and a 'terrible mush of humour and sentimentality', implying that it patronized both young people and families and failed to represent the realities of life as written about by writers of the left such as Heslop himself.[42] On the other hand, another character, who was Cameron's political rival with aspirations above his class, was described by Heslop as being, 'one of that new breed of men, who read diligently, who owned a radio and who was not greatly interested in the footling vaudeville programmes of the BBC'.[43] Wireless programmes had both the potential to alienate and inspire and to provide writers with opportunities

---

[38] George Orwell ([1937] 1962), *The Road to Wigan Pier*, Harmondsworth, Middlesex: Penguin, pp. 80–1.
[39] Orwell, *The Road to Wigan Pier*, p. 81. Williams, *British Writers and the Media*, p. 108. Orwell later worked for the BBC during the war. See Henry Mead (2014), '"Keeping our little corner clean": George Orwell's cultural broadcasts at the BBC', in Matthew Feldman, Erik Tonning and Henry Mead, eds., *Broadcasting in the Modernist era*, London: Bloomsbury Academic, pp. 169–94.
[40] Scannell and Cardiff, *A Social History of Broadcasting*, pp. 364–5.
[41] Simon Frith (1983), 'The Pleasures of the Hearth: The Making of BBC Light Entertainment', in Formations Editorial Collective, eds., *Formations of Pleasure*, London: Routledge & Kegan Paul, p. 121. Emphasis in original. See also David Cardiff (1988), 'Mass Middlebrow Laughter: The Origins of BBC comedy', *Media, Culture & Society* 10 (1): 41–60.
[42] Harold Heslop ([1935] 1984), *Last Cage Down*, London: Wishart Books, p. 194; Williams, *British Writers and the Media*, p. 65.
[43] Heslop, *Last Cage Down*, p. 42.

to highlight the distinctions between the cultural capital of the social classes. However, there were critics both within and outside the Corporation ready to make their feelings known.

Satirizing radio: Making fun of the new medium

The BBC had, by the mid-1930s, entrenched its position as the country's leading radio broadcaster. Indeed, 'During the interwar years the BBC became the pre-eminent social and cultural conduit for the nation, bringing programmes as diverse as political debates, dance band concerts and poetry readings into the home'.[44] However, it faced sustained competition from the European stations and became a figure of fun in a number of films of the period. Will Hay's send-up of Lord Reith in the movie *Radio Parade of 1935* was called Lord Garlon (a play on the words Garland / Wreath / Reith). The radio station was the *National Broadcasting Group* which gave the acronym NBG – at the time widely understood to mean 'No Bloody Good'.[45] Hay played a befuddled character who preferred to avoid any contact with both his listeners and his staff. He arrived in his office at eight o'clock and only came out to change the sign on his office from 'Do not disturb' to 'Out' (Figure 3). He imagined himself suave and debonair, did Hitler impressions in his private bathroom, but resorted to lazy management by letting others – notably his strong-willed daughter – have their own way.

In a comment on the BBC hierarchy, a comedy song-and-dance routine was performed in the film by two music hall stars of the day, Lily Morris and Nellie Wallace, dressed as charladies. They cleaned the corridor outside the management offices, including one door marked 'Capt. Esme St. J. Entwistle G.C.M. Ret, 4th Assistant to the D.G. (Very Private)'. This joke reflected the number of BBC staff who had served in the First World War and, as already mentioned, later found work in BBC management.[46] Indeed, Will Hay declared in the film, 'An organization of this kind must be run on strict military lines! We can't be bothered with new ideas'. The entertainer was previously involved in a musical review in 1922 at the Apollo Theatre in London called *Listening In*, where he played Professor Broadcaster struggling to get a wireless receiver to

---

[44] Murphy, *Behind the Wireless*, p. 16.
[45] Jeffrey Richards (2010), *Cinema and Radio in Britain and America, 1920–1960*, Manchester: Manchester University Press, p. 160. The film was released in the United States as *Radio Follies*.
[46] Elmes, *Hello Again*, p. 31. See also Georgina Born (2004), *Uncertain Vision: Birt, Dyke and the Reinvention of the BBC*, London: Secker & Warburg, p. 69.

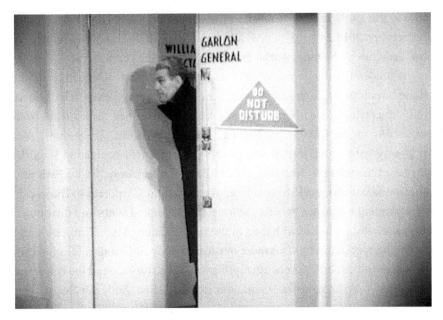

Figure 3 Will Hay as Lord William Garlon, the reclusive director general of the NBG radio station. *Radio Parade of 1935* (1934), Dir. Arthur B. Woods, UK: British International Pictures.

work properly.[47] It was another comment about poor reception, rather than a critique of actual programme content.

It is, today perhaps, remarkable that a ninety-minute cinema such as *Radio Parade of 1935* should contain so many criticisms of the relatively young BBC. Film historian John Ellis said it suggested both that the Corporation was not universally popular at the time and that 'The film assumes that its audience will respond favourably to the image of a top-heavy bureaucracy'.[48] However, the BBC was evidently confident enough of its own cultural position by this time to be able to let such satire pass. Indeed, an occasional BBC radio series, briefly mentioned in the previous chapter, called *Airy Nothings*, poked fun at the Corporation and at characters on both sides of the microphone.[49] Later, a number of shows on

---

[47] Seán Street (2009), *The A to Z of British Radio*, Lanham, MD: The Scarecrow Press, p. 163.
[48] John Ellis (2000), 'British Cinema as Performance Art: *Brief Encounter*, *Radio Parade of 1935* and the Circumstances of Film Exhibition', in Justine Ashby and Andrew Higson, eds, *British Cinema, Past and Present*, London: Routledge, p. 103. It seemed that the movies could get away with satirizing the BBC, whereas the West End stage could not. A 1936 musical revue was banned by the Lord Chamberlain's office because it featured a character resembling Reith. See McIntyre, *The Expense of Glory*, pp. 223–4.
[49] Cardiff, 'Mass Middlebrow Laughter', p. 53. Also see Scannell and Cardiff, *A Social History of Broadcasting*, p. 254.

radio in the 1970s and 1980s satirized the organization (see Chapters 7 and 8), and between 2014 and 2017 a BBC TV comedy *W1A*, discussed in Chapter 10, also made fun of the inner workings of the Corporation's bureaucracy.

The finale of *Radio Parade of 1935* had a variety concert televised in colour by the broadcasting company, in defiance of the owners of vaudeville theatres who – mirroring contemporary reality – had earlier banned their artistes from performing on the wireless.[50] Satirizing a monopoly, in this case the BBC, was fairly easy game, and with many listeners tuning in to competing English-language transmissions from the likes of Radio Luxembourg, Radio Paris and others, cinemagoers would have enjoyed the jibes at the Corporation. The weekly entertainment magazine *Variety*, published in the United States and distributed internationally, remarked with faint praise that 'To attempt to fully review a film containing specialities by 40 or more musical comedy and vaudeville luminaries is about as impossible a task as attempting to write a story around the respective specialities'.[51] Writing in the 1980s, the film historian Andy Medhurst went further and called the film 'a hamfisted mess'.[52] In fact, the movie offered a useful contemporary representation of the early BBC and captured some of the popular opinions of the broadcaster during the 1930s.

Sing as You Swing (1937) was another British film that satirized the Corporation. In the movie Clapham and Dwyer – a popular male comedy duo – played themselves, and in a case of art imitating life they were sacked, 'for saying a vulgar word'.[53] They were working for the fictional 'British Visionary Distributing Broadcasting Company' (the acronym BVD, when spoken quickly, sounded similar to 'BBC'). The boss of the BVD was an arrogant character – incidentally, another ennobled leader: 'Lord Bogham' played by an uncredited actor – who early on was seen sitting in his Art Deco office and declaring, 'What mint sauce is to lamb, I am to the listening public.' The narrative trope was now firmly established of a leader of a broadcasting organization requiring a peerage. In an act of rebellion, the film's ensemble of artists and singers signed up to a competing foreign radio station and flew out from Croydon Airport near London to the fictional European country of Sopenberg (which was an

---

[50] Asa Briggs (1961), *The History of Broadcasting in the United Kingdom, Volume I, The Birth of Broadcasting*, Oxford: Oxford University Press, p. 251.

[51] Jolo [Joshua Lowe] (1935), 'Film Reviews: Radio Parade of 1935 (British Made)', *Variety*, 1 January 1935, p. 18.

[52] Andy Medhurst (1986), 'Music Hall and British Cinema', in Charles Barr, ed., *All Our Yesterdays: 90 Years of British Cinema*, London: BFI Publishing, p. 174.

[53] The duo were banned for five months by the BBC in 1935 for a risqué joke. See Seán Street (2006), *Crossing the Ether*, pp. 61–2.

intentional homophone of 'Luxembourg') to take part in 'The Dog Biscuit Hour', a special Sunday light entertainment show. The radio show was not broadcast due to power supply problems, but instead – and again prophetically – a television version was broadcast for the benefit, no doubt, of the viewing cinema audience.

Another movie, *Head over Heels* (1937), was not directly about the BBC, but instead it featured a foreign station broadcasting to England. It has been regarded by one recent critic as 'disappointing', with a 'trite storyline of a romantic triangle in a redundant Parisian setting'.[54] The film starred Jessie Matthews, mentioned in Chapter 2, who was by then at the height of her popularity. She played a nightclub singer called Jeanne, who had to choose between two men: one was her on-stage partner, the lothario Marcel (Louis Borel); the other was faithful Pierre (Robert Flemyng). Jeanne was intrigued by Pierre, who said he worked at a radio station, and she initially assumed he was an announcer. However, she quickly lost interest when he explained he was an engineer in the control room:

> Pierre: You see [. . .] I'm working on an automatic programme selector. It's based on a system of time and wavelength incorporating a synchronizing electric timer coupled to the tuning circuits of a sensitive supersonic heterodyne receiver. What do you do?
> Jeanne: Sing – and dance.

Jeanne's assumption – and the likely response of the contemporary viewer – was that to work in radio was to be on-air, and so be a famous personality. However, she later got her break, thanks to Pierre (whom she did eventually fall for), on Radio Seine (a fictionalized version of Radio Paris), where she sang two songs and performed a live radio commercial in the Art Deco studios. This was another visual trope in the movies of this period: that a studio had to look 'modern' and stylish, when in reality it was often a functional space devoid of any character.[55] *Head Over Heels* gave the clear message that commercial radio in the 1930s had become normalized, and that the BBC faced sustained competition for audiences.[56] Her song mentioned soap, shirts, cheese, girdles, chewing gum and toothpaste and suggested that sung advertisements were an innovative change from – as a character in the film said – the 'boring voices of the announcers' who usually promoted the products.

---

[54] Richards, *Cinema and Radio*, pp. 166–7.
[55] Richards, *Cinema and Radio*, p. 147.
[56] Street, *Crossing the Ether*, pp. 7–8.

Radio in the public space: Communal listening and soundscapes

In *South Riding*, Holtby understood that radio listening could be done pretty much anywhere: both in the home and outdoors – where it could be overheard by many. In her portrayal of 1930s rural poverty, she described an isolated shanty settlement called The Shacks, where the radio was often playing.[57] Those living there were in transit: homeless and moving through, or bankrupt and sliding down the social scale. The first time the reader learned about The Shacks was during the warm weather of early summer: 'Gramophones blared, loud-speakers uttered extracts of disquieting information about world politics or unemployment in cultured voices.'[58] This was a reference by Holtby to the incongruity of the BBC's current affairs speech output in this scene of poverty, as well as to the gathering tensions across Europe in the 1930s. Radio in this period had clearly become part of rural life. Later in the same scene Lydia Holly, the gifted child of poor parents, who eventually gained a scholarship to the grammar school, read *A Midsummer Night's Dream* to herself whilst in the background, 'She only heard, as a gentle and appropriate accompaniment to Shakespeare's words, the Light Orchestral Concert played on the wireless belonging to two young men living in "Coachways".'[59] Steadily the sounds from the radio began to mix with the physical landscape, and Holtby imagined an almost idyllic pastoral scene: 'Below the magic of Shakespeare's uncomprehended words, the wood near Athens, the silvery sweetness of Mendelssohn from the wireless, the benign warmth of afternoon sun on her arms and shoulders, below all these present pleasures lay the lovely glowing assurances of future joy.'[60] As the 'Overture' to *A Midsummer Night's Dream* played on the wireless, Holtby managed to create a description of a soundscape which recreated for the reader the complexity of the listening experience: the way in which the radio had both intruded into, and transcended across, distinctions between low, middle and highbrow. It was second-hand listening, to someone else's radio set, which both created an ambient atmosphere and turned the radio into 'a domestic utility for relaxation and enjoyment'.[61] Returning to The Shacks later in the novel, the reader found

---

[57] Holtby, *South Riding*, pp. 47–55, 245, 260.
[58] Holtby, *South Riding*, p. 48.
[59] Holtby, *South Riding*, p. 50.
[60] Holtby, *South Riding*, p. 51.
[61] Paddy Scannell and David Cardiff (1982), 'Serving the Nation: Public Service Broadcasting Before the War', in Bernard Waites, Tony Bennett and Graham Martin, eds, *Popular Culture: Past and*

the middlebrow utopia destroyed: a married couple, the Mitchells, were on their way down the social scale as unemployment and poverty beckoned and they were forced to live in this slum:

> To Nancy Mitchell, keeping herself to herself in Bella Vista, this halcyon life [of summer- time at The Shacks] added insult to life's injury. The girls in bathing suits, the boys sunning themselves naked to the waist, the braying of jazz from portable wireless sets and the frizzling of sausages over Primus stoves jarred her strained nerves and pinched with acid disapproval her once pretty face.[62]

In Holtby's narrative, the radio was still playing in the background. But this time the scene took place on a Thursday afternoon, and jazz music during the daytime on the radio would quite possibly signify a non-BBC station, either Radio Luxembourg on long wave (it moved to 208 metres medium wave in 1951) or Radios Paris and Normandy on medium wave.[63] Here in this rural setting the sound of such music reminded readers that the BBC had failed to meet the needs of lowbrow listeners. Some forms of jazz were, for a substantial period of time, avoided by the BBC as being too vulgar and undignified a musical genre for its airwaves.[64]

A stage play by Louis MacNeice with music by Benjamin Britten called *Out of the Picture* (1937), written before MacNeice joined the Corporation, was another example of the radio being 'everywhere'. The play, staged in London by the Group Theatre, an experimental company of actors, began and ended with the noises from a radio receiver placed on the stage. At the start of act one, scene one, it provoked an immediate reaction from a leading character, a struggling artist, as he turned off the wireless: 'These mechanical appliances! They like the sound of their own voice.'[65] The play reflected on the growing threats to international peace and the spectre of death. The year before, the Group Theatre company worked on a staging of W. H. Auden and Christopher Isherwood's *The Ascent of F6* (1936).[66] A reviewer of a 1938 production said, 'Brilliant use

---

Present - A Reader, Beckenham, Kent: Croom Helm, p. 186.
[62] Holtby, *South Riding*, p. 245.
[63] Holtby, *South Riding*, p. 246. Street, *Crossing the Ether*, pp. 69 and 143. See also D. L. LeMahieu (1988), *A Culture for Democracy: Mass Communication and the Cultivated Mind in Britain Between the Wars*, Oxford: Oxford University Press, pp. 274-8.
[64] Fildes, 'Winifred Holtby', pp. 99-100. See also Paddy Scannell (1981), 'Music for the Multitude? The Dilemmas of the BBC's Music Policy, 1923-1946', *Media, Culture & Society*, 3(3): 243; Street, *Crossing the Ether*, p. 69.
[65] Louis MacNeice (1937), *Out of the Picture: A Play in Two Acts*, London: Faber and Faber, p. 9.
[66] W. H. Auden and Christopher Isherwood ([1938] 1958), *The Ascent of F6*, London: Faber & Faber. See Michael Sidnell (1984), *Dances of Death: The Group Theatre of London in the Thirties*, London: Faber and Faber, pp. 184-206. The play also included Auden's original version of his 'Funeral Blues',

is made of wireless commentators to parody the official platitudes of pomp and power, and at times the full technique of revue is employed with skilful effect.'[67] The plot of *The Ascent of F6* included a suburban couple, Mr and Mrs A, who followed events by listening to the radio – signified by a curtained-off section of the theatre stage. Auden and Isherwood had put the wireless into the heart of the narrative, and the theatre audience was able to see both the broadcasters and the listeners' reactions on stage. It was a parable about the use and abuse of power, reflecting the growing tensions of the 1930s, and was a satire of imperialism, patriotism and war itself.

The Ascent of F6 was, like the novel by Rex Warner *The Wild Goose Chase* (1937), a fantasy which attempted to express left-wing principles to audiences and readers alike.[68] Both included mentions of the dangers of the misuse of broadcasting, and later critics observed that 'Leftists' science-fiction visions of how radio might shape the future were always cautionary'.[69] Warner's book, his first novel, was about a quest by three brothers in a strange foreign country ruled by an authoritarian leader. Two of the young men stopped at a farmer's house and listened to the 'All-you- need News' on a receiver authorized and issued by the government. The bulletin surprised them by broadcasting details of their entry into the country and suggested that the authorities had a sophisticated surveillance system in operation. The radio announcer continued, 'Rumours that there is any danger to the financial stability of the country are malicious and should be discounted by all men and women of good will. Never has the country been in so prosperous a state.'[70] The brothers were credulous, but the farmer listening with them shook his head and urged them not to believe what they had just heard.[71] Later in the novel, one of the brothers was shown into a 'machine room' by the ruler who explained that the equipment was indeed a form of complex CCTV system, similar to George Orwell's *Nineteen Eighty-Four* (1949), which was being developed to watch and listen to every citizen in the country.[72] Warner's novel reflected concerns about the rise of fascism in

---

a poem which later was used as 'Stop All the Clocks' in the British film *Four Weddings and a Funeral* (1994).
[67] J. M. D. Pringle (1938), 'The Ascent of F6, at the Prince's theatre, Manchester', *The Manchester Guardian*, 5 July. Available online: https://www.theguardian.com/books/2019/jul/05/ascent-of-f6-a uden-isherwood-mountaineering-play-review-1938 (accessed 24 May 2021).
[68] Andrew Cramp ([1937] 1990), 'Introduction', in Rex Warner, ed., *The Wild Goose Chase*, London: Merlin Press, p. xv.
[69] Williams, *British Writers and the Media*, p. 63.
[70] Warner, *The Wild Goose Chase*, p. 81.
[71] Warner, *The Wild Goose Chase*, p. 82.
[72] Warner, *The Wild Goose Chase*, pp. 224–5.

Europe and worries about the build-up to war. Further works by W. H. Auden, Christopher Isherwood and Rex Warner are discussed in the next chapter.

A more light-hearted account of the effects of public listening to the wireless appeared in the George Formby film *Feather Your Nest* (1937). Formby was cast as a clumsy assistant in a gramophone record factory who broke a master disc of a new singer. To cover his mistake, he recorded his own version which became a great success and led to the hunt for the anonymous star who had recorded the song. In the *denouement* of the film, it was heard on the pub radio, and, in order to emphasize the physicality of the public broadcast, the wireless was filmed in a central position opposite the bar, between the fireplace and the window. The actors were drawn towards it as they recognized Formby's voice singing on the record. The wireless announcer said:

> You have just heard 'Leaning on a Lamp Post', the most successful record of the year. If the gentleman who made this record is listening, would he please communicate immediately with the manager of the Monarch Gramophone Company who is prepared to offer him a substantial contract.

It showed the radio as a public service in finding missing persons, and in a clever piece of cinema cross-media marketing, the song featured at least five times in the seventy-eight-minute movie, serving as an extended promotional vehicle for Formby's talents. The fact that it had appeared on the radio in the film was a veiled joke reflecting that other songs by Formby had been banned from the BBC for their *double entendre* lyrics.

One radio drama which promoted the career of an American actor and director was a version of the novel by H. G. Wells, *The War of the Worlds*. Orson Welles directed and starred in a 1938 radio version, broadcast in the United States on the night before Halloween, and he gained a certain notoriety for subsequent newspaper reports of panic by listeners. The critic Keith Williams said Welles's broadcast, from the script by Howard Koch (CBS, 1938), presented a form of hyperreality that created mass hysteria in a credulous listenership through 'the simulated immediacy of a live news commentary on an extra-terrestrial invasion for Hallowe'en'.[73] It presented radio as a drama, within a radio play. Fascination with this radio play has endured, and was mentioned by the Brazilian sculptor Cildo Meireles, discussed in Chapter 10, as an inspiration for many of his pieces including one about the performativity of radio. Welles's work

---

[73] Williams, *British Writers and the Media*, p. 61. See also Richards, *Cinema and Radio*, pp. 26–7.

as both a director and an actor showed how deeply he understood the mechanics of radio drama. However, some have questioned the actual level of mass panic generated by the broadcast. Welles's lack of specific denial, and a subsequent reliance on inaccurate reporting, helped to generate further uncertainty.[74] Many listeners may have understood the programme to be a work of fiction, just as others may well have misheard it for any number of reasons from poor reception to inattention and distraction.

Radio in the public space: Royal broadcasting

The epilogue of *South Riding* presented a fictionalized version of a real event: the BBC's royal silver jubilee service broadcast of 6 May 1935. Events were relayed to loudspeakers placed in the public park. In terms of seeking to create a national identity and unity, the BBC and the monarchy appeared to be well suited to each other.[75] However, even whilst many in the crowd in Holtby's novel listened with their family and friends, others paid little attention.[76] Here she was highlighting the differences and divisions, not the unity: 'The low roar outside St. Paul's [in London] reached them, accompanied by the scream of the sea against the pebbles and the cry of swooping gulls [in Yorkshire].'[77] Radio presented the happenings in the capital as a secondary, vicarious, activity for listeners elsewhere in the country.[78] Shortly afterwards, there was a technical problem, the broadcast link failed and prayers had to be said by the local leaders instead of listening to those from London. By having the relay break, Holtby provided a critique of what was seen as the BBC's pomposity and self-importance. Paddy Scannell, in his consideration of the 1937 broadcast of the coronation of King George VI, noted that Mass Observation's account of that day showed a wide range of responses to the event, not all of them reverential,

---

[74] A. Brad Schwartz (2015), *Broadcast Hysteria: Orson Welles's* War of the Worlds *and the Art of Fake News*, New York: Hill and Wang, p. 223. See also W. Joseph Campbell (2010), *Getting It Wrong: Ten of the Great Misreported Stories in American Journalism*, Berkeley, CA: University of California Press, pp. 26–7.

[75] Jean Seaton ([2015] 2017), '*Pinkoes and Traitors*': *The BBC and the Nation, 1974–1987*, 2nd edn, London: Profile, p. 147. See also Thomas Hajkowski (2010), *The BBC and National Identity in Britain, 1922–1953*, Manchester: Manchester University Press, p. 83.

[76] Holtby, *South Riding*, pp. 505–10. Mark Pegg, using archival research, described the events around the country: 'During the Jubilee celebrations of 1935, radio was often used as a highlight after a traditional street party or fete', and 'The day revolved around the radio set: chapels and churches changed their ceremonies to suit broadcasting times'. Pegg, *Broadcasting and Society*, p. 192.

[77] Holtby, *South Riding*, p. 507.

[78] Holtby, *South Riding*, p. 510. Williams, *British Writers and the Media*, p. 61.

and all outside the control of both the broadcaster and the organizers of local listening events.[79] The implication was that despite the best attempts of the BBC the solemnity of a royal event, such as that described by Holtby, had failed to be communicated effectively to the masses listening elsewhere in the country. In her novel she included a description of the BBC radio commentator Stephen King-Hall, who, Holtby said, had a 'bland informal voice [. . .] describing the scene as he saw it from St. Paul's Cathedral'.[80] The radio historian Andrew Crisell suggested that the Corporation regarded its royal broadcasts of the 1930s as being the pinnacle of its output, thereby ignoring a need to report and reflect upon the poverty and social problems of the period.[81] Holtby, in her fictional account, had chosen the BBC's royal coverage to be a technical disaster. The mass medium of radio had not lived up to its promise in terms of public listening.

There was an echo of this ability of the wireless to promise unreal expectations in the film *Radio Lover* (1936). This British comedy told of a singer Joe Morrison (played by Wylie Watson) with a beautiful voice but an ugly face. He was, he reckoned, perfect for radio but was forced to employ another to mime when he appeared on stage and in film. Indeed, he admitted his own physical failings: 'The voice is a voice of the lover, but the face is a pain in the neck.' *Radio Lover* highlighted the illusions radio could create. The cinema viewer was placed in a powerful position to be able to observe the subterfuge, and hence derive humour from the situation. This movie provided an early version of what was later to become the audio joke in the Hollywood film *Singing in the Rain* (1952), starring Gene Kelly and Debbie Reynolds, where the voice of Reynolds was paired with the looks of Jean Hagen (playing the character Lina Lamont). In both films, the deception was revealed with comic results.

Finally, this chapter has offered readings of novels and movies from the mid-1930s, each of which has revealed a range of listening practices. The wireless was part of the home, where radio programmes could stimulate a conversation and offer consolation during times of illness or loneliness. It had also become a background to activities in public spaces to deliver new sounds in the outdoors, in residential areas, as well as in public parks and municipal gardens. In cinemas,

---

[79] Scannell, *Radio, Television and Modern Life*, pp. 77–8.
[80] Holtby, *South Riding*, p. 507. Certainly, he had a military crispness to his delivery, and a posh voice, but others credited him with a witty delivery which lent him a certain simplicity and warmth. See Elmes, *Hello Again*, p. 67. An audio excerpt of his appearance on the BBC's *Desert Island Discs* in 1961 is available online: https://www.bbc.co.uk/sounds/play/p009y6fy (accessed 24 May 2021).
[81] Crisell, *An Introductory History*, p. 45.

it had allowed audiences to see people like themselves listening to the radio. The next chapter continues to consider how radio listening was portrayed in other media. It takes in the war years when the BBC became both a public voice in the midst of the conflict and an imagined nation builder. The Second World War was to mark the beginning of radio's change.

4

The home front

Modernism, war and its aftermath, 1938 to 1949

The wireless comes of age

This chapter examines how, as the war approached, cinema and popular literature increasingly recognized radio's centrality in everyday society. Listeners, both civilians and troops, could hear trusted news and morale-boosting entertainment on the radio, just as they could also find propaganda from broadcasters both at home and abroad, 'in the sense that, for the first time, belligerent nations mobilized wireless broadcasting on a global scale for both domestic and international persuasion and information'.[1] By the end of hostilities, 'broadcasting as a whole had gained influence during the war not only in Britain but in all parts of the world'.[2] This period was bookended by two events in the history of the BBC. In June 1938, John Reith left the corporation; two years later he took up posts with the government, including a short time as minister of information.[3] By 1949, when this chapter concludes, new national BBC stations were well established in the form of the Home, the Light and the Third. For listeners in other countries, what had begun in 1932 as the BBC's Empire Service in English became in 1939 the Overseas Service. The Arabic Service started in January 1938, and was the BBC's first foreign language broadcast. By 1943 there were forty-three language services, mostly on short wave. In 1965, they together, formally, became known as the BBC World Service.

---

[1] Ian Whittington (2018), *Writing the Radio War: Literature, Politics and the BBC, 1939–1945*, Edinburgh: Edinburgh University Press, p. 2; see also Asa Briggs (1970), *The History of Broadcasting in the United Kingdom, Volume III, The War of Words*, London: Oxford University Press, p. 4.

[2] Asa Briggs ([1979] 1995), *The History of Broadcasting in the United Kingdom, Volume IV, Sound and Vision*, Oxford: Oxford University Press, p. 26.

[3] Ian McIntyre (1993), *The Expense of Glory: A Life of John Reith*, London: HarperCollins, pp. 250–66.

Radio, Modernism and James Joyce

If *South Riding* (see Chapter 3) was the key middlebrow text on radio listening, then James Joyce's *Finnegans Wake* (1939) can be considered the highbrow equivalent. Just a few months before the outbreak of the war came the full publication in book form of what was regarded by many academics as the epitome of the Modernist novel, perhaps because of its impenetrable vocabulary, the strange sentences and confusing narrative which at the same time appeared to reference, critique, satirize and respond to contemporary events across Europe. Some editions included line numbers on each page to help guide the reader who used one of the many study aids published. Joyce made references to Hitler, to Irish religious and cultural traditions, to inventors such as Marconi and to European fables including *Tristan and Iseult*. There were quotes from the Bible, the Koran and the Egyptian Book of the Dead, as well as references to Popeye and the Keystone Cops.[4] It served also to describe radio listening during the 1930s, and indeed for the entire analogue era which lasted well into the early years of the twenty-first century. Joyce abandoned conventional narrative styles and invented many of the words used in the text. Opinions as to the storyline varied. Some considered it to be about our own perceptions of life and the universe; some suggested that the major part of the book may have been based around a séance with different voices interrupting and interjecting.[5] Others thought it prefigured cyberspace and virtual reality.[6] I take the view that it was a novel which focused on radio listening and that, 'Certainly, Joyce realized the abnormality of radio, and crafted a vocabulary equal to any duplicitous broadcast signal, muted or twisted by static'.[7] This interpretation allows his technique of disjointed subject matter and unexpected interruptions to represent radio listening of the era.[8] However, even supporters of this reading have sounded a

---

[4] The comic and author Ben Elton, in his 1999 novel *Inconceivable* (see Chapter 9), said 'A road map of Birmingham is easier to follow' (Elton, p. 88).
[5] Finn Fordham (2011), 'Finnegans Wake: Novel and Anti-novel', in Richard Brown, ed., *A Companion to James Joyce*, Oxford: Blackwell, p. 88; Jane Lewty (2002), 'Broadcasting Modernity: Eloquent Listening in the Early Twentieth Century', PhD diss., University of Glasgow.
[6] David Trotter (2013), *Literature in the First Media Age: Britain Between the Wars*, Cambridge, MA: Harvard University Press, p. 12 and note 38 on p. 294.
[7] Lewty, 'Broadcasting modernity', PhD diss., pp. 111–2.
[8] James A Connor (1993), 'Radio Free Joyce: *Wake* Language and the Experience of Radio', *James Joyce Quarterly*, 30/31: 825–43. See also Jane Lewty (2009), '"What They Had Heard Said Written", Joyce, Pound, and the Cross-Correspondence of Radio', in Debra Rae Cohen, Michael Coyle and Jane Lewty, eds, *Broadcasting Modernism*, Gainesville, FL: University Press of Florida, p. 206.

note of caution: 'Thematically, any technology can be traced through the Joycean maze.'[9]

Joyce wrote *Finnegans Wake* between 1923 and 1939 whilst living in Paris. It was likely that he tuned into what he called Radio Athlone (later known as Radio Éireann), which would have been an audible yet a weak signal with some interference especially after dark.[10] As well as listening to Irish radio he would also have been able to pick up the BBC, the English language programmes of the commercial stations across Europe and, as a multilinguist, he would have been capable of listening to a range of other broadcasters. One critic has observed:

> Radio air was full of noises, wandering signals, high altitude skips, and superheterodyne screeches, and anyone who listened to it had gradually to attune himself or herself to a cacophony of voices speaking all at once. For Joyce the exile, Joyce the *aficionado* of popular culture, the invention of radio was not something to be ignored.[11]

What he was doing in *Finnegans Wake* was attempting to mimic the sensation of listening to a radio, possibly a valve set tuned to a distant medium wave station in the evening, 'picking up airs from th'other over th'ether'.[12] Thus, his characters were connected together by their interactions with the shifting patterns of listening and reception throughout the book. Radio listening between the wars on valve sets, powered by batteries or increasingly by mains electricity, to medium-, long- and short-wave stations was often a haphazard affair. A supplement in *The Times* newspaper to coincide with a wireless exhibition at London's Olympia reminded listeners about the technical difficulties of picking up radio broadcasts. It said, 'It is very much to be doubted if more than a small percentage of listeners get the best out of their receiving sets. [. . .] The fault lies almost invariably with the individual, not with the set.'[13] The article went on to identify problems such as poor aerial and grounding, inaccurate manual tuning, mismatched loudspeaker impedances and a set powered by batteries with the wrong voltages. Listening in was clearly a challenge. Complaints about wireless interference appeared in

---

[9] Jane Lewty (2008), 'Joyce and Radio', in Richard Brown, ed., *A Companion to James Joyce*, Oxford: Blackwell, p. 393.
[10] Lewty, 'Broadcasting Modernity', pp. 111–2; Connor, 'Radio Free Joyce', p. 827. Radio Athlone began on 413 metres but changed to 513 metres after a reallocation of European-wide frequencies in the early 1930s.
[11] Connor, 'Radio Free Joyce', p. 826. Emphasis in original.
[12] James Joyce ([1939] 2012), *Finnegans Wake*, Ware, Hertfordshire: Wordsworth, p. 452 line 13 (hereafter referred to as *FW*).
[13] F. Goddard (1934), 'Handling of the Set: Results Good and Bad', *The Times*, Broadcasting Number, 14 August, p. viii.

George Buchanan's novel *Entanglement* (1938), when a young rich girl and her technically naïve father entered a radio shop and approached the sales assistant:

> 'We want,' she said in a still voice, 'a new radio-set,' and added the name of a particular manufacturer.
>
> Charles [Her father], who moved calmly beside her, said: 'Our last one made crashing noises. Absolutely frightful. Do, like a good man, see that we get a decent one.'[14]

Which must have delighted the shopkeeper. Poor reception was also commented upon in other sources mentioned in this chapter, suggesting that listeners consistently struggled with the technology. The enduring problems of tuning analogue radios was later to become a symbol, a trope, of the first few decades of radio. The 2017 film, *On Chesil Beach* (based on an Ian McEwan novel of 2007), was set in 1962. The opening scene of the newlyweds at the centre of the narrative had the young husband attempting, and failing, to tune a radio in their honeymoon suite to a station playing rock and roll music. It was a metaphor for their doomed relationship, and for film audiences it was a reminder of how life in the early 1960s was: involving a haphazard way of listening to music on the radio and marriages troubled by a lack of communication.

The literary historian James Connor identified numerous examples of radio interference in *Finnegans Wake*. Firstly, it contained unexpected 'words that sound like the background soup of static'.[15] This was often a low-level electrical interference which came and swelled for no reason, for example in the middle of a sermon:

> Bothallchoractorschumminaroundgansumuminarumdrumstrumtrumina humptadumpw aultopoofoolooderamaunsturnup![16]

And whilst Joyce included incoherent syllables, it did contain traces of recognizable words, just as if it were transient interference being heard over the radio. This was one of ten long-form words in the novel which became known as 'thunderwords'.[17] Two types could be identified: firstly, the aforementioned example which was often heard on AM radio and was likely to have been

---

[14] George Buchanan (1938), *Entanglement*, London: Constable, p. 51.
[15] Connor, 'Radio Free Joyce', p. 832.
[16] *FW*, p. 314 lines 8–9.
[17] Connor, 'Radio Free Joyce', p. 842 note 22. He observed that these words were first identified by Marshall McLuhan, and further analysis was developed by McLuhan's son. See Eric McLuhan (1997), *The Role of Thunder in Finnegans Wake*, Toronto: University of Toronto Press, pp. 152–71.

caused by low-level interference fading in and out in a sibilant manner with the inclusion of 'th' and 'sch'. The second type was full of hard consonant sounds, like an electric crackle caused by distant lightning in cloud formations. An example appeared without warning in the middle of the very first page of Joyce's novel:

> bababadalgharaghtakamminarronnkonnbronntonnerronntuonnthunntrovar rhounawnsk awntoohoohoordenenthurnuk![18]

Both noises were part of the radio listening experience of the era.[19] Additionally, Joyce included the sound of tuning across a series of stations, which created an effect of cutting spoken words in half as the dial was turned.[20] In this example, the act of tuning the radio ended up with the sound of a weather and shipping forecast:

> Am. Dg.
>
> Welter focussed.
>
> Wind from the nordth. Warmer towards muffinbell, Lull.[21]

Instead of descriptions, Joyce appeared to use his own vocabulary of invented, adapted or truncated words to create a written form of the sound of the wireless. In doing so, he was making the act of listening to the radio a very real and immediate part of the text of the novel.

The final piece of evidence offered to suggest *Finnegans Wake* was a radio novel was the circularity of the whole text. Famously, the first and last sentences appeared to join together. The final words ended in an incomplete sentence without a full stop:

> Given! A way a lone a last a loved a long the[22]

whilst the novel started without a capital letter, as if halfway through:

> riverrun, past Eve and Adam's, from swerve of shore to bend of bay, brings us by a commodius vicus of recirculation back to Howth Castle and Environs.[23]

Together the two phrases offered a circular continuity and seemed to demonstrate how messages heard on a radio programme could come and go. Connor suggested

---

[18] *FW*, p. 1 lines 15–17.
[19] Connor, 'Radio Free Joyce', p. 842 note 22.
[20] Connor, 'Radio Free Joyce', p. 833.
[21] *FW*, p. 324 lines 23–25.
[22] *FW*, p. 628 lines 15–16.
[23] *FW*, p. 3 lines 1–3.

of the start of the book, 'We begin in the middle of a message, as if that [radio] station, whatever it may be, has been on all along, and we are now just picking it up.'[24] Finnegans Wake, then, encapsulated the experience of contemporary radio listening. It presented, in its own impenetrable manner, what listening to news, entertainment and even propaganda might look like if written down. In doing so it provided the context for listening in the 1930s. Sometimes Modernist literature mentioned contemporary technology just in order to appear up to date.[25] However, it is plausible to suggest that Joyce found the sounds and noises of radio, particularly of long-distance listening on medium, long and short wave in the 1930s, to provide just the right aural inspiration for his novel. It gave the basis for a fluid use of language and the juxtaposition of disparate ideas, woven into what was not so much a linear narrative as a multidimensional soundscape in text form. Whether he did it intentionally, however, remains a matter of speculation.[26] But therein lies the enduring fascination of the text.

Radio news: Journalism and the build-up to war

Until the declaration of war, the BBC continued to broadcast its first news bulletins of the day only in the evening. However, from the beginning of hostilities in September 1939 radio news summaries were on air from seven o'clock in the morning and at hourly intervals at breakfast, lunch and evening.[27] The nine o'clock evening news had an estimated audience reach of between 43 and 50 per cent of the population.[28] Radio newsreaders also lost their anonymity, and for the duration of the war they introduced themselves by name so that listeners could confirm they were listening to the Corporation and not a foreign propaganda broadcast.[29] Works of drama and fiction mentioned the growing tension of the late 1930s, including *On the Frontier* (1938), a play by W. H. Auden and Christopher Isherwood (*The Ascent of F6* (1936) was discussed in Chapter 3). In this production, the theatre stage was split so that the audience

---

[24] Connor, 'Radio Free Joyce', p. 834.
[25] Lewty, '"What They Had Heard Said Written"', p. 200.
[26] Connor, 'Radio Free Joyce', p. 835.
[27] Richard Havers (2007), *Here is the News: The BBC and the Second World War*, Stroud, Gloucestershire: Sutton Publishing, p. 8.
[28] Briggs (1970), *The History of Broadcasting Vol III*, pp. 47–8.
[29] Hugh Chignell (2011), *Public Issue Radio: Talk, News and Current Affairs in the Twentieth Century*, Basingstoke, Hampshire: Palgrave Macmillan, p. 53.

could see both 'houses' of two warring families. Each had a radio set, and at the beginning of act two both broadcast conflicting accounts of the increasing unrest.[30] Finally, at the end of act three scene one, one of the radios emitted a chilling call to action:

> [*tonelessly, like a time-signal*]. Kill, Kill. Kill, Kill, Kill! [*Continues to the end of the scene.*][31]

This was reminiscent of the stridency of Hitler's speeches, and foreshadowed the use of radio in 1994 to stir up interracial hatred during the Rwanda massacre (see Chapter 9). In a similar vein *Autumn Journal* (1939) was a book-length poem written by Louis MacNeice between August and December of 1938, in which he reflected on the growing political and diplomatic tensions during those months: 'There is no time to doubt / If the puzzle really has an answer. Hitler yells on the wireless'.[32] He contrasted this with the everyday sounds outside his London home as Britain prepared for war, and he articulated a concern that the BBC might become a similar source of unchecked propaganda for the Allies' cause.[33] This echoed a passing comment W. H. Auden had made in his poem 'Letter to Lord Byron' (1936). It was an extended, sometimes wry, reflection upon contemporary events, and Auden worried then about the 'Rumours of War, the B.B.C. confirming 'em'. Both poets showed evident concern about the growing threat of military conflict in Europe.[34]

A stark warning also appeared in *The Professor* (1938) by Rex Warner. One literary historian called the novel 'a grim and spare anti-fascist fable', which chronicled the last days of a humane leader of a European country facing instability and invasion.[35] The story was a 'political fable' which demonstrated that 'the strength of a broadcast medium was also its weakness', because it can be interrupted and switched off.[36] The leader's speech was listened to avidly:

---

[30] W. H. Auden and Christopher Isherwood ([1938] 1958), *On the Frontier*, London: Faber & Faber, pp. 142-3. See: Keith Williams (1996), *British Writers and the Media, 1930-1945*, Basingstoke, Hampshire: Macmillan, p. 69.
[31] Auden and Isherwood, *On the Frontier*, p. 170.
[32] Louis MacNeice ([1939] 1998), *Autumn Journal*, London: Faber and Faber, p. 22.
[33] Williams, *British Writers and the Media*, pp. 67, 69-70. For a discussion of the role of the BBC during the Second World War, see Tom Mills ([2016] 2020), *The BBC: Myth of a Public Service*, London: Verso, pp. 77-83.
[34] W. H. Auden ([1936] 1986), 'Letter to Lord Byron', in W. H. Auden, *The English Auden: Poems, Essays and Dramatic Writings 1927-1939*, ed. Edward Mendelson, London: Faber and Faber, p. 197.
[35] Debra Rae Cohen (2009), 'Annexing the Oracular Voice: Form, Ideology, and the BBC', in Debra Rae Cohen, Michael Coyle and Jane Lewty, eds. (2009), *Broadcasting Modernism*, p. 149.
[36] Trotter, *Literature in the First Media Age*, p. 199.

In other streets, too, the sight would have been the same, while in hundreds of thousands of homes families were gathered around radio sets in large or small rooms, staring at the instruments, whether home-made or expensively manufactured, as though those arrangements of wood, glass and wire were oracles, gods, or idols.[37]

However, he had misjudged the impact of his speech, and political opponents had jammed the broadcast and taken over the studios of the 'Central Radio Station' by force.[38] Here was a critique of Reithian principles, which Warner felt kept broadcasters aloof from the general public. These standards, he thought, were now in danger of being abandoned as the broadcaster tried to please the masses.[39] Indeed, as the war began the BBC realized that it needed to provide popular entertainment to encourage both the troops and the population at home – as will be explained in the following text.

Meanwhile, a somewhat unflattering snapshot of the radio industry was to be found in the comedy film *Let's Be Famous* (1939), released in March just six months before the declaration of war. It featured Jimmy (Jimmy O'Dea) as an Irish shopkeeper and Betty (Betty Driver, who later starred in *Coronation Street* (ITV) from 1969 to 2011) as a girl from Liverpool. They each travelled to London thinking they were to appear on national radio: she on a commercial station, he on the BBC. The movie was a farce about the rivalry between stations to hire the best talent.[40] The BBC producers were portrayed as calculating, metropolitan types, whilst the booking agents for the commercial station, a fictional Radio France, were charming and friendly. The timing of the film's release was unfortunate. The key storyline about competition in the radio industry was soon overtaken by the outbreak of war. Radio Luxembourg closed on 21 September 1939; Radio Normandy's English broadcasts stopped in that same month; and Radio Paris was commandeered by the French Vichy Government in June 1940. In the film, Jimmy's fellow villagers tried to listen to him, but had trouble tuning the wireless. One said, 'Ah, wait now. That set was made in Ireland. Maybe it won't work on English stations'; to this, another replied, 'Like Rafferty's? That can only get Athlone and Moscow.' At a stroke, the technical problems of tuning in a wireless in the 1930s was encapsulated in

---

[37] Rex Warner ([1938] 1986), *The Professor*, London: Lawrence & Wishart, p. 184.
[38] Warner, *The Professor*, p. 193.
[39] Williams, *British Writers and the Media*, p. 68.
[40] Jeffrey Richards (2010), *Cinema and Radio in Britain and America, 1920–1960*, Manchester: Manchester University Press, pp. 154–55.

portrayals of racial stereotypes of the rural Irish and, perhaps unintentionally, referenced Joyce's *Finnegans Wake*.

The wireless and entertainment during the war

A move towards popular programming had already started before the war; world events simply hastened the changes to the BBC's output as the Corporation adopted a more pragmatic attitude towards listeners' tastes and quietly dropped some of its assumptions of cultural leadership.[41] Mass listening meant radio, and the BBC in particular, consolidated its place in British society. However, the programmes were not to everyone's taste, and it took the BBC some months to strike the right tone as a broadcaster of mass appeal. For example, Graham Greene declared his dislike of cinema organ music in *Brighton Rock* (1938), his novel about provincial gangs and downmarket journalism. He used a description of a wireless receiver playing in a cheap restaurant on Brighton's seafront:

> In Snow's the [lunchtime] rush was over and the table free. The wireless droned a programme of weary music, broadcast by a cinema organist – a great *vox humana* trembled across the crumby stained desert of used cloths: the world's wet mouth lamenting over life. The waitress whipped the cloths off as soon as the tables were free and laid tea things.[42]

Greene was suggesting that organ recital programmes by the likes of Reginald Foort and Reginald Dixon were lacking in artistic merit, despite the fact they had mass appeal. The author was, in this novel, 'concerned to use popular forms for serious purposes', and evoked the sound of a radio to denote the dreary life

---

[41] David Cardiff and Paddy Scannell (1981), 'Radio in World War II', in *The Historical Development of Popular Culture in Britain*, U203, Block 2, Unit 8, Milton Keynes, Buckinghamshire: Open University Press, pp. 31–78. See also Andrew Crisell (2002), *An Introductory History of British Broadcasting*, 2nd edn., London: Routledge, p. 59; Stephen Barnard (1989), *On the Radio: Music Radio in Britain*, Milton Keynes, Buckinghamshire: Open University Press, p. 17.

[42] Graham Greene ([1938] 1971), *Brighton Rock*, London: Penguin, p. 26. Greene's opinion mirrored the BBC's distinction between genres of the period. Scannell and Cardiff later noted, 'Dance band music, the cinema organ, musical reviews and operettas were not classified as music and were produced by the Variety Department. The Music Department dealt with serious music.' Paddy Scannell and David Cardiff (1982), 'Serving the Nation: Public Service Broadcasting before the War', in Bernard Waites, Tony Bennett and Graham Martin, eds, *Popular Culture: Past and Present – A Reader*, Beckenham, Kent: Croom Helm, p. 183.

of the lower middle classes.[43] A similar disdain for light classical music played on a theatre organ was shared by the writer Rose Macaulay, who complained:

> morning, noon and night, doses of organ. (On this Sunday when I write, there are four goes of this disagreeable musical instrument; yes, this disgusting noise is to return on the air like a windy elephant no less than four times.)[44]

In fact, she thought that the first few weeks of war broadcasting had, for her educated taste, been depressingly lowbrow. She continued:

> it seemed for a time as if what the BBC was doing was to go all canteen, in the intervals between news bulletins and Government notices. That stage is, I think, wearing off a little; good music is seeping back, though still not in great quantity.[45]

However, it was likely that Greene and Macaulay were in a minority. Research gathered a few years previously in 1935 in York suggested that cinema organ music was 'very popular', especially amongst working-class radio listeners.[46]

Cinema, together with radio, became increasingly popular as mass audiences sought entertainment and diversion. British film studios contributed several significant wartime releases with narratives linked to broadcasting and to radio personalities.[47] Indeed, one film historian argued that radio and music hall variety stars were 'mobilised into the wider effort of propaganda. [. . .] Whether one sees this process in the official terms of boosting morale or in the more analytic sense of securing hegemony, the films made by variety artists during the war played a significant part in shaping audience attitudes'.[48] An example of this 'mobilization' was the film *Band Waggon* (1940), based on characters in the BBC radio comedy which ran from 1938 to 1939. The film included a mixture of crosstalk, physical pratfalls and good humour and, like the radio version, had 'Big Hearted' Arthur Askey and Richard 'Stinker' Murdoch living in a flat on the

---

[43] Simon Frith (1983), 'The Pleasures of the Hearth: The Making of BBC Light Entertainment', in Formations Editorial Collective, eds, *Formations of Pleasure*, London: Routledge & Kegan Paul, p. 102.
[44] Rose Macaulay (1939), 'War and the BBC', *The Spectator*, 20 October, p. 10.
[45] Macaulay, 'War and the BBC', p. 10. See also Melissa Sullivan (2012), 'A Middlebrow Dame Commander: Rose Macaulay, the "Intellectual Aristocracy", and *The Towers of Trebizond*', *The Yearbook of English Studies*, 42: 168–85.
[46] Ross McKibbin (1998), *Classes and Cultures: England 1918–1951*, Oxford: Oxford University Press, p. 465.
[47] Richards, *Cinema and Radio*, p. 182.
[48] Andy Medhurst (1986), 'Music Hall and British Cinema', in Charles Barr, ed., *All Our Yesterdays: 90 Years of British Cinema*, London: BFI Publishing, p. 177.

roof of Broadcasting House.[49] That fantasy of something bizarre happening on the roof of the building was continued by Terry Wogan, who presented the BBC Radio 2 breakfast show from 1972 to 1984 and again between 1993 and 2009. He joked about, 'the "dance of the BBC virgins" that supposedly took place on the roof of Broadcasting House each morning'.[50] At the beginning of the movie, Arthur Askey said, 'My ambition is to be a radio star, and have a lovely house out in the country and always turn up half an hour late for rehearsal', which was a sarcastic swipe at fellow radio personalities of the era. Film historians such as Jane Stokes have observed that Askey's work repeatedly lampooned the Corporation:

> *Band Waggon* and *Make Mine a Million* [see next chapter] played on Askey's well- established public persona as a popular performer prepared to speak his mind and challenge authority. The films saw Arthur and his chums taking on the broadcasting establishment in the interests of the taste of ordinary folk.[51]

The movie showed the Corporation's director general as a dour Scot called Sir Angus MacBeath, reminiscent of Will Hay's performance mentioned in the previous chapter. The film also portrayed the head of music as a 'stuffy, pompous, monocled establishment figure who actually hate[d] music'.[52]

Arthur Askey starred in another movie *Back-Room Boy* (1942), and although not based on a radio show, it again satirized the BBC. In particular it poked fun at the regular timekeeping created by the use of the Greenwich Time Signal, a service that had started in February 1924. Pulses generated at the Greenwich Observatory were sent to Broadcasting House, where they were turned into the tones known as 'the pips'.[53] *Back-Room Boy* opened with an establishing shot of the exterior of Broadcasting House, by now a common movie trope signifying 'radio' in British films. There then followed a scene in 'the newsroom', suggesting how important journalism now was – with the editor handing bulletin scripts

---

[49] Paddy Scannell and David Cardiff (1991), *A Social History of British Broadcasting, Volume One: 1922–1939, Serving the Nation*, Oxford: Basil Blackwell, p. 272.
[50] Mark Lawson (2016), 'Terry Wogan: The Intriguingly Subversive National Treasure', *The Guardian*, 31 January. Available online: https://www.theguardian.com/media/2016/jan/31/terry-wogan-intriguingly-subversive-national-treasure (accessed 24 May 2021).
[51] Jane Stokes (2000), 'Arthur Askey and the Construction of Popular Entertainment in *Band Waggon* and *Make Mine A Million*', in Justine Ashby and Andrew Higson, eds, *British Cinema, Past and Present*, London: Routledge, p. 126.
[52] Richards, *Cinema and Radio*, p. 69.
[53] Seán Street (2009), *The A to Z of British Radio*, Lanham, MD: The Scarecrow Press, pp. 127–8. See also Peter Jefferson (2011), *And Now the Shipping Forecast: A Tide of History around our Shores*, Cambridge: UIT Cambridge, pp. 204–15.

to his secretary Betty Moore (Joyce Howard) to give to the announcer. Moore's boyfriend was Arthur Pilbeam (Askey), who was responsible for 'making' the pips. A four-minute sequence then followed in which Askey made an arrogant entrance into the building, and ostentatiously donned a white glove to use a Morse key to generate the time signal. After this he turned and left his 'office' in the Broadcasting House basement. The scene spoke both to the self-importance of the broadcaster, which is that his 'job' was of 'national importance', and to the BBC's recently found obsession with timekeeping. This was principally the result of the introduction of continuity announcers who, as now on Radio 4, made sure that programmes started at exactly the right time and, if necessary, gave information about other shows in order to fill out time until the top of the hour.[54] Eventually Askey's fiancée left him because of his dedication to 'the pips'. As a result, he revolted against the officialdom around him and miskeyed them. Again, broadcasters decades later reworked Askey's comedy: this time it was the DJ Noel Edmonds, host of the Radio 1 breakfast show in the 1970s, who had one of his alter-ego characters, Flynn, in charge of 'the pips'. They included 'Lofty' the long final pip, who often needed discipline from Flynn to stay in order. Both can be read as reactions to the constraints of BBC working practices and of the strictures of timing output to the second.[55]

The impact of radio timekeeping on everyday life in this period was highlighted by John Stewart Collis, an academic and writer who was born in Dublin and spent the Second World War as a volunteer farm labourer in the south of England. He chronicled his work with observations about the environment and people around him and the passing of the traditional methods of agriculture. He found the physical work quite a challenge, and repeatedly mentioned how he listening to the BBC after a day's work: 'These were long days. By the time I had pushed my bicycle back up the hill, it was generally just in time to hear the Nine o'Clock News – news a thousand miles away. It would be eleven o'clock before I got into bed.'[56] Even so, Collis recognized that the concept of time introduced by the Corporation was alien to rural life:

---

[54] Briggs (1970), *The History of Broadcasting, Vol. III*, p. 53. See also Jefferson, *And Now the Shipping Forecast*, pp. 84–6. Peter Jefferson was a BBC continuity announcer from the 1970s until the late 2000s.

[55] For example, see an article by a former BBC broadcast duty manager, Mike Todd (2008), 'The Greenwich Time Signal', 18 September. Available online: http://www.miketodd.net/other/gts.htm (accessed 24 May 2021).

[56] John Stewart Collis ([1973] 2009), *The Worm Forgives the Plough*, London: Vintage Books, p. 106.

in the actual prosaic matter of knowing the hour of the day I had no watch and worked outside the whole clock-world and dwelt far from the frame of mind of the BBC announcer who says, 'It is just coming up to half a minute to eight'. But I did not quite dispense with a clock. I used the lofty, golden time-piece of the sun and a tree which cast a clear, clean shadow with its trunk.[57]

Coherent timekeeping also meant that radio shows were scheduled at the same time every week helping to build substantial audiences, as was the case with *ITMA* (1939–49).[58] The acronym stood for 'It's That Man Again', and the 1943 film version traded on its radio roots, declaring in the opening credits 'The radio sensation with twenty million listeners'. Tommy Handley played the mayor of a town called Foaming-at-the-Mouth, where his comic fraud, arrogant dissembling and disreputable behaviour reflected his radio character. In the process he gambled with the town's finances in a game of poker and won a derelict bombed-out London theatre. The film served to let audiences see radio stars on the cinema screen. In itself, it emphasized for many viewers that the fast-paced verbal style of the radio version was more enjoyable than the cinema experience. The inclusion of physical comedy and song-and-dance sequences – required for the film narrative – appearing contrived.[59]

Two other movies were also spun out of radio shows in the war years. *Hi Gang* (1941) was based on a BBC radio series starring an American couple, Ben Lyon and Bebe Daniels, and was intended to imitate the wise cracking of American comedy shows. The radio series was broadcast between 1940 and 1949, and then transferred to television on the BBC (and later, ITV) as *Life with the Lyons*. There was also a touring stage version. The film was made with an eye to distribution in the United States, offered British audiences a glimpse of the exotic world of American radio and was potentially 'an important means of cementing Anglo-American friendship in the early days of the war'.[60] The original radio show mixed scripted comedy with songs and guest stars. The movie spin-off opened with the credits, 'By permission of the British Broadcasting Corpn. [*sic*]: Radio's Greatest Success'. Lyon and Daniels played rival radio reporters for two fictional New York stations. Ben Lyon worked for the General Broadcasting Company (GBC), whilst Bebe Daniels was a journalist with the Liberty Broadcasting Company (LBC). From the first scene it was clear to British cinema audiences that radio

---

[57] Collis, *The Worm Forgives the Plough*, p. 272.
[58] Briggs (1970), *The History of Broadcasting, Vol III*, p. 109.
[59] Richards, *Cinema and Radio*, p. 75.
[60] Richards, *Cinema and Radio*, p. 71.

reporters in the United States were comfortable with including in their on-air talk mentions of programme and station sponsors. This was a style of address that British listeners would have last heard when Luxembourg and Normandy were on the air but was a continued anathema to the licence fee-funded BBC. Ben Lyon saw a BBC van and joked, 'Why, that's the Bigger Babies Company!' The film closed with a cinema version of their radio variety show, and what had by now become a narrative trend for the final half hour of these film adaptations.

Another radio show which transferred to the screen was *Happidrome*. It was broadcast from 1941 to 1947 on Sunday evenings, which caused some debate amongst the BBC's board of governors.[61] It went out on the Forces Programme, live from a theatre in North Wales, which meant that some stars had a round trip of 500 miles each week to take part. *Happidrome* 'contrasted sharply with the wisecracking of *Hi Gang*', and instead was a 'cheerful and unsophisticated' traditional variety show interlinked with comedy sketches by a trio of hapless staff of a fictional variety theatre.[62] The movie version (1943) opened with the three, played by northerners Harry Korris, Cecil Frederick and Robbie Vincent, remarking how they were currently playing to millions on the wireless. One then added, 'It's not so long since things were different. We've come a long way, lads, we've come long way.' The rest of the movie charting their imaginary rise to success. The film was a light morale booster, again allowing audiences to enjoy the opportunity to see radio stars on the screen.

Propaganda, exhortation and cinema's representations of radio listening

The BBC resisted pressure from politicians and the government to become an outlet for propaganda that answered completely to the Ministry of Information.[63] Instead, the Corporation sought to tread a fine line, and 'Considerable constraints of censorship and propaganda meant that, throughout the upheavals of the war, the BBC played a double role: it both channelled official policies and information, and reflected the concerns and aspirations of a broad swath

---

[61] Briggs (1970), *The History of Broadcasting, Vol. III*, p. 555.
[62] Richards, *Cinema and Radio*, p. 72; Briggs (1970), *The History of Broadcasting, Vol III*, p. 575 and 314.
[63] Briggs (1970), *The History of Broadcasting, Vol. III*, pp. 1–6, 33.

of the British public'.[64] There was an understanding that rather than face any direct interference from the ministry, the BBC was able to self-censor effectively throughout most of the war and hence maintain some form of independence.[65] However there were signs of strains between the broadcaster and the ministry, satirized by J. B. Morton, writing as 'Beachcomber' in the *Daily Express*, who thought that 'The tiff between the Ministry of Information and the B.B.C. reminds me of one of those rows at a girls' school', a remark reminiscent of George Orwell's diary entry in 1942 that the BBC itself was, at times, 'something halfway between a girls' school and a lunatic asylum'.[66] The Corporation from the outset of hostilities decided upon a policy of reporting and broadcasting the truth as best it could, and, despite a number of occasions when the government prevented it from relaying specific events, it built up enormous trust both at home and abroad for its authoritative reporting of the war.[67]

Elsewhere, and in a more overt form of propaganda, the technology of the wireless was highlighted in the film *Freedom Radio*. It dramatized the use of 'clandestine' radio as part of the underground resistance in Germany by opponents of the Nazi regime.[68] It was reportedly based on an anonymous 1939 novel called *Freedom Calling!*.[69] Cinema historians pointed out that, during the war film was able to visualize listeners being united by radio in contrasting ways: 'For the 1941 British film *Freedom Radio*, this awareness fulfilled a different function where isolated individuals [were] also seeking to relate to a wider community – but this time in *resistance*. Radio allow[ed] isolated individuals to come together, forming an oppositional grouping.'[70] The cinema audience never saw the face of the Nazi broadcasters. In contrast, the viewer was allowed to develop a relationship with the resistance radio operators by watching them on screen, and thus regard them as trustworthy sources of information.[71] As the clandestine station was being planned, the hero (Clive Brook) said, 'There might be some use in talking – through a microphone [on the wireless].

---

[64] Whittington, *Writing the Radio War*, p. 3. See also Jean Seaton ([2015] 2017), *'Pinkoes and Traitors': The BBC and the Nation, 1974–1987*, 2nd edn, London: Profile, pp. 289–90.
[65] Briggs (1995), *The History of Broadcasting, Vol IV*, p. 27; McKibbin, *Classes and Cultures*, p. 461.
[66] J. B. Morton (1944), *Captain Foulenough & Company*, London: Macmillan, p. 154. The George Orwell comment is quoted in Briggs (1970), *The History of Broadcasting, Vol. III*, p. 22.
[67] Crisell, *An Introductory History of British Broadcasting*, p. 61.
[68] Briggs (1970), *The History of Broadcasting, Vol. III*, p. 61.
[69] Jo Fox (2005), '"The Mediator": Images of Radio in Wartime Feature Film in Britain and Germany', in Mark Connelly and David Welch, eds, *War and the Media: Reportage and Propaganda, 1900–2003*, London: I.B. Tauris, p. 97.
[70] Fox, '"The Mediator": Images of Radio', p. 96. Emphasis in original.
[71] Fox, '"The Mediator": Images of Radio', pp. 98–9.

It's the only way we'll get them to listen.' It was a cumbersome and somewhat self-evident comment, and an anonymous contemporary reviewer said the movie lacked 'psychological subtlety and depth'.[72] The release of the film came at a time when domestic audiences were already worn down with a plethora of anti-Nazi messages, and had by 1941 come to realize that Germany would not be defeated quickly.[73] Movies made with the approval of the British government's Ministry of Information often included radio as part of their patriotic narratives: *In Which We Serve* (1942) had the ship's crew hear the declaration of war relayed from the radio across the boat's loudspeakers; *One of Our Aircraft is Missing* (1942) saw members of the Dutch underground secretly listening to broadcasts; *Millions Like Us* (1943) included the enduring trope of a family listening to the evening news together; and *The Way Ahead* (1944) had British soldiers serving in North Africa listening to the programmes on the short-wave transmitters of the BBC's Overseas Service.[74]

British-made films of the era recreated the impact that listening to popular music on the radio had on troops of both the Allied and the Axis powers. *The True Story of Lili Marlene* (1944) was a Crown Film Unit drama-documentary production about a song that was appropriated by both the British and the Germans. A fictionalized version of events appeared in *Lilli [sic] Marlene* (1950), which had a cameo appearance from the BBC radio star Richard Murdoch, mentioned earlier. Both films highlighted how the one song sung repeatedly on the wireless could unify troops, as viewers of each movie heard the music variously in German, in French and, finally, in English.[75] Similarly, a film starring Vera Lynn became a symbol of imagined nation-building to such an extent that decades later in April 2020 Queen Elizabeth II made reference to it during a televised address to the nation during the Covid-19 pandemic. Vera Lynn was not universally liked in the 1940s, particularly amongst some within BBC management who reckoned she sang overly sentimental songs when the troops should instead be listening to stirring tunes. However, servicemen and women, and the young working classes, appeared to take her to their hearts.[76] That was reflected in the movie *We'll Meet Again* (1943), which amounted to

---

[72] '"Freedom Radio." At the Regal: The Cinema' (1941), *The Spectator*, 31 January, p. 12.
[73] Fox, '"The Mediator": Images of Radio', p. 100.
[74] Charles Barr (1986), 'Broadcasting and Cinema: 2: Screens Within Screens', in Charles Barr, ed., *All Our Yesterdays: 90 Years of British Cinema*, London: BFI Publishing, pp. 206–24.
[75] Richards, *Cinema and Radio*, pp. 186–8. The 1950 *Lilli Marlene* movie also included a performance of the song 'We'll Meet Again', reflecting how culturally significant both pieces of music were.
[76] Briggs (1970), *The History of Broadcasting, Vol. III*, pp. 578–9.

Figure 4 Peggy Brown (Vera Lynn, right) tries to impress BBC secretary Miss Bohne (Betty Jardine, left) with her newly pressed 78-rpm demo disc. *We'll Meet Again* (1943), Dir. Phil Brandon, UK: Columbia Pictures.

a biopic of the singer and her radio request programme, *Sincerely Yours*. The film showed the Corporation's music department run by a 'kindly, wise and paternalistic executive' (Mr Hastropp, played by Frederick Leister), attended to by a 'comically anxious and officious secretary' (Miss Bohne played by Betty Jardine).[77]

Reflecting wartime conditions, Hastropp and Miss Bohne worked from an office with bare brick walls and lined with sandbags (Figure 4). Miss Bohne was curt with telephone callers and said to her boss after trying to dismiss someone on the line, 'Really, some people seem to think they've bought the BBC just because they have a wireless licence.' The two together took charge of Peggy Brown's (Vera Lynn's) career as she became 'the forces sweetheart' and went on to broadcast shows which linked soldiers with their families back home. The urge to look forward to more hopeful times was evident in *This Happy*

---

[77] Richards, *Cinema and Radio*, p. 189.

Breed (1944), a film directed by David Lean. It was another movie that sought to create and reflect a 'core national identity'.[78] The screenplay was written by Noel Coward, and later critics described it as 'deeply complacent and politically conservative'.[79] However, it was extremely successful at the box office, and the cinemagoing public undoubtedly enjoyed it as an invented saga, set between 1919 and 1939 which resonated with so many of their own lives.[80] In the last third of the film, the radio, left on and unattended in the dining room, played music by a military band and prompted a stern response. The elderly grandmother sat next to it, first reading a newspaper and then ostentatiously doing her knitting whilst complaining: 'Wish somebody'd turn that wireless off. It's getting on my nerves.' The scene, amid a family crisis, showed the radio being ignored. Later, the wireless was used as a narrator, bringing into the dining room news of the death of King George V and allowing the cinema audience to see the faces of the actors as they reacted to the solemn news, this time attending closely to the radio news bulletin.

Within the space of thirty minutes, this film had presented the wireless as both something to be ignored and something to be listened to carefully.

After the war: Auntie's media choices expand

By the end of the Second World War, the BBC was quick to promise listeners a return to regional output, fresh programming and opportunities to have a choice of listening.[81] In 1945, the Home Service continued as the main national network, and what had been the Forces Programme (started in 1940) was renamed the Light Programme. In 1946, the Third Programme opened. For the first time, the BBC was broadcasting separate radio services of broadly low-, middle- and highbrow content. No longer would it transmit on a single frequency a variety of programmes which it thought would appeal to the nation; no longer would there be clashes of style, for example, between a comedy show followed by a symphony recital.[82] The listener could now '*choose* to be "improved"' rather than having

---

[78] Andrew Higson (2000), 'The Instability of the National', in Ashby and Higson, eds, *British Cinema*, p. 44.
[79] McKibbin, *Classes and Cultures*, p. 444.
[80] McKibbin, *Classes and Cultures*, pp. 442–3.
[81] Briggs (1970), *The History of Broadcasting, Vol. III*, p. 714.
[82] Street, *The A to Z of British Radio*, p. 13.

improvement thrust upon her'.[83] However, a small amount of programming was repeated on other networks.

Some plays and recitals were rebroadcast between the Light and the Home, and the Home and the Third.[84] Within a year the Light was attracting mass audiences, and the overall effect of widening choice was that it perpetuated the BBC's monopoly.[85] The BBC had, in effect, divided and dominated the radio spectrum, 'While the launch of the Third Programme in 1946 would ensure a forum for highbrow content for decades to come, the tripartite division of broadcasting services served to institutionalize cultural hierarchies while splitting the attention of the national radio public.'[86] That split attention was something which did not go unnoticed amongst writers and humourists. Take, for example, a comedy drama given this billing in the *Radio Times*:

> *How to Listen*, Third Programme, Sunday 29 September 1946, 6.00pm. Including How Not To, How They Used To, and How You Must. By Stephen Potter, with selected examples, by Joyce Grenfell, of Third Class Listening. The whole demonstrated for this exclusive occasion by especially selected members of the 'How' Repertory Company.[87]

It was the first programme, broadcast live, on the Third Programme's opening night, and was repeated several times over the next few months.[88] It was a satire of radio listening, or rather non-listening, which mocked the perceived pomposity of the cultured classes – and BBC drama producers in particular: a brave choice with which to open the new radio station. The narration of the drama panned from the BBC studio, across to various homes where people were in states of inattention, and from a young man chatting up a girlfriend, to a middle-aged group playing a game of cards, to two old ladies hard of hearing making a cup of tea, to a listener dealing with persistent static interference (again, reminiscent of James Joyce). The radio producer complained that his audience was not listening to his carefully crafted work. It was an almost perfect satire of the exclusivity of the newly created Third Programme; that

---

[83] Crisell, *An Introductory History of British Broadcasting*, p. 69. Emphasis in original.
[84] Crisell, *An Introductory History of British Broadcasting*, p. 68.
[85] Briggs (1995), *The history of Broadcasting, Vol IV*, p. 60 and 77.
[86] Whittington, *Writing the Radio War*, p. 191.
[87] 'How to Listen' (1946), *Radio Times*, issue 1200, 27 September, p. 4. Available online: https://genome.ch.bbc.co.uk/4a6f0c1eabde45478ec087c5adfaef95 (accessed 24 May 2021).
[88] Julian Potter (2004), *Stephen Potter at the BBC: 'Features' in War and Peace*, Orford, Suffolk: Orford Books, pp. 178–81.

'good' listeners should check the *Radio Times*, mark up the programmes they wanted to hear and then pay strict attention to the entire broadcast. Indeed, the Third was aimed at 'attentive and critical listeners' but was seriously hampered by its patchy reception on medium wave.[89] The station did not get VHF/FM transmission until 1955, and post-war BBC management and transmitter engineers were well aware of the technical limitations of the medium-wave frequencies used by the station when it first opened. The Potter and Grenfell creation was accurate in its reflection of the realities of radio listening, just as James Joyce's had been in 1939.

The three national stations, the Home, the Light and the Third, still known at this time as either a 'service' or a 'programme', continued the BBC's radio hegemony, despite the reappearance of Radio Luxembourg in 1946. There were no news bulletins on the Third until 1963, and programmes often overran so as not to interrupt a symphony or a live play.[90] The other two stations, especially the Home Service, were timed to the 'pips' and had around ten news bulletins and summaries per day. One of the most popular programmes was the *Brains Trust* (1941–61), which started on the Forces Programme and later transferred to the Home Service. It was an unscripted discussion show, the first of its kind and recorded 'live' each week.[91] The children's author, Richmal Crompton, satirized the self-importance of its panel members in her 1945 short story *William and the Brains Trust*.[92] The author contrasted perceptions of highbrow and lowbrow entertainment and told how the schoolboy hero William persuaded a visiting speaker, a fictional Professor Knowle from the BBC programme, to appear at the village RAF concert evening. Instead, a popular impressionist arrived to do his act as 'Prof. Know-all', to a rather baffled audience expecting to hear an erudite lecture by a radio personality. Crompton made clear that the radio show was not a programme likely to engage mischievous young boys: 'William was not particularly interested in all this. He had listened once to the BBC *Brains Trust* on the wireless and had been so bored that he had taken care never to listen again.'[93] In her story, the impressionist was puzzled as to why his audience was

---

[89] Briggs (1995), *The History of Broadcasting, Vol IV*, pp. 62–3. See also Humphrey Carpenter (1996), *The Envy of the World: Fifty Years of the BBC Third Programme and Radio 3, 1946–1996*, London: Weidenfeld and Nicholson, pp. 22–4.
[90] Carpenter, *The Envy of the World*, pp. 214–16.
[91] Paddy Scannell (2003), 'The *Brains Trust*: A Historical Study of the Management of Liveness on Radio', in Simon Cottle, ed., *Media Organisation and Production*, London: Sage, pp. 99–112.
[92] Richmal Crompton ([1945] 1989), *William and the Brains Trust*, London: Macmillan Children's Books, pp. 1–19.
[93] Crompton, *William and the Brains Trust*, p. 2.

so quiet and failed to laugh, whilst the real professor – who had turned up at another venue in front of an audience expecting a comic – found he had to answer banal questions such as, 'Where do flies go in the winter?', receiving 'a frenzied burst of applause' when he explained the reason.[94] It being a children's story, the two characters met and eventually became firm friends – and William was excused for causing the mix-up.

In November 1947, Princess Elizabeth, the future queen, and Prince Philip were married with the wedding service broadcast on the radio. Five years later, her coronation was a major highlight of the new post-war television service from the BBC. A film that provided a promise of the new Elizabethan era to come was *Helter Skelter* (1949). This comedy portrayed BBC radio providing mass entertainment that was a world away from what was perceived as the Reithian seriousness of its interwar years. Some critics dismissed the film for its 'unimaginative direction and undistinguished script'.[95] However, it presented a snapshot of the new energy to be found in the contemporary broadcasting industry. The movie began with a parody of the opening words of *In Town Tonight*, a Saturday evening BBC radio celebrity chat show, in order to offer the viewer vignettes of characters in the film: 'We bring you some of the interesting people who are "On the Prowl Tonight"', as the movie frame stopped and started on each character in order to give a knowing post-modern effect to the narrative. It was a film with a zany surreal humour and approach to storytelling that anticipated the anarchic comedy of *The Goon Show* on radio (1951-1960), and later *Monty Python's Flying Circus* (BBC TV 1969–74).

Helter Skelter had a somewhat slender plot, concerning an heiress, Susan Graham (played by Carol Marsh, who appeared previously in a film version of *Brighton Rock*), trying to find a cure for her hiccups. She linked up with a radio star Nick Martin (David Tomlinson), who was in the midst of an emotional crisis and unable to cope with both his insistent fans and the nightly transmission deadline of his show: '6.45 on the Light Programme'. The cinema audience watched a scene showing the recording of Martin's programme, with an energetic sound effects operator, brusque scriptwriter and unenthusiastic producer.

---

[94] Crompton, *William and the Brains Trust*, p. 16.
[95] Steve Chibnall and Brian McFarlane (2009), *The British 'B' Film*, London: Palgrave Macmillan/British Film Institute, p. 73.

Contemporary radio stars had cameo appearances, including Jimmy Edwards, Harry Secombe and Jon Pertwee. Terry-Thomas performed a sketch as a hapless presenter and disc jockey. On the wall of his studio was a sign:

> REMEMBER THE LISTENER. All Announcers should bear in mind that when they are on air they are in contact with millions of listeners who are in the habit of clinging to every word and might possibly re-act to the least suggestion of crisis during the presentation of a programme. Therefore, in the interests of the listener, DO NOT PANIC!

This appeared to contradict the complaints of inattention featured in Potter and Grenfell's *How to Listen* mentioned earlier. When the gramophone record Terry-Thomas was due to play was accidently broken, he gazed at the sign on the wall before rolling his eyes and responding with the understatement, 'So sorry listeners for the delay but I've just discovered a slight technical hitch.' It added to the overall tone of this movie, which presented BBC radio as a haphazard affair staffed by oddballs who still managed to make engaging programmes.[96]

Above all, the Corporation in this period was cast as an endearing institution. As if to emphasize such a sentiment, this was the era of linguistic change for audio broadcasting: from 'wireless' to 'radio'. Seán Street, an academic and radio producer, reckoned that this started around 1944 when talk began of a 'Radio Industry' rather than a 'Wireless Industry'.[97] This change emerged with the manufacture of 'utility *radio* receivers', backed by government support, which provided cheap and simple sets for the mass wartime market.

However, the BBC's output continued to be known as either 'services' or 'programmes', and it was not until 1967 when they became 'radio stations', as in Radio 4 or Radio 2. The immediate post-war era was probably when the BBC gained the pet name, 'Auntie'. Opinions varied as to its origins, but one source suggested Arthur Askey claimed to have coined the word 'Auntie' sometime during his long career.[98] The historian Asa Briggs narrowed the time period down: 'The BBC had not been known as "Auntie BBC" before the Second World

---

[96] See also the description of the BBC in *Human Voices* (1980) by Penelope Fitzgerald, discussed in Chapter 7. Terry-Thomas also appeared in a cameo role in a radio-related movie, *Brass Monkey* (1948), as an entertainer discovered by the radio talent-scout Carroll Levis. Levis had, between the mid-1930s and late 1950s, appeared variously on Luxembourg, Normandy and the BBC.
[97] Seán Street (2005), *A Concise History of British Radio 1922–2002*, 2nd edn, Tiverton, Devon: Kelly Publications, p. 78. Capitalized in the original.
[98] Stokes, 'Arthur Askey', p. 126.

War', and he regarded the term to imply less of a lovable family relation and more of a slightly overbearing one: 'Now the term was coming into general use at a time just before George Orwell was to forecast the two-way screen and the arrival into the home of a very different relative, Big Brother.'[99] This slightly uneasy feeling towards radio will be discussed in the next chapter. Meanwhile, other unconfirmed sources suggested that it could have been the radio DJ Jack Jackson in the 1950s who used the epithet 'Auntie', but this writer can find no independent confirmation of this. Finally, it is likely that the term 'Beeb' emerged later in the 1970s. Peter Sellers in a special reunion of *The Goon Show* called the Corporation the 'Beeb Beeb Ceeb', and the turn of phrase was quickly taken up by the DJ Kenny Everett.[100] Such linguistic changes placed the BBC firmly at the heart of British culture and society. The next few decades, and the emergence of the baby boomer generation, would change radio, pop music and the entertainment industry in decisive and dramatic ways.

---

[99] Briggs (1995), *The History of Broadcasting, Vol IV*, p. 195. *Nineteen Eighty-Four* by George Orwell was published in 1949.
[100] 'The Last Goon Show of All' (1972), *The Goon Show*, BBC Radio 4 and simulcast on BBC 2, 5 October. James Hogg and Robert Sellers (2013), *Hello, Darlings! The Authorized Biography of Kenny Everett*, London: Bantam, p. 57.

5

The new Elizabethans and new questions, 1950 to 1968

Post-war radio: From change to revolution

This chapter continues the theme of how radio listening – as opposed to its production which is highlighted in Chapters 7 to 9 – has been portrayed by writers and musicians. The period between 1950 and the end of the 1960s marked a shift in the way radio was written about and filmed. Seán Street identified this in two phases: firstly, the years from the end of the war to 1959 which, for him, formed an era in radio of both 'change and eternal values'; and secondly, the decade of the 1960s which he described as a time of 'radio revolution'.[1] This transition meant that from the domesticated Auntie BBC of the 1950s, radio became the illegal 1960s' pirate Caroline. But even so, radio's dominance continued to decline as television increasingly became the entertainment source of choice. One example of this was reflected in a children's weekly comic, *Radio Fun*, which had been published since 1938 and at its height featured some of the major British (mostly BBC) radio stars of the day. After the war, its content began to change as it included fewer names associated with British radio and increasingly more film stars, such as Clark Gable from the United States and Norman Wisdom from the United Kingdom. By the 1950s, there now appeared features on television comedians such as Benny Hill, and pop stars including Petula Clark and Elvis Presley. *Radio Fun* eventually became only a name: it changed owners in 1959, and after over a thousand issues it disappeared when it merged with the children's weekly *Buster* in 1961. Meanwhile, the BBC moved from the 1950s to the 1960s with a new confidence and what appeared to be a strengthened cultural monopoly. Alasdair Milne, a future director general, joined the Corporation in 1954 as a trainee and found it to have an air of

---

[1] Seán Street (2005), *A Concise History of British Radio 1922–2002*, 2nd edn, Tiverton, Devon: Kelly Publications, pp. 87 and 105.

'supreme self-confidence'.[2] The sociologist Tom Burns observed in 1963 and 1973 a growing sense of professionalism and authority amongst the staff he interviewed, in departments including engineering, schools broadcasting and light entertainment.[3] The transformation into a new assertive character was manifest in a fresh stridency in its journalism, a decline in deference and a new desire to question authority.[4] Britain was not, however, the only European country facing social and cultural change in the post-war decades.

The end of the ancient regime

This chapter begins with a French film that harked back to – and embodied – the continuities of a gentle, almost pre-modern, existence and which cast a comedic light on the radio listening habits of the previous twenty years. *Les Vacances de Monsieur Hulot* (1953) was filmed at a resort in Brittany, chosen for its unspoilt character. It reflected Jacques Tati's interest in the tensions between tradition and modernity which would also feature in his later films such as *Playtime* (1967) and *Trafic* (1971).[5] However, *Les Vacances de Monsieur Hulot* was the only one to include scenes with characters listening to a radio. The movie reflected a period when French society was emerging from a primarily agricultural economy to become a modern decolonized republic. In a quiet corner of the hotel lounge sat a man in a beret staring so closely at a wooden valve radio set on a table that at first glance he could have been watching a television. He ignored the physical comedy of Hulot's entry along with the gusts of wind through the opening and closing lobby door. On the film soundtrack was the radio music, high in the mix even though the receiver was not the centre of visual focus. The man, whose beret was a trope of his nationality, was the only one listening to the broadcast.

The other guests heard it but ignored it, preferring to carry on reading their books, or playing cards. Indeed, there was little dialogue in the movie and, 'the writer-star-director [was] more interested in sight gags, sound effect jokes,

---

[2] Milne was director general from 1982 to 1987. Alasdair Milne ([1988] 1989), *DG: The Memoirs of a British Broadcaster*, London: Coronet, p. 6.
[3] Tom Burns (1977), *The BBC: Public Institution and Private World*, London: Macmillan, p. 126.
[4] Hugh Chignell (2009), 'Change and Reaction in BBC Current Affairs Radio, 1928–1970', in Michael Bailey, ed., *Narrating Media History*, London: Routledge, pp. 37–9.
[5] David Parkinson (1995), *History of Film*, London: Thames and Hudson, pp. 183–4. See also Kristin Ross (1995), *Fast Cars, Clean bodies: Decolonization and the Reordering of French Culture*, Cambridge, MA: MIT Press, p. 30.

and the inimitable mannerisms of his hero', all of which helped it to gain an international audience.[6] Tati's approach to cinema sound was unusual and involved adding most of it at the post-production stage. According to one critic, 'When Jacques Tati applie[d] unorthodox audio practices deliberately to give his characters rather weak, unintelligible voices, matching in audio scale the long shot he generally film[ed] in, he [got] a uniquely perturbing effect.'[7] Moviemaking techniques involving radio sound are discussed in detail in Chapter 9, but here the act of paying attention to a radio programme became an unnerving experience amongst the physical comedy of the hotel lobby scene.

Later, a middle-aged English guest, a single lady assumed to be a widow or spinster, looked yearningly for entertaining music from the radio which broadcast nothing but depressing news about trade, employment and politics.[8] Her eyes lit up when Hulot played a record of energetic jazz on his gramophone: a representation of how boring and worthy post-war French radio could be compared to other European broadcasters. At the end of the evening, the transmission of the Radiodiffusion-Télévision Française's *Programme Parisien* closed with the national anthem. Hotel guests began to rise out of respect, but someone switched the radio off, and instead they milled about in embarrassed confusion, all half-standing for a split second before each deciding to go to bed. The French were, thus, watching themselves projected onto the cinema screen as polite middle-class holidaymakers on the Brittany coast with an English woman amongst them enthusiastic for some fun and excitement.[9] In this manner, movies were continuing to show cinema audiences (as mentioned in Chapter 3) that radio listening was a cultural practice.

The brave new future: Radio and the Festival of Britain

Two post-war examples portrayed the radio, both listening to it and appearing on it, set against the contemporary backdrop of the Festival of Britain of

---

[6] Jamie Russell (2003), 'Review: *Monsieur Hulot's Holiday (Les Vacances de M Hulot)* (1953)', 1 July. Available online: http://www.bbc.co.uk/films/2003/07/01/les_vacances_de_m_hulot_1953_review.s html, (accessed 24 May 2021).
[7] Michel Chion (1999), *The Voice in Cinema*, trans. Claudia Gorbman, New York: Columbia University Press, p. 82.
[8] Ross, *Fast Cars*, p. 171.
[9] By complete co-incidence, John Reith's biographer described the first BBC director general's behaviour, on a 1923 foreign holiday, as 'slightly reminiscent of a Jacques Tati film'. Reith had attempted to mend a broken tap in his hotel bedroom with a coat hanger and suitcase. Ian McIntyre (1993), *The Expense of Glory: A Life of John Reith*, London: HarperCollins, p. 131.

1951 which celebrated the nation's science, technology and hope for the future. A further three films from this period put radio – and the BBC in particular – in dark narratives which involved law-breaking and murder. Firstly, *London Entertains* (1951) and *The Happy Family* (1952) both mentioned the Festival and showed the BBC as a male-dominated organization with a metropolitan bias and an obsession with celebrity. *London Entertains* opened with the radio and TV personality Eamonn Andrews picking up a copy of the *Radio Times* folded back at page eleven, showing his picture at the top of the second column next to a listing for his show on the Light Programme at two o'clock in the afternoon on a Sunday in May 1951, called *Welcome Stranger*. The programme listing in the magazine said:

> Eamonn Andrews, with a BBC mobile recording unit, welcomes to London people from home and overseas who are here for the Festival of Britain. Produced by Phyllis Robinson.[10]

This suggested that radio and the BBC were at the heart of modernity at the Festival. The film moved from a factual travelogue of London sights through to a fictional tourist escort agency run by young women recently graduated from a Swiss finishing school. Whilst not prurient, it did feature recurring casually offhand sexist comments and *double entendres* from Andrews and others. The film was only forty-five minutes long, relied on stock footage for its establishing shots, and was made as a cheap supporting feature to be played out before the main movie.[11] As if to foretell the future of radio comedy, it included scenes with 'Those crazy people, the Goons', as the opening credits described them. The four original Goons were shown warming up an audience with improvised jokes, and then later performing their radio show from their scripts. The impression was that these comedians were not visual but aural performers: there was little of interest to look at on the screen during their scenes, and the recording consisted of them addressing the microphones rather than either the studio or the cinema audience. For the sake of the movie, there were cutaways of a theatre audience laughing. On the other hand, the BBC was cast on the side of tradition in a movie *The Happy Family*, released the following year. It was a story of a working-class household in conflict with the authorities who wanted to demolish their house

---

[10] 'Welcome Stranger' (1951), *Radio Times*, issue 1436, 18 May, p. 11. Available online: https://genome.ch.bbc.co.uk/3aa57773c78b4110bff6c43a21d33c99 (accessed 24 May 2021).

[11] Steve Chibnall and Brian McFarlane (2009), *The British 'B' Film*, London: Palgrave Macmillan/British Film Institute, p. 119.

to make way for an access road to the Festival site on the south bank of the River Thames in London. It was 'an engaging Ealing-esque comedy' starring Stanley Holloway as the head of the family.[12] The narrative had a fictional BBC reporter Maurice Hennessey (played by Tom Gill) finding himself inside the house as the family barricaded itself against the demolition crews. He was a toff with a plumy accent who wore a bowtie, dark suit and carnation in his lapel, to contrast with Holloway's South London accent, shabby cardigan and pipe. Hennessey was both ambitious and enthusiastic and began a running commentary on the events for radio listeners, not dissimilar in style to a cricket commentary.[13] The standoff between the barricaded family and the developers made a mid-bulletin story in the one o'clock radio news summary, and the correspondent achieved his ambition by being named on-air. In this invented story, the BBC was on the ground and reporting live about local concerns. Even though it appeared to be on the side of the little people, its reporters remained deeply patronizing towards the lower classes. In the end harmony was established, their house was saved and building plans for the Festival site were modified, symbolizing an imagined post-war unity of British society.[14]

Radio on film: Continuity with an edge of suspicion

Three movies that linked the radio industry to narratives about murder (a connection last seen in Chapter 2) were released in these years. Somewhat disconcertingly perhaps for the BBC, these films featured either real shows or actual genres of programme heard on-air. One had a killer use a radio broadcast to announce his crimes, another saw a detective working with his listeners in order to solve a case and the third had a blackmail victim kill his tormentor and then die himself, later giving his admission of guilt on the radio from beyond the grave.

The first of these, *The Twenty Questions Murder Mystery* (1950), saw reporters working to uncover the identity of a killer who had been sending clues to the

---

[12] Jeffrey Richards (2010), *Cinema and Radio in Britain and America, 1920–1960*, Manchester: Manchester University Press, p. 165. Stanley Holloway starred in an ITV sitcom, *For the Love of Ada*, mentioned in Chapter 6.
[13] Richards, *Cinema and Radio*, p. 165.
[14] Ross McKibbin (1998), *Classes and Cultures: England 1918–1951*, Oxford: Oxford University Press, p. 535.

eponymous radio quiz show *Twenty Questions* (1947–76). The movie allowed cinemagoers to watch behind the scenes, as an audience waited to enter the Paris Theatre in Lower Regent Street, long a venue used by the BBC for live recordings. Once inside, the journalist Richard Dimbleby was seen introducing himself and the panellists to the live audience. There were shots of cloth-covered tables, large microphones on stands, Bakelite headphones worn over the back of the head so as not to spoil the brilliantined hair for the cinema cameras, as well as studio clocks and cue lights that switched on as the second hands reached the top and transmission began. These images denoted the Corporation in action. Later, film critics observed that in these post-war years 'It was often an association with BBC radio that offered the opportunity for the low-budget film to improve its status'.[15] Indeed, *The Twenty Questions Murder Mystery* was an example of this strategy, and the opening credits said the movie was presented 'With the 20 Questions Team (by arrangement with Maurice Winnick)'. The latter was a dance band leader who introduced the show to Britain from the United States. The movie also again allowed cinema audiences to watch themselves listening to the radio, including a woman at home enjoying the broadcast whilst knitting. Her husband was seen in the kitchen putting on his tie in front of a mirror. Somewhat ominously, this man, who had failed to pay attention to the radio, ended up as the serial killer's first victim. The film gave the message to its cinema audiences that radio had such a major importance in society, and commanded mass attention from the British public, that a murderer could use it to fulfil his warped need for publicity over the airwaves.

The second example was *The Armchair Detective* (1951), which was a movie spin-off from a BBC radio series that mixed book reviews with dramatizations and was a regular fixture on the Light Programme from 1942 until the late 1950s presented by Ernest Dudley. The movie had Dudley solving a mystery and proving the innocence of a radio singer. It was poorly received by critics who called it 'unremarkable', and who thought the radio show was 'better heard than seen'.[16] Dudley later had five stories turned into British comic book versions in the *Super-Detective Library* series, published by Alfred Harmsworth's Amalgamated Press, between 1953 and 1955. None of them mentioned the radio in their narratives. At the opposite end of the critical spectrum was *The*

---

[15] Chibnall and McFarlane, *The British 'B' Film*, p. 41.
[16] Richards, *Cinema and Radio*, p. 112. Chibnall and McFarlane, *The British 'B' Film*, p. 127.

Voice of Merrill (1952).[17] This was an 'ingenious murder mystery', which began as a low-budget B-movie but was, like *The Twenty Questions Murder Mystery*, promoted as a co-feature because of its high production values.[18] The complex plot concerned the wife of a writer who wanted to promote her lover's literary career through a BBC radio series actually written by her husband. In order to establish the connection, the opening credits played over familiar exterior shots of Broadcasting House in London. Jonathan Roach (James Robertson Justice) was the author of a twelve-week radio serial called *The Voice of Merrill* written under a pseudonym. To complicate matters, the story was read live by Hugh Allen (played by Edward Underdown, Figure 5), who was the lover of Roach's wife Alycia (Valerie Hobson).

The cinema audience saw the author listening attentively at home, whilst in the studio Allen's slightly crumpled suit contrasted with the elegant cut of a BBC announcer's clothes. The scene was intercut with shots of transmitter masts, of

Figure 5 Hugh Allen (Edward Underdown, left) reads the *Merrill* story as his lover Alycia Roach (Valerie Hobson, far right, out of focus) looks on from behind the control room glass. *The Voice of Merrill* (1952), Dir. John Gilling, UK: Tempean Film.

---

[17] *The Voice of Merrill* was released in the United States as *Murder Will Out*.
[18] Richards, *Cinema and Radio*, p. 172; Chibnall and McFarlane, *The British 'B' Film*, p. 86 and 134.

pages from the *Radio Times*, of back-lit valve radio tuning dials and of listeners' letters to the programme. In the film, the author Roach died of natural causes, and shortly afterwards the final radio broadcast contained his confession to being a killer himself: of a woman in the opening scenes of the movie who had been blackmailing him. It was a complex resolution to a story that had been produced to give a film noir feel. The implication was that writers and broadcasters who worked for the BBC were a scheming, duplicitous lot who would stop at nothing in order to advance their own careers. The final moral note came as Alycia, the adulterous wife, died in a road accident.

The film closed with a camera tilt up the exterior of Broadcasting House, as if the Corporation had sat in judgement of the wrongdoers. These films pointed to an immediate future when the BBC would no longer be regarded as part of an innocent radio medium, intent on mere public service broadcasting. It would now be engrained both in life and in sudden unexplained death; and whilst it carried its traditions of public service into the 1950s and into the new Elizabethan age, it was increasingly seen and portrayed as being involved in the darker sides of modern life.

The beginning of the turn: From Auntie to inquisitor

From the outset of British radio broadcasting in 1922, the medium had enjoyed a mostly positive image. Any light-hearted criticism of the BBC had come in the form of friendly digs at its vague air of pomposity and self-importance. On film, its London headquarters from 1932, Broadcasting House, was used as an Art Deco symbol of the medium's modernity. Commercial radio stations including Radio Luxembourg, and before the war Radios Paris and Normandy, had been represented as slightly racy yet charming organizations also based in sumptuous Art Deco buildings. All in all, the radio had so far received a mostly positive representation. That was to change in the mid-1950s, and the pivot point came in the years between the publication of two novels by Evelyn Waugh. It happened between his 1952 book, *Men at Arms*, where radio was a pervasive but benign presence in the narrative, and *The Ordeal of Gilbert Pinfold* (1957), where the BBC in particular took on a haunting psychotic presence in the mind of the novel's protagonist.

Evelyn Waugh was not a particular fan of some of the post-war BBC programmes. He 'ordered his wife to buy a wireless set just to hear the Third

Programme', when it came on air in 1946.[19] He was said to be unimpressed with what he heard, but even so he recognized the importance of broadcasting. *Men at Arms*, for example, referred to it as the 'wireless' whenever it appeared in the narrative, consistent with its wartime setting. He used 'radio' only in the context of 'radio-telegraphy'. At the beginning of the novel, listening to broadcasts was a way to keep in touch with the latest information: 'Funny how one keeps twiddling the thing these days. I never had much use for it before', remarked Guy Crouchback's brother-in-law.[20] As the story progressed, the wireless kept appearing as characters were variously attentive to its sound or ignored its constant thrum in the background. One danced around the Army billiards room, 'with raised hands in little shuffling dance steps' to the sounds of jazz on the radio.[21] Waugh also recognized in *Men at Arms* that the receiver was sometimes an intrusion to be avoided. He mentioned what was probably the BBC's Forces Programme playing in the officers' mess after a campaign to have a set installed was finally successful despite initial opposition.[22] Once there, it was often left on to play out Churchill's speeches, news about air raids and the general progress of the war.[23] However, 'When the news was over, music began. Guy found an arm-chair as far from the wireless as possible', in order to avoid the sound of the BBC.[24] Later, Waugh sarcastically wrote how Guy enjoyed a trip to visit a friend in hospital, 'where there was no wireless to aggravate the suffering'.[25] The portrayal of radio in this novel was as an ambivalent piece of technology: it was necessary for the latest information but gave sadness and upset when it relayed bad news, and the character Guy relished his moments away from the noise of the wireless.

Men at Arms was part of the Sword of Honour trilogy, with the other two, *Officers and Gentlemen* and *Unconditional Surrender*, published in 1955 and 1961. In between writing this series, Waugh had a medical and emotional crisis which led to a nervous breakdown. Substance abuse and a shortage of money added to his troubles. When the BBC in 1953 offered to pay him for three

---

[19] Asa Briggs ([1979] 1995), *The History of Broadcasting in the United Kingdom, Volume IV, Sound and Vision*, revised edn, Oxford: Oxford University Press, p. 66.
[20] Evelyn Waugh ([1952] 1964), *Men at Arms*, Harmondsworth, Middlesex: Penguin, p. 21 (hereafter referred to as EW-MaA).
[21] EW-MaA, p. 46.
[22] EW-MaA, p. 93.
[23] EW-MaA, p. 169.
[24] EW-MaA, p. 170.
[25] EW-MaA, p. 235.

interviews on the radio about his life and work, he accepted.[26] The first session was recorded at Waugh's home for the programme *Personal Call*, to be broadcast on the Overseas Service. The second comprised two interviews at Broadcasting House, which were edited together for a programme called *Frankly Speaking*, for the Home Service, where he was questioned by a panel of three interviewers. One of Waugh's biographers, Martin Stannard, considered the interviews to have been acceptable and not particularly confrontational, but they played on Waugh's mind.[27] In particular, he appeared to worry about self-deprecating comments he had made which he thought highlighted his own shortcomings: as a father, a husband and a writer, remote from both his reading public and his own family and friends.

Waugh's novel *The Ordeal of Gilbert Pinfold* (1957) chronicled his own mental breakdown and his obsession with the outcome of those recent radio interviews. It was the story of a man bedevilled by voices in his head, peculiar obsessions and a persecution complex which made him think the BBC was intent on his destruction. The novel marked the turning point in the way radio was written about and presented by authors, filmmakers and artists. On one level, it was a novel about artistic impotence, but it was also a cautionary tale about the newly strident journalism of the post-war BBC.[28] This was the first time that radio in general, and the Corporation in particular, had been represented as a traumatic adversary causing mental distress. Waugh's novel began and ended with references to Sunday morning conversations Pinfold had with his neighbour in the village about radio programmes they had each listened to during the previous week. At the start he was merely bored by the conversation; on the last page of the novel, Pinfold could not even bring himself to face his neighbour.[29] In this manner, the whole story turned on talk about radio listening and the emotional effect it could have.

Pinfold accepted a request at the beginning of the novel to take part in a radio programme, and the BBC sound engineers arrived to set up their recording equipment in his library: 'The fee was . . . liberal [and] in an idle moment Mr Pinfold agreed and at once regretted it.'[30] But his fears increased when the lead BBC interviewer, called Angel, started his questioning:

[26] Martin Stannard (1992), *Evelyn Waugh: No Abiding City, 1939–1966*, London: J. M. Dent, p. 334.
[27] Stannard, *Evelyn Waugh*, p. 336.
[28] Stannard, *Evelyn Waugh*, p. 349.
[29] Evelyn Waugh ([1957] 1998), *The Ordeal of Gilbert Pinfold: A Conversation Piece*, London: Penguin, p. 7 and 132. Further references denoted EW-OGP.
[30] EW-OGP, p. 13.

> The commonplace face above the beard became slightly sinister, the accentless, but insidiously plebeian voice, menacing. The questions were civil enough in form but Mr Pinfold thought he could detect an underlying malice. Angel seemed to believe that anyone sufficiently eminent to be interviewed by him must have something to hide, must be an impostor whom it was his business to trap and expose, and to direct his questions from some basic, previous knowledge of something discreditable. There was the hint of an under-dog's snarl.[31]

The name Angel was a reference both to a character in Thomas Hardy's *Tess of the D'Urbervilles*, who drove Tess to despair, and to the angels at the gates of heaven ready to interrogate and deliver God's judgement upon sinners.[32] Pinfold's subsequent brooding about the interview turned into an obsession, and during an ocean cruise to recuperate, he imagined voices, radio programmes and people in his head, including psychotic episodes when he hallucinated that Angel and his family had joined him on the sea voyage to torment him, and that the occupants of the cabin next door were playing excerpts from the Third Programme at high volume in order to disturb his peace of mind. One critic regarded it as an 'oddly compelling text', and 'a dazzling verbal construct', which mirrored Waugh's own experiences at the time when his mental health worsened.[33] However, in real-life Waugh was not completely opposed to appearing again on the BBC and having to face more personal questions. In fact, in 1960 he agreed to take part in a television interview with John Freeman in a series called *Face to Face*. It was a programme that later became renowned for Freeman's ability to reduce guests, including Gilbert Harding and Tony Hancock, to nervous wrecks using a mixture of intense politeness and incisive questions. The Evelyn Waugh programme had no such effect on its subject, and the two had the following exchange on-air about the inspiration for the *Pinfold* novel:

> Freeman: Have you in fact a particular deep feeling about the BBC? (NO) Because it comes again into a number of your books, which is why I asked, always in a slightly pejorative context.
>
> Waugh: Well, everyone thinks ill of the BBC, but I don't think I'm more violent than anybody else.[34]

---

[31] EW-OGP, p. 14.
[32] Richard Jacobs (1998), 'Introduction', in EW-OGP, p. x.
[33] Jacobs (1998), 'Introduction', p. xiii.
[34] Quoted in Richard Jacobs (1998), 'Appendix', in EW-OGP, p. 164.

Waugh's *Pinfold* story was adapted for the Third Programme earlier that same year. The drama was well received by critics but the novelist himself, reportedly, refused to listen to it.[35]

Radio's newfound troubled reputation continued in a film about a professional hitman who attempted to plant a bomb in a portable receiver in a hotel lounge to kill a pompous cabinet minister who was staying there with his mistress. *The Green Man* (1956) was a black comedy about an enthusiastic assassin, Harry Hawkins (Alastair Sim). He purchased a radio set from a small shop run by Arthur Lowe and employed a dour Scottish technician (John Chandos as Angus McKechnie) to modify the wireless. In a subtle reference to Lord Reith and the BBC's pre-war heritage, Hawkins said to the electrician, 'You know, it's that fearsome combination of eager beaver and Scots non-conformist that makes your company so hard to bear, Angus.' The satire continued with Hawkins's next-door neighbour, who was a BBC announcer (Colin Gordon as Reginald Willoughby-Cruft): a character who was well dressed, strait-laced and somewhat off-hand – with a double-barrelled name to complete the trope of a haughty Corporation employee. The hero of the story was a travelling vacuum cleaner salesman (George Cole as William Blake) who eventually threw the radio set containing the bomb into the sea, thus saving everyone's life.

Death, intrigue and horror: Radio's dark side

Lying, corruption and control were some of the other themes presented in movies featuring radio in the late 1950s. *The Key Man* (1957, released in the United States as *Life at Stake*) was a British B movie in the style of an American hardboiled detective film. The investigator was a radio reporter, with a weekly show. The viewer heard the pips for seven o'clock in the evening, and the radio announced: 'This is Radio Cosmopolis bringing you *Crimes of the Times*, reconstructions from international police files presented by Lionel Hulme [played by Lee Paterson] and produced by Lawrence "Larry" Parr [played by Colin Gordon].' Lee Paterson was a Canadian actor who made a living playing tough American types in British movies in the 1950s and 1960s. The fictional Radio Cosmopolis was an attempt to make this film appeal to a transatlantic

---

[35] *The Ordeal of Gilbert Pinfold: A Conversation-Piece* (1960), BBC Third Programme, 7 June. See, Jacobs (1998), 'Introduction', p. xxxvi. See also Stannard, *Evelyn Waugh*, p. 430.

audience in order to get away from any BBC dominance, even though Scotland Yard was mentioned, and the street scenes were clearly shot in London. The story was a tale of chequebook journalism and sensationalist undercover reporting. The BBC would never have entertained the former, and it was not until the 1970s that it embarked on investigative journalism programmes with Roger Cook and *The Cook Report* on BBC Radio 4.[36]

Television had already been alluded to in a number of movies, for example it appeared as part of the plot in *Radio Parade of 1935* (1934) and *Sing as You Swing* (1937) – both discussed in Chapter 3 – and *Band Waggon* (1940, in Chapter 4), the latter of which had featured a secret TV station run by Nazi spies. These representations took on the feel of science fiction at times as they looked vaguely towards the future. But now, from 1955 British viewers had two channels to watch: the BBC and ITV. The coming of commercial television was the subject of the movie *Make Mine a Million* (1959), a comedy starring Arthur Askey and Sid James. Its release was timely because 'advertising was seen [by the British working class] as a symbol of the end of post-war austerity'.[37] In the movie, the BBC was transformed into the fictional National Television Corporation, whose directors were 'haughty and self-satisfied', whilst the commercial station was the popular TAA Commercial Network. The film suggested that BBC employees, such as Askey's character as a make-up artist, were buyable and corruptible. Radio was highlighted towards the end of the movie during a chase sequence when Askey broadcast his movements on national radio from the back of a Post Office van he had been using for his pirate television broadcasts, the van having been hijacked by an armed gang.

A work of science fiction that used radio as a key plot device was *The Day of the Triffids* (1951) by the British author John Wyndham. The entire story turned on one radio-related event. William (Bill) Masen was in hospital recovering a week after having been blinded by a sting from a benign triffid plant. As a consequence, he missed the opportunity to watch a subsequent meteor shower and could only follow it on the wireless:

The announcer, giving an account of the phenomenon in the six o'clock news, advised everyone that it was an amazing scene, and one not to be missed. He

---

[36] See Chapter 8 for a spoof of BBC radio investigative journalism, *Delve Special*, starring Stephen Fry. Another fictional radio detective was *Shoestring* (BBC TV, 1979) mentioned in Chapter 7.
[37] Jane Stokes (2000), 'Arthur Askey and the Construction of Popular Entertainment in *Band Waggon* and *Make Mine a Million*', in Justine Ashby and Andrew Higson, eds, *British Cinema, Past and Present*, London: Routledge, p. 130.

mentioned also that it seemed to be interfering seriously with short-wave reception at long distances, but that the medium waves on which there would be a running commentary were unaffected.[38]

Wyndham cast doubt into the reader's mind by suggesting that some menacing electromagnetic force was operating. William, in his temporary blindness in the hospital ward, mused as to why the radio even bothered to cover the event, especially since everyone was outdoors to watch the meteor shower for themselves:

> I tried listening to the radio, but it was making the same 'ooohs' and 'aaahs' helped out by gentlemanly tones which blathered about this 'magnificent spectacle' and 'unique phenomenon' until I began to feel that there was a party for all the world going on, with me as the only person not invited.[39]

It was a comment by the author, perhaps, on the quality of some BBC commentaries he may have recently listened to. One critic said Wyndham's novel re-created for the reader a feeling of insecurity, whereby 'as we become more certain, so the world portrayed becomes a less secure one'.[40] The radio here was instrumental in creating an imperfectly described and terrorized future world, and in the case of William the broadcast was unable to supply him with any useful information. When he later removed the bandages from his eyes, he discovered that almost everyone had been permanently blinded and that the Triffids had come to life and were beginning to take over. The radio broadcast was an integral part of the creation of that unstable and threatening world, and the auditory took on a new significance with the unfolding horror of the apocalyptic events.

As if to counter these negative images, the BBC attempted to provide a positive portrayal of itself in 1959 with a film documentary which it distributed to cinemas to be shown as a supporting feature to the main movie, as well as transmitting it on television.[41] *This is the BBC* was a montage of radio and

---

[38] John Wyndham ([1951] 1954), *The Day of the Triffids*, Harmondsworth, Middlesex: Penguin, p. 13. The novel was adapted into a movie (1962); two BBC radio plays, one on the Light Programme (1957) which was re-recorded for Radio 4 in 1968, and a version on the BBC World Service (2001); and two BBC TV versions (BBC 1, 1981 and BBC 1, 2009). Each, like the novel, employed the narrative device of using the radio to give information to characters blinded by the triffids. The 2009 TV adaptation also included a scene with twenty-four-hour satellite news coverage, reflecting the advances in contemporary media technology.
[39] Wyndham, *Day of the Triffids*, p. 14.
[40] C. N. Manlove (1991), 'Everything Slipping Away: John Wyndham's *The Day of the Triffids*', *Journal of the Fantastic in the Arts*, 4 (1): 29–53.
[41] Asa Briggs (1995), *The History of Broadcasting in the United Kingdom, Volume V, Competition*, Oxford: Oxford University Press, pp. 234-7. The film was premiered at the Odeon Leicester Square,

television vignettes across a twenty-four-hour period, and was similar to the 1937 documentary *BBC: The Voice of Britain* (see Chapter 2). It presented a series of images, but this time mostly of the inside of BBC studios and buildings, from Broadcasting House to Lime Grove television studios, to transmitter stations. The idea of 'news priority' was introduced to viewers with a breaking story of a missing aeroplane and the mobilization of reporters and camera crews to cover the events, reflecting journalism's fresh sense of professional authority in both BBC radio and television.

However, even if the BBC had been able to successfully demonstrate its positive side, there were still writers and poets prepared to cast a gloomy shadow over the media. Philip Larkin's poem *Broadcast* was written in 1961 and first published in the BBC's literary magazine *The Listener*, before being included in his 1964 collection *The Whitsun Weddings*. Larkin imagined he was at home one Sunday, as a classical music concert by the BBC Symphony Orchestra played on the radio. It began with the national anthem and the sounds of the audience rustling and coughing as they settled into their seats. Larkin thought of the one person who he knew was in the audience. In the typical English manner of understatement and deprecation, he imagined how she was wearing unfashionable shoes and that one of her gloves had fallen to the floor. He considered the 'glowing wavebands' of his radio and concluded by imagining the chasm between him and this one special person: 'Leaving me desperate to pick out / Your hands, tiny in all that air, applauding.'[42] Larkin was writing about his friend Maeve Brennan, who was there that evening at the City Hall in Hull.[43] Radio was both a connector and an isolator: disconnecting the homebound Larkin from his friend, and the audience in the hall. For the poet, it symbolized love unfulfilled, unrequited, un-sustained and unrewarded. If Larkin represented the serious lonely man, then perhaps Tony Hancock was the comic incarnation of such a character. In an episode of his sitcom *Hancock* called 'The Radio Ham', first shown on TV in 1961, he had taken up the hobby of amateur radio. Viewers saw Hancock returning to his bedsit with two new valves for his transmitting equipment:

London, in November 1959, and went on general release on 1 January 1960. It was broadcast on TV on 29 June 1960, when Television Centre opened.

[42] Philip Larkin ([1961] 1988), 'Broadcast', in Anthony Thwaite, ed., *Collected Poems*, London: The Marvell Press and Faber and Faber, p. 140.

[43] Maeve Brennan (2002), *The Philip Larkin I Knew*, Manchester: Manchester University Press, pp. 57–8.

Now then, where are me radio valves? Ah you little beauties! We'll soon have the watts throbbing through you, and your filaments glowing red hot! Carrying the thoughts and words of mankind to the four corners of the world. Oh there's nothing like a 19DS/87B! Look at you: a triumph of technological engineering. A work of art! They can keep their Mona Lisa, give me the inside of a wireless set any day.[44]

The suggestion was that amateur radio enthusiasts were obsessive, sad, lonely individuals, just like the Hancock character, and that their conversations with fellow hobbyists across the world were banal and inconsequential. He picked up a BBC news bulletin, immediately identifiable by its professional sounding voice, and complained about hearing it on the amateur wave bands. Later, Hancock's repeated attempts to respond when he heard a distress signal from a sinking boat ended in his apparent failure to either get the details written down or relay them to the relevant rescue authorities. It was a sustained comic representation of listening gone wrong. The message of the comedy was that radio was inherently small-minded and parochial, despite its international reach. Hancock's character was a consistently depressive, downbeat character suited to the representation of solitary listening to the radio. The week before, his show had satirized *The Archers*, the long-running BBC radio soap opera. Written by Hancock's regular scriptwriters, Ray Galton and Alan Simpson, 'The Bowmans' had a studio recording descend into chaos as Hancock misbehaved. It suggested that radio soap opera was a benign façade.[45]

A jumpin' little record I want my jockey to play

Both the 1950s and the 1960s were a time when society and ways of looking at it were in transition. It was an era when popular culture was becoming globalized and the pre-war attitudes towards the British class system and deference were changing. Works by Raymond Williams and Richard Hoggart each prompted the development of what would become 'culturalism' and subsequently the academic discipline of British cultural studies.[46] To borrow terms from what was this emerging area of study, popular culture was beginning to be regarded as less banal and lowbrow, and instead was being seen as a form of subaltern resistance and

---

[44] 'The Radio Ham' (1961), *Hancock*, BBC TV, series 7, episode 3, 9 June.
[45] 'The Bowmans' (1961), *Hancock*, BBC TV, series 7, episode 2, 2 June.
[46] Raymond Williams (1961), *The Long Revolution*, London: Chatto & Windus; Richard Hoggart (1957), *The Uses of Literacy*, London: Chatto & Windus.

semiotic reinvention.[47] These cultural changes came as technology allowed radio receivers to be increasingly portable, both through developments in electronic circuits and in dry-cell batteries.[48] The technology itself inspired a number of songs, including 'Tiny Blue Transistor Radio' (1965) by Connie Smith, 'Made in Japan' (1972) by Buck Owens and 'Magic Transistor Radio' (1973) by the Beach Boys. Van Morrison's 'Brown Eyed Girl' (1967) also remembered the youthful joys of listening to the transistor radio outdoors in the sunshine and fresh air.[49] The British jazz singer and writer George Melly reflected in an essay on the importance of pop culture, and how the portable radio had been instrumental in the way music was used and integrated into a mobile, youthful, society:

> It evolved at the same time as pop, another illustration of the chicken-or-egg rule which seems to operate so consistently in pop culture, and the transistor is a personal object like a wrist-watch or fountain pen. It both transmits and reflects the life-style of its owner.[50]

Likewise, the American guitarist and singer Chuck Berry was adamant that radio had a part to play in youth culture. 'Roll Over Beethoven' (1956) was an insistent song about a young man urgently wanting his local radio station to play rock 'n' roll. The imperatives came in the form of an injunction for the classical composer to turn in his grave. It was a song that captured both generational rebellion and the joy of music. He was clear that the radio should be the place to hear rock 'n' roll. However, any change in the programming of new musical genres on the radio, particularly at the BBC in Britain, was gradual. The Corporation mostly played only limited amounts of pop music in the 1950s and early 1960s, and when it did, it was heavily mediated and monitored.[51] The BBC still held to the vestiges of its pre-war notion that it was dispensing some

---

[47] Joe Moran (2005), *Reading the Everyday*, Abingdon, Oxfordshire: Routledge, p. 12.
[48] Michael Brian Schiffer (1993), 'Cultural Imperatives and Product Development: The Case of the Shirt-Pocket Radio', *Technology and Culture*, 34 (1): 98–113. Seán Street (2009), *The A to Z of British Radio*, Lanham, MD: The Scarecrow Press, p. 273. Robert Chapman (1992), *Selling the Sixties: The Pirates and Pop Music Radio*, London: Routledge, p. 26,
[49] Henry Schlesinger (2010), *The Battery: How Portable Power Sparked a Technological Revolution*, New York: HarperCollins, p. 256.
[50] George Melly ([1970] 1972), *Revolt into Style: The Pop Arts in Britain*, Harmondsworth, Middlesex: Penguin, p. 187.
[51] Dick Hebdige (1982), 'Towards a Cartography of Taste 1935–1962', in Bernard Waites, Tony Bennett and Graham Martin, eds, *Popular Culture: Past and Present – A Reader*, Beckenham, Kent: Croom Helm, pp. 202-3. In this period, the Corporation was also restricted by agreements with musicians and publishers about the amount of gramophone records it could play. See Stephen Barnard (1989), *On the Radio: Music radio in Britain*, Milton Keynes, Buckinghamshire: Open University Press, pp. 26–8, and 104–07. Also see, Chapman, *Selling the Sixties*, pp. 18–26.

Victorian ideal of 'cultural values' as a service to society.[52] It was not until the offshore pirates from 1964 onwards that music on the radio appeared to engage directly and consistently with youth culture and that, as the historian Eric Hobsbawm later remarked of this period, '"youth" was seen not as a preparatory stage of adulthood but, in some sense, as the final stage of human development'.[53]

Radio Luxembourg, its English service by now on 208 metres medium wave every evening from dusk, played a mixture of music as well as weekly American evangelical programmes by the likes of Billy Graham and Oral Roberts, and quiz and talent shows fronted by Michael Miles and Hughie Green both adopting mid-Atlantic accents. From the mid-1950s there were increasingly more hours of teenage-orientated pop record shows, including a rebroadcast of Alan Freed's rock 'n' roll show from the United States every Saturday night. A satirical song by the British singer Paddy Roberts talked about some of the personalities on a commercial station such as Radio Luxembourg. 'The Big Dee Jay' (1959), delivered in Roberts's deadpan half-spoken delivery, ridiculed the inflated egos of some of the star presenters, in particular those who fronted programmes sponsored by individual record labels. There were, however, others who were the prophets of doom: from the United States came a salutary lesson of what could happen if a radio presenter let his (and it was still at this time a gendered profession) fame go to his head and affect his behaviour. 'B.J. the D.J.', by Stonewall Jackson (1964), was a country song that warned of the dangers of celebrity life. The young presenter's mother learned about the death of her son in a car accident only because he was not on air for his usual breakfast show. In this song, the DJ had become a pathetic egotist concerned more about his own fame and alure than about any connection with the listeners.

From rock 'n' roll to pirate radio

Life was apparently a lot safer in Britain. A number of films from the early 1960s mixed rebellious pop culture and pirate radio into a safe mediated representation

---

[52] Paddy Scannell and David Cardiff (1982), 'Serving the Nation: Public Service Broadcasting before the War', in, Waites, Bennett and Martin, eds, *Popular Culture: Past and Present*, pp. 186–7. See also Paddy Scannell (1981), 'Music for the Multitude? The Dilemmas of the BBC's Music Policy, 1923–1946', *Media, Culture & Society*, 3 (3): 243–60.

[53] Eric Hobsbawm (1994), *Age of Extremes: The Short Twentieth Century 1914–1991*, London: Michael Joseph, p. 325.

of what might otherwise have been a dangerous medium if it were allowed free reign. Firstly, the movie *Climb Up the Wall* (1960), which was a compilation of film and music clips hosted by Jack Jackson, a trumpeter and dance band leader who became a disc jockey after the war.[54] His radio programmes were a feature of Saturday lunchtimes on the Light Programme from the 1950s to the 1970s, and he was also part of the Radio 1 line-up when it started in 1967. The film offered a taste of his approach to interacting with the music: the manner in which he edited, played and replayed audio clips from well-known comedy shows before introducing the record itself, and how he talked across the multiple pre-recorded voices as if in a conversation with them. This audio editing style influenced Kenny Everett and Noel Edmonds, who both used versions of this technique in each of their 1970s shows on BBC Radio 1. This movie put Jackson in front of the camera, and the radio was visualized with him appearing to operate a vertical panel with a screen and multiple dials to bring film clips in and out. It had the effect of taking away the chemistry of what he achieved on radio by concentrating instead on the technology that he was controlling. Tantalizingly the cinema viewer could see a radio control room through a glass partition that was full of machinery, with ten-inch tape reels hanging on the wall. The film was a sixty-five-minute B-movie touching the edges of the new rock 'n' roll and expresso coffee craze of the early 1960s and featured early British pop stars such as Russ Conway, Glen Mason and Craig Douglas miming to their hits. It also included some very short clips of the young Goons, including Michael Bentine and Peter Sellars performing solo turns, which were originally shot for another movie, *Down Among the Z Men* (1952), and reused here.[55] In *Climb Up the Wall*, Jackson wrote most of his own links and appeared with his son Malcolm. Even if his delivery was upbeat and wacky, he was seen onscreen as a white middle-aged father figure in neatly pressed trousers with a well-mannered son by his side. Father and son were mediating both the energy of radio and the rebelliousness of pop music into an acceptable cultural product for all the family.

The depiction of British pop stars would continue with perhaps one of the most iconic British movies of the era, which prophetically mentioned pirate radio three years before Caroline took to the airwaves. *The Young Ones* (1961) was a musical vehicle for Cliff Richard, and the story concerned a youth

---

[54] Chibnall and McFarlane, *The British 'B' Film*, p. 59. See also Chapman, *Selling the Sixties*, p. 238.
[55] *Down Among the Z Men* (1952) and *Climb Up the Wall* (1960) both had production and distribution links to E. J. Fancey's film businesses. See Chibnall and McFarlane, *The British 'B' Film*, p. 59 and pp. 117–21.

club which faced demolition to make way for an office block. Easy tropes helped to drive the narrative: the older generation thought the youth were aggressive and violent when in reality they were polite, well-dressed and eager to please; in return the older generation were shown as selfish and obsessed by money. Resolution was achieved in the story through intergenerational understanding.[56] *The Young Ones* was an example of how 'teenage culture is a contradictory mixture of the authentic and the manufactured'.[57] Having found an abandoned north London theatre, the actual Finsbury Park Empire which closed in 1960, they used it to stage their fundraising show to save the youth club. Nicky (Cliff Richard) came up with the idea of using pirate radio to promote the show: 'Wait a minute! I've got an idea. Does anyone know how we can get hold of an old radio transmitter?' The group had a brief attempt at guessing and concluded, somewhat implausibly, that they could find one in a junk shop. 'If we do get one do you know how to work it?', asked Cliff/Nicky. Melvyn Hayes, who played Jimmy, said, 'Yeah, just plug it in and turn it on'. The implication was that broadcasting was a remarkably simple procedure and did not require a bureaucratic institution such as the BBC.

The next day they broadcast live from a market stall in the street to advertise their show. The authorities quickly attempted to track the pirate broadcasts down but were frustrated by their own incompetence. It turned out that the signal was interfering with the ITV transmitters. On the other channel, a BBC newsreader somewhat sanctimoniously said, 'The BBC transmitters are of such strength that it is impossible for them to be interrupted', to which the pirates switched frequency and said, 'Want a bet?!' It was a light-hearted dig at the pomposity of the BBC. The suggestion was that radio could be used for illegal purposes and that the price for breaking the law was not arrest and a court appearance, but national fame. Three years after the film's release, the offshore pirates became symbolic of youthful rebellion within the commercial confines of the pop music industry. Cultural historian Robert Chapman said:

> until the pirates came along the listeners had 'no body' to represent them. Even though the station owners were largely interested in their purchasing power they also recognized the prestige to be gained from such sentiments. As consumers the audience's existence had meaning. Listeners were participants in a new

---

[56] John Hill (1986), *Sex, Class and Realism: British Cinema 1956–1963*, London: BFI Publishing, p. 104.
[57] Stuart Hall and Paddy Whannel ([1964] 2009), 'The Young Audience', in John Storey, ed., *Cultural Theory and Popular Culture: A Reader*, 4th edn, Harlow, Essex: Pearson Longman, p. 47.

emerging youth culture but 'no body' had so far given them much of a voice. They were simply presented with a litany of prohibition, a discourse on all that was forbidden.[58]

The Who and the Small Faces: Mod style goes offshore

The main arguments against the offshore pirates were their lack of music copyright payments, and the interference of their transmitters with both established broadcasters and the emergency service frequencies.[59] The British government implemented legislation to outlaw the stations, eventually curtailing their operations in 1967. Before then a movie called *Dateline Diamonds* (1965) linked pop music, crime and the offshore station Radio London into a single narrative. It featured the band the Small Faces and included a cameo performance by the DJ Kenny Everett.[60] The cinema audience was shown how the system of getting on board the boat worked, as a journalist arrived at Harwich docks asking for the 'tender to the radio ship'. Later, the Small Faces turned up at the docks in their minibus, also wanting a passage to the actual MV *Galaxy*, the home of Radio London. Back on land, the movie showed an entire family listening to the station and suggested that the pirates were both popular during this era and met an appetite from the public. Tom Jenkins, a police detective (played by Conrad Phillips), was seen both at home and in his car listening in as Dale Meredith (played by Burnell Tucker) gave news of a diamond robbery. The robbers were shown listening to the same broadcast, whilst the detective's daughter had the station on at home on her transistor radio. The teenager was clearly a fan, as she sent letters and record requests to the DJs and waited to hear her name mentioned on-air.[61] The plot had diamond robbers smuggling the proceeds of their crime to Amsterdam via the Radio London boat in boxes of seven-inch reels of audio tape – unbeknown to the radio station – which had tenders arriving from both Britain and the Netherlands. It was a plausible idea and connected offshore broadcasting to illegal activities.

---

[58] Chapman, *Selling the Sixties*, p. 54.
[59] Richard Rudin (2007), 'Revisiting the Pirates', *Media History*, 13 (2–3): 238. Chapman, *Selling the Sixties*, p. 32.
[60] James Hogg and Robert Sellers (2013), *Hello, Darlings! The Authorized Biography of Kenny Everett*, London: Bantam, pp. 57–8.
[61] Radio London, which intentionally copied American pop radio styles, was a major competitor of Radio Caroline. See Chapman, *Selling the Sixties*, pp. 74–93.

The links to crime and international espionage were in evidence in an episode of the British television series *Danger Man*, which was set on-board another offshore pirate station.[62] Instead of a boat, the fictional Radio Jolly Roger was based on a disused British sea fort built on stilts off the coast of Kent. In real life, the Red Sands Fort was used by Radio 390, which was thanked in the closing credits.[63] The viewer was shown the mechanics of arriving at the fort by motor launch, the layout of the connecting walkways and the interior of radio studios (shot separately in the television studio). The star, John Drake (Patrick McGoohan), was deployed undercover to investigate the owners of the station who were sending state secrets to a nearby submarine. Again, pirate radio was seen to be involved not just in 'illegal' broadcasting but in international criminal activities. This theme resurfaced in an episode of the British TV crime series *Special Branch* in 1974, featuring a storyline about land-based pirate radio, mentioned in the next chapter. As parliamentary opposition grew towards the offshore pirates, a group of British musicians recorded a single *We Love the Pirates* in 1966 under the name of The Roaring 60's. It was written by Geoff Stephens, John Carter and Terry Kennedy, and sung in the style of the Beach Boys, with close male harmonies and jangling guitars. It was not a hit despite being played on a number of the offshore stations at the time as a call to arms for supporters.

In the summer of 1967, the offshore pirates were outlawed by act of parliament. Just before Christmas that year, The Who released a concept LP which paid tribute to stations such as Caroline and London. The band, like the Small Faces, had benefitted greatly from the pirates playing and promoting their records.[64] *The Who Sell Out* was an LP of songs interspersed with the band's renditions of radio commercials and some of the actual jingles from Radio London, as if the whole thing were a broadcast programme. Versions of some of the jingles on the album were heard again in the 2017 TV comedy *Hospital People*, discussed in Chapter 10. Radio Caroline continued broadcasting in 1967 and was later joined by Radio Northsea International in the 1970s and Laser 558 in the 1980s, all allegedly supplied from non-British ports.[65] Also, in 1967 the BBC launched

---

[62] *Danger Man* (1966), ITV/ITC, 'Not so Jolly Roger', series 3, episode 23, 7 April. The series was known in the United States as *Secret Agent*. It was shown in the UK from 1960 to 1968.
[63] Radio 390 broadcast middle-of-the-road music, similar to the Light Programme, from September 1965 until July 1967. See Chapman, *Selling the Sixties*, pp. 138–43.
[64] Richard Barnes ([1982] 2000), *The Who: Maximum R&B*, London: Plexus/Eel Pie, pp. 47–8 and 66.
[65] For a memoir of working onboard Caroline in the 1980s and 1990s, see Steve Conway ([2009] 2014), *Shiprocked: Life on the Waves with Radio Caroline*, Dublin: Liberties Press. For an account of

Radio 1 and renamed its existing national stations as Radios 2, 3 and 4. In addition it opened what would become a network of forty local radio stations. Independent commercial radio did not begin in Britain until 1973.

The memory of the offshore pirates would be the subject of a nostalgic film four decades later called *The Boat That Rocked* (2009, see Chapter 10). In the meantime, a romanticized form of radio's past was already available in 1968 in the action movie *Where Eagles Dare*, which included scenes of British and American spies using short-wave radio. The writer Geoff Dyer was ten years old when he first saw the film, and fifty years later, in 2018, he published a humorous reflection on the movie. He argued that Richard Burton's repeated declaiming of the radio callsign 'Broadsword calling Danny Boy', when trying to communicate to his headquarters in England from the depths of the mountains in enemy territory, had become 'embedded in the national psyche'.[66] Just as the BBC repositioned itself as both the nation's national and local broadcaster in 1967, so too the very medium was seen in the movie *Where Eagles Dare* as central to the idea of Britishness through Burton's mellifluous enunciations. This imagined national identity would soon come under foreign cultural influences. The next chapter explores the deepening links between American and British portrayals of radio listening.

---

working on both the offshore and the new UK commercial stations in the 1970s, see Clive Warner (2018), *Adventures in the Luminiferous Aether*, Kindle edn, Citiria Publishing.

[66] Geoff Dyer (2018), *'Broadsword Calling Danny Boy': On Where Eagles Dare*, London: Penguin, p. 22 and 79. See also Alasdair Pinkerton (2019), *Radio: Making Waves in Sound*, London: Reaktion Books, pp. 181–2.

6

Britain and the fascination with American radio nostalgia, 1969 to 1979

Don't touch that dial: Transatlantic inspiration

The previous chapter charted the first two decades after the war and the changes in the way the BBC in particular was represented in film, novels and popular music: how its image altered from an endearing and slightly overbearing Auntie into a self-assured broadcasting behemoth determined, amongst other things, to mediate any growing influence of youth culture and pop music. This chapter now explores how views about radio continued to develop as the 1970s saw an influx into Britain of American movies and songs that talked about the medium. It gave the British a glimpse of a different radio culture. On the one hand, it was, according to the movies and songs in this chapter, a problematic type of broadcasting still connected with murder threats. Yet on the other it represented, in this decade, the beginning of a turn to nostalgia – specifically for the immediate past of the teenage years of the baby boomers now reaching the first peak of their creative outputs. The British reaction to these 1970s movies and music about American radio was at first muted but, as domestic Independent Local Radio (ILR) funded by commercials established itself, negative critiques eventually emerged from the likes of The Clash, The Selecter and Elvis Costello.

The American influence

In a sense, the influence of American culture on British radio broadcasting had always been present. During the inception of the BBC in the 1920s, firstly as a company under a government licence, later as a public corporation through a royal charter, it was the view that Britain should have a strictly regulated system diametrically opposite to what was perceived to be a commercial free-for-all in the United States and 'a chaos of wavelengths' of competing radio station transmitters.[1] Such a view had been confirmed at the time after visits by British radio executives. As commercial stations in Europe opened in the 1930s, they came under the influence of American advertising agencies in both programming and production, particularly at Radios Normandy, Luxembourg and other stations broadcasting to Britain.[2] During the Second World War, there were opportunities, albeit limited, to tune in to the American Armed Forces Network broadcasting locally to troops stationed at bases in Britain. Whilst on the BBC, popular American variety stars appeared on air, including Bob Hope and Jack Benny. Some, like Ben Lyon and Bebe Daniels (see Chapter 4), had enduring careers in British radio and TV into the 1950s. Behind the microphone, the American influence led to professional methods being introduced such as continuity announcers, strict timekeeping and consistent programme scheduling. All proved to be popular with British listeners, even if the audience did not immediately realize the source of such techniques.[3]

After the war American culture continued its allure: British movie audiences in the 1950s enjoyed the latest Hollywood releases, and for some members of the new post-war generation, 'American culture represented a force of liberation against the grey certainties of British everyday life.'[4] As radio sets became transistorized, listening to the radio after dark alone in a teenage bedroom became easier. Luxembourg played pop, and, as mentioned in the previous chapter, some of its key presenters adopted mid-Atlantic accents. In the 1960s, Radio London (see Chapter 5) intentionally set out to emulate American pop radio formats and presentation styles, and became, alongside Caroline, one of the most popular offshore pirate stations of the era. For cultural historians, the outcome of such a prolonged exposure to American culture meant that it had become by the 1970s 'sedimented in British common sense', and in 1973 an

---

[1] Asa Briggs (1961), *The History of Broadcasting in the United Kingdom, Volume I, The Birth of Broadcasting*, Oxford: Oxford University Press, p. 97. Simon Dawes (2017), *British Broadcasting and the Public-Private Dichotomy: Neoliberalism, Citizenship and the Public Sphere*, Cham, Switzerland: Palgrave Macmillan, pp. 141–4.

[2] Seán Street (2006), *Crossing the Ether: Pre-War Public Service Radio and Commercial Competition in the UK*, Eastleigh, Hampshire: John Libbey, pp. 85–94; Asa Briggs (1965), *The History of Broadcasting in the United Kingdom, Volume II, The Golden Age of Wireless*, Oxford: Oxford University Press, p. 365.

[3] David Cardiff and Paddy Scannell (1981), 'Radio in World War II', in *The Historical Development of Popular Culture in Britain*, U203, Block 2, Unit 8, Milton Keynes, Buckinghamshire: Open University Press, pp. 68–9.

[4] John Storey (2006), *Cultural Theory and Popular Culture: An Introduction*, 4th edn, Harlow, Essex: Pearson Education, p. 7.

estimated half of all movies screened around the world were made in America.[5] However, the contemporary British radio industry still sounded to some as if it was two decades behind its North American counterpart. The ILR stations which opened from 1973 onwards were tightly regulated, burdened with legal requirements and beholden to a public authority which determined the technicalities of transmission.[6] As a result of the conflicting imperatives of public service broadcasting and commercial success, they were restrained (until the 1990s) to the point of sounding like public service broadcasters that happened to play commercials.[7] ILR in Britain in this period was a pale imitation of the variety and vibrancy of the American industry. As a result, there was a certain fascination with the American films, songs and novels which highlighted an industry that itself was beset with its own particular issues. I mention the American examples which follow not to seek to describe here the American radio industry of the 1970s in detail, but rather – by remembering that these texts circulated in Britain during this period – to consider how they may have influenced the ways in which radio, broadly conceived, was regarded in the years that followed. At the end of this chapter, therefore, is a collection of British cultural responses, each of which was tinged both with critiques of contemporary UK commercial radio formats and in particular the music policies of the stations. These were to form the foundations of British reactions to radio for the next forty years.

Play Misty for Me: The radio as a threat to life

The first example was a Hollywood movie which emphasized the level of suspense and threat connected to radio. *Play Misty for Me* (1971) was Clint Eastwood's first film as a director. He also took the lead, playing a DJ on a local music station – actually KRML, close to where Eastwood lived on the Californian coast. British audiences could observe that there existed local radio stations which played album tracks and genres such as rock and jazz, unlike in

---

[5] Dick Hebdige (1982), 'Towards a Cartography of Taste 1935–1962', in Bernard Waites, Tony Bennett and Graham Martin, eds, *Popular Culture: Past and Present - A Reader*, Beckenham, Kent: Croom Helm, pp. 203 and 215.
[6] Guy Starkey (2011), *Local Radio, Going Global*, Basingstoke, Hampshire: Palgrave Macmillan, pp. 45–6.
[7] D. P. Allen (2011), 'Independent Local Radio (ILR) in the West Midlands, 1972–1984: A Comparative Study of BRMB Radio and Beacon Radio', PhD diss., University of Worcester, pp. 6, 12 and 97; Tony Stoller (2010), *Sounds of Your life: The History of Independent Radio in the UK*, New Barnet, Hertfordshire: John Libbey, pp. 24 and 32.

the UK where the distinctions were the broad categories of 'pop' (Radio 1), 'easy-listening' (Radio 2) and classical (Radio 3), with limited space for 'specialist' genres in the evenings such as folk, and brass bands. The movie began with Dave Garver (Eastwood) getting into his open-top sports car, pressing the AM (medium wave) pre-set button on his radio and listening as KRML played a stirring rock track – a musical contrast to his own evening jazz show.

Eastwood portrayed his late-night DJ character as a type of lothario: who picked up women in bars and traded his on-air position for free drinks in restaurants. There was a similarity in this laid-back macho characterization that was also present in the movie *FM*, and the TV series *WKRP*, both mentioned later in this chapter. Eastwood portrayed a public personality who became the target of a psychopath. Viewers saw him go on-air for his five-hour show (8.00 pm to 1.00 am) with little sign of preparation and no use of headphones in the studio. This was a visualization of the working DJ which was, and still is, commonly seen in movies and TV dramas. However, later in the film Garver was seen at home at a typewriter apparently preparing scripts and looking at album covers, a recognition that freeform American radio relied on the creative talents of DJs to select appropriate music to play and that the profession was more akin to a craft than a trade because it pervaded the DJ's entire daily time. The film also demonstrated how pre-recorded radio shows could, and did, deceive audiences as Eastwood put on a tape when he left the studio during the final brutal moments of the film.

Elsewhere, the image of the somewhat chaotic and solitary existence of a DJ was highlighted in the song 'W.O.L.D.', by Harry Chapin, which was a hit in Britain in 1974. It was about a morning DJ regretting his life of fame behind the microphone, and how he had given up his marriage and personal happiness for work in such a transient industry. Just a few years before this single was released, Randy Newman had identified radio's connection to substance abuse and riotous parties. His song 'Mama Told Me Not to Come', by Three Dog Night (1970), linked the sound of the radio in the third verse to the bad experiences of a drug-induced evening at a party where the radio could be heard playing loud music as his girlfriend collapsed in a drink and drug-induced stupor. However, even as the hedonism of the late 1960s and early 1970s was in full swing, there were those post-war creatives, some by now in their mid-twenties, intent on looking back to their own teenage years, to the days of rock 'n' roll. It was the beginning of a turn to nostalgia that would persist for decades to come and would be firmly linked to images of the radio.

Baby boomer radio: How youth cultures came of age

The central example of this tendency was the film *American Graffiti* (1973), which unashamedly harked back to the early 1960s, with the promotional strapline 'Where were you in '62?' Cultural analysts have identified the movie as one of the key nostalgic films of the era. It was also, like *Play Misty for Me*, a movie that dealt with the listener's creation of the imagined DJ character. Talking about his inspiration for the movie, George Lucas explained that he was fascinated with

> The intimate nature of people's familiarity with disc jockeys who they've never met, who were basically a fictitious fantasy character that they become very friendly with because they listen to them all the time on the radio, especially if they're cruising at night. There's this fantasy character that actually becomes part of your life.[8]

The movie began with the sound of a jingle, anchoring the radio – and American rock 'n' roll radio in particular – as part of the narrative. The voice of the DJ Wolfman Jack become a persistent motif in the soundtrack between and behind scenes as if in a remote conversation with the on-screen characters.[9] Film dialogue served to underline how much the characters enjoyed listening to his shows, and the DJ was built up during the first part of the film into a mythical unseen personality. The movie followed a group of young people preparing to move on from college and into adult life. Visually, it showcased brightly coloured classic cars, era-specific clothes and a persistent soundtrack of rock 'n' roll music: the youth culture that Lucas, the director and co-writer, grew up with in small-town California.

Cultural theorists have since sought to explain this turn to nostalgia, especially Fredric Jameson in the 1980s, who detected an attempt to recover an immediate past that was somehow missing from mid-1970s society.[10] Jameson felt that *American Graffiti* and other films of the period including *Rumble Fish*, *Body*

---

[8] George Lucas (1998), 'The Making of American Graffiti' [DVD bonus material (2003), *American Graffiti*], Universal Studios Home Video.
[9] Gene Fowler and Bill Crawford (2002), *Border Radio: Quacks, Yodelers, Pitchmen, Psychics, and Other Amazing Broadcasters of the American Airwaves*, Austin, TX: University of Texas Press, pp. 259–74.
[10] Fredric Jameson (1984), 'Postmodernism, or the Cultural Logic of Late Capitalism', *New Left Review*, 146, July–August: 66–7. Available online: https://newleftreview.org/issues/i146/articles/fredric-jameson-postmodernism-or-the-cultural-logic-of-late-capitalism (accessed 26 May 2021). A similar critical view was also taken by Simon Reynolds (2011), *Retromania: Pop Culture's Addiction to its Own Past*, London: Faber & Faber, pp. 292–4.

Heat and *Chinatown* were postmodern reactions to contemporary economic and political events. However, Jameson's concern appeared to be a lack of historically critical depth, and that this engagement with the recent past of the early 1960s was somehow shallow or lacking in seriousness. As a result, for him, it was an example of postmodern pastiche. Jameson had his critics, and I agree with academics such as Vera Dika, who suggested that such movies may have instead been symptomatic of a much more direct engagement, whereby producers and audiences were looking for a (re)presentation of their remembered recent past. It was not a shallow reaction but instead, as Dika said, the film was intended to 'have a lived resonance' for people who came to adulthood during the eleven years from 1962 to 1973. These were the years between when the movie was set and when it was released.[11] On the one hand, the film did indeed appear to oversimplify the past, but on a deeper level it also presented a conflict between lived memory and imagined memory. It was much more than mere pastiche, and the movie used nostalgia positively to 'ruminate', 'reclaim' and 'redefine' the past.[12] Another critic, Fred Davis, writing in the late 1970s, observed through his readings of popular culture, including comics, film and music, that nostalgia was central in forming and maintaining an individual's identity and their own place in society. He suggested that nostalgia was a type of recollection that was formed in the present, often in order to deal with current anxieties.

However, like Jameson after him, he suggested that movies such as *American Graffiti* lacked a 'genuine' nostalgia.[13] What had become evident was that any desire to look to the past was motivated by a complex set of influences and concerns, both by individuals and society at large. By recalling the past and rediscovering former selves through such fictional films, people could attempt to deal with, and understand, the present. Vera Dika agreed that George Lucas's movie was able to fulfil this need, and that '*American Graffiti* ha[d] the structure of irony, producing a feeling of nostalgia but also of pathos and registering the historical events as the cause of an irretrievable loss'.[14] However, this attempt to regain a lost past was here a white nostalgia. Racial diversity was absent from this and other films, novels and songs of the period included in this chapter.

---

[11] Vera Dika (2003), *Recycled Culture in Contemporary Art and Film: The Uses of Nostalgia*, Cambridge: Cambridge University Press, p. 91.
[12] Michael D. Dwyer (2015), *Back to the Fifties: Nostalgia, Hollywood Film, and Popular Music of the Seventies and Eighties*, New York: Oxford University Press, pp. 51 and 58.
[13] Fred Davis (1979), *Yearning for Yesterday: A Sociology of Nostalgia*, New York: Free Press, pp. 86–90.
[14] Dika, *Recycled Culture*, p. 91.

The radio in *American Graffiti* took on a central role, supplying both the musical soundtrack and a way to resolve the romantic thread of the story. The emotional highpoint of the movie was a very European cinematic moment, a *coup de foudre*, when Curt Henderson (Richard Dreyfuss), sitting in the back seat of a car at a set of lights, saw a mysterious blonde woman in a white Thunderbird coupe who appeared to mouth inaudibly 'I love you' at him before driving away. In an attempt to find her he eventually went to the radio station, denoted in the film as an out-of-town utilitarian building next to a tall transmitter mast, with the intention of sending a message over the air. He was disappointed to find just one person in the studio at such a late hour. It was an overweight bearded white man who first complained that the freezer had broken down, and then denied that he was the Wolfman, claiming that the shows were pre-recorded elsewhere and relayed to multiple stations such as this one. As Curt left the studio, he saw the man talking at the microphone and realized with a wry smile that he had been deceived: this was the Wolfman himself. The point being that reality and artifice in radio were shown to be confused and confusing.[15] Wolfman was previously heard on the soundtrack saying to one of his phone-in callers, 'Gonna make all your dreams come true, baby!' as if he had hyperreal abilities. The film's narrative suggested that an imaginary 'Wolfman' radio character could resolve Curt Henderson's romantic yearnings. The DJ, a larger-than-life personality, had elsewhere inspired, and been mentioned in a number of American pop songs including the following: 'The WASP (Texas Radio and the Big Beat)' by The Doors (1971), Grateful Dead's 'Ramble On Rose' (1972), Todd Rundgren's 'Wolfman Jack' (1972), The Guess Who with their 'Clap for the Wolfman' (1974) and Tammy Wynette's 'I'd Like to See Jesus on The Midnight Special' (1978). The latter, somewhat incongruously, imagined Wolfman Jack introducing Jesus as one of the acts performing a song on the American music TV show of the same name.

Another evocation of the recent past came with the song 'Yesterday Once More' by the Carpenters (1973). It was a co-written by Richard Carpenter recalled a youth remembered through favourite songs of the era, yet somehow lost. If Lucas's *American Graffiti* was an attempt to deal with the uncertainties of growing up in the early 1960s, then the Carpenters were sharing an almost-Proustian theme of longing for what may be termed 'a golden age' of radio, an

---

[15] This was an example of Michel Chion's *acousmêtre* effect, the hidden/revealed voice in cinema, discussed in detail in Chapter 9.

imagined listening seeking to recapture lost time. 'Yesterday Once More' was a hit as a seven-inch single; however, the album version segued into a twenty-minute medley of 1950s and 1960s oldies with scripted 'radio' interjections that attempted to recreate the overexcited DJ presentation clichés of a contemporary radio show. It perhaps unintentionally mirrored *The Who Sell Out* (1967), mentioned in the previous chapter.

Other songs of the era, all with varying touches of nostalgia, included 'Rock and Roll' by The Velvet Underground (1970). Written by Lou Reed, it was musically a genre away from the Carpenters, but even so, it yearned for a return to youthful innocence. It spoke of a girl called Jenny, apparently just five years old, who had a certain ennui about her life with her materialistic parents. One day she tuned into a big-city radio station that was playing rock 'n' roll music. The song was a joyous shout for liberty and rebellion, fuelled by the music of contemporary youth culture which literally saved her young life. 'Radar Love' by Golden Earring (1973) represented the European response: a band from the Netherlands performing in the American hard-rock vein, mentioning a country music singer from the 1950s and 1960s, Brenda Lee, who was heard playing on the radio. It was an anthemic song with a simple call and response pattern between the vocals and the guitar. The recalling of the past times of recent youth also permeated 'Roadrunner' by Jonathan Richman and the Modern Lovers (recorded in 1972 and released in 1976). Again, this was a call and response song, with 'Radio on' being the persistent answer to every line of the chorus. For one critic, writing forty years later, '"Radio on!" [was] the mantra for anyone who ever believed in the power of pop music to open up worlds of possibility'.[16] Richman's simple song quickly became one of the iconic themes of the punk rock movement, and was covered somewhat chaotically, but with a certain amount of charm, by the Sex Pistols in 1979.

Even as punk rock was on the ascendency in Britain, an American film went on general release which at first appeared musically anachronistic. *The Last Waltz* (1978), directed by Martin Scorsese, featured some of the biggest musical acts of the 1960s and 1970s; artists who had made their names in the album-oriented rock (AOR) market (of which more later) but by the end of the decade were losing their popularity.[17] It was a cinematic record of a 1976 farewell concert by The Band, led by Robbie Robertson. The group, which originated in Canada, rose

---

[16] Sean L. Maloney (2017), *The Modern Lovers*, London: Bloomsbury Academic, p. 6.
[17] Dika, *Recycled Culture*, p. 87.

to prominence in the United States first as Bob Dylan's backing band and then as artists in their own right. This movie was identified as another type of nostalgia film which, because of its high professional cinematic quality, broke from the tradition of rough-and-ready live concert footage. According to one cultural historian:

> The rock concert event is thus seen through the patina of the glossy image, which fixes it, as it were, and so quite consciously relegates it to the past. Through the calcification of the image, *The Last Waltz* chronicles the end of The Band and, symbolically, the end of a cultural era.[18]

Like Lucas's *American Graffiti*, Scorsese's *Last Waltz* demonstrated a fondness for radio. In the latter it was an appearance by the Belfast-born Van Morrison that provided a glimpse of the nostalgia and memories evoked by the mention of listening to the radio. Visually, as remarked upon in the introduction, Morrison was not at his telegenic best; however, the message was clear in the words he sang with deeply felt emotion. He linked listening to songs on the radio with a romantic tryst with his lover, and memories of late adolescence and early adulthood as a baby boomer in the early 1960s (Morrison was born in 1945; 'Caravan' was first released in 1970).[19] The camera caught him lost in the music. There was a gospel, quasi-religious quality to Morrison's repetition that evoked a spiritual connection and was a reason, perhaps, why the British novelist Nick Hornby once said that he wanted the song played at his own funeral.[20] It was music which presented an imagined past of the joyful simplicity of a teenager listening to music on the radio: a way to lose your own soul in the ecstatic moment. Morrison returned to the studio and the subject of the radio with the title track of his album *Wavelength* (1978), which spoke of the radio making connections. It was both a romantic love song and a hymn to the spirited energy of pop radio. Morrison sang that his radio could bring happiness and lift his melancholy when he was feeling sad and far from home. He also included veiled nostalgic mentions of a Ray Charles song from 1954 ('Come Back Baby') and, indirectly, his own 1967 hit – referred to in Chapter 5 – 'Brown Eyed Girl' (both

---

[18] Dika, *Recycled Culture*, p. 86.
[19] Brian Hinton (2000), *Celtic Crossroads: The Art of Van Morrison*, 2nd edn, London: Sanctuary Publishing, p. 107.
[20] Nick Hornby (2003), *Songbook*, New York: Riverhead Books, p. 93.

lyrics mentioned romantic encounters in the grass).[21] The theme re-emerged in 1990 in his duet with the Irish poet Paul Durcan, discussed in Chapter 8.

This nostalgia was expressed by Ed Ruscha in his painting *Smells Like Back of Old Hot Radio* (1976). Ruscha was an American conceptual artist closely associated with the pop art movement. Some of his most famous pieces were paintings of words or phrases in plain bold capital letters, as in *Smells Like Back of Old Hot Radio*, which consisted of the phrase in white words against a brown background. As a work of pop art, it presented a word image of old technology, of a wireless receiver with valves which emitted heat as they worked to amplify the signals. For the viewer, it had the transcendental effect of conjuring up the evocative aroma of such an old piece of equipment. Ruscha was underlining that modern transistor radios neither smelt nor got hot when in use.[22] This connection with the past had previously been used in Britain by the American writer Ray Bradbury in a radio drama broadcast by BBC Radio 3 in 1968.[23] The one-hour play, *Leviathan '99*, was set in the future but the narrative harked back to the mid-nineteenth-century novel *Moby Dick* by Herman Melville. Both were stories of obsessive quests. Bradbury's tale had a spacecraft hurtling back through time in order to chase an elusive comet. He used archive sounds to evoke the past of thirty years ago from 1938, which according to one interpretation was 'representing a cloud of transmissions that the Captain's rocket ship would encounter on its way to meet the great white comet'.[24] The drama suggested that transmissions from the past were still out there in space and included songs, royal commentaries and political speeches: 'No sound, they say, is ever truly lost, [and] we tuned up echoes of forgotten wars and peaceful summers', declared Ishmael the narrator (Denys Hawthorne) as they flew through time and space.

On British television, a contemporary sitcom managed to strike a nostalgic note by featuring two elderly characters, both played by well-known actors and broadcasters. Irene Handl had a long and successful career from the late

---

[21] Hinton, *Celtic Crossroads*, p. 211.
[22] Another of Ruscha's radio-related text-based paintings sold for a record US$ 52.5 million in 2019. See '"Some artists do roses, but I work primarily with words" - Ed Ruscha's *Hurting the Word Radio #2* (1964)' (2019), Christies, 4 November. Available online: https://www.christies.com/features/Ed-Ruscha-Hurting-the-Word-Radio-2-1964-10108-3.aspx (accessed 24 May 2021).
[23] *Leviathan '99* (1968), Ray Bradbury, BBC Radio 3, 18 May.
[24] Phil Nichols (2006), 'A Sympathy with Sounds: Ray Bradbury and BBC Radio, 1951– 1970', *Radio Journal: International Studies in Broadcast & Audio Media*, 4 (1–3): 119. The idea of sound both lingering and travelling through time has been used by other authors. See David Lowenthal (2015), *The Past Is a Foreign Country - Revisited*, Cambridge: Cambridge University Press, p. 62.

1930s onwards in film and television. Wilfred Pickles was a BBC newsreader during the Second World War and his radio show, *Have a Go*, was a touring quiz programme which ran on the BBC from 1946 to 1967. Together they played a couple of pensioners, Ada and Walter, in *For the Love of Ada* (ITV, 1970–1). In the episode 'The Honeymooners Return', they moved in together after marrying, only to find that Ada preferred *Coronation Street* (a sly plug for the ITV soap) whilst Walter preferred to listen to BBC Radio 3.[25] 'He thinks more of his old radio than he does of me', complained Handl's character. It suggested that listening to radio programmes was the preference of old men, and that the medium was trapped in the past in the days when it used to be known as 'the wireless'. The turn to radio nostalgia, which began in the 1970s with George Lucas's *American Graffiti*, came to be repeated both in the 1980s and in the new century, and is discussed further in Chapters 8 and 10. This persistent desire to look to the past over the following decades suggested that, for these successive post-war generations at least, cultural nostalgia was as relevant as any attempt to represent the contemporary authenticity of radio listening in what was quickly becoming a media-saturated age.[26]

Format radio: The persistent popularity of American country music

In the 1970s, British music-lovers heard American pop and rock stars sing about country music radio stations. It was intriguing, because at that time such specialist broadcasters did not exist in the UK, and only became available with the advent of DAB, internet radio and music-on-demand services in the 2000s. The Byrds's 'Drug Store Truck Drivin' Man' (1969), written by Roger McGuinn and Gram Parsons, was a song about a real-life country DJ, Ralph Emery, who was once critical of the band on-air. McGuinn and Parsons responded in forthright terms, and it was a form of public retaliation from young musicians offended by the encounter. It was itself performed as a pastiche of country and Western music, complete with pedal steel guitar and close harmonies set in a waltz-time rhythm.

---

[25] 'The Honeymooners' Return' (1971), *For the Love of Ada*, ITV, series 3, episode 1, 15 March.
[26] Olivia Angé and David Berliner (2015), 'Introduction: Anthropology of Nostalgia - Anthropology as Nostalgia', in Olivia Angé and David Berliner, eds, *Anthropology and Nostalgia*, New York: Berghahn, p. 4. Stephen Brown (2018), 'Retro Galore! Is There No End to Nostalgia?', *Journal of Customer Behaviour*, 17 (1–2): 9–29.

'Turn Your Radio On', by Ray Stevens (1971), was a version of a southern gospel song from the 1930s, reflecting on the rise of Christian preachers on American stations.[27] For Joni Mitchell in 1974, the radio represented the soundtrack of wasted, listless time as she sat at home expecting her lover to drive up to see her. In 'Car on a Hill' (from her album *Court and Spark*), she equated listening to the radio as a boring inevitability of passing empty time. One critic summarized this as being 'left with a sense of a life reduced to waiting for something that never comes'.[28] She was trapped in space and time with only the radio to distract her. Mitchell had also made reference to the radio in other songs. On her 1971 album *Blue*, the track 'This Flight Tonight' had a short sequence in the third verse where she imagined the radio playing a sentimental song, and the audio was compressed to make it sound as if an AM radio station was playing it. In 1972, Mitchell had, on her *For the Roses* LP, directly addressed the medium with a single called 'You Turn Me On, I'm a Radio', which sarcastically suggested that, in itself, the track was a perfectly constructed song for playing on-air.[29] She was implying that American music radio was becoming formulaic and predictable, and to highlight this point she demonstrated that phrases about broadcasting, such as 'reception', 'static', 'the lines are open' and 'signal', could be turned into song-lyric clichés, some of them as *double entendres*.

When it came to visual critiques of American radio, a film and a TV series from this era each encapsulated the mood and played to small but significant British audiences who were both intrigued and fascinated. The movie *FM* (1978) attempted to celebrate the programming format of rock stations and the changes underway. It showed the conflict between art and money: a station and its staff apparently trying to balance musical and commercial decisions. For British viewers, it was somewhat perplexing as the music and behaviour bore little similarity to the UK radio industry, where both BBC and ILR stations were driven by public service requirements. In comparison, the title song of the movie, Steely Dan's 'FM (No Static at All)' told a different story. It suggested, according to one critic, that tight radio formatting was cynically constructed by the industry in order to win profits ahead of listener engagement. 'Its subtitle ['No Static at All'] sounded less like a technical boast than an admission that nothing on the airwaves was likely to surprise anyone. The overlapping voices

---

[27] Fowler and Crawford, *Border Radio*.
[28] Sean Nelson (2007), *Court and Spark*, New York: Bloomsbury Academic, p. 69.
[29] Nelson, *Court and Spark*, pp. 23 and 35–6.

in the refrain mimicked a generic station ID'.[30] The song, featuring a smooth orchestral string section and mellow saxophone solo, was an ironic counterpoint to the predictability of the output of music stations that played popular AOR tracks in strict rotation in order to gain advertisers and hence maximize profits for the station owners. Such FM stations reflected the move, from the 1960s and into the 1970s, away from 45-rpm singles to a new culture of 33-1/3-rpm albums. In the United States, AM stations continued, for a time, to play the 'oldies, but goodies' from the 1960s.[31] In Britain, ILR stations began splitting frequencies from the mid-1980s, typically offering pop music on FM and golden oldies on AM.

The TV sitcom *WKRP in Cincinnati* (1978–82), although unrelated, had a similar look and feel to the movie *FM*.[32] Both were products of their times and reflected the American radio industry in the 1970s, with studio technology arranged for self-op broadcasting: standard in American radio stations, and only just being introduced in British radio stations after the launch of BBC Local Radio, and Radio 1, in 1967 and the ILR stations from 1973 onwards.[33] The opening credits of the TV sitcom featured a song constructed in the style of a sung jingle, the lyrics of which echoed Harry Chapin's single about an itinerant radio DJ mentioned earlier. The series was regarded as providing realistic settings, albeit without the actors using headphones in the studio, and had an attention to detail in the dialogue.[34] Individual episodes included storylines about outside broadcasts, audience ratings, listener complaints, competition from other stations and the challenge of selling advertising slots. All of which would have had resonances with British audiences, as the ILR network expanded over the course of the 1970s and 1980s.

One digression is offered here, to both highlight how American ideas about radio were affecting broadcasters outside the Anglophone world – and to provide a bridge to the reactions to come from British cultural creators. It was the use of radio in a novel by the Brazilian writer Clarice Lispector, *The Hour of the Star*, which was published in Portuguese in 1977 with a movie version in

---

[30] Don Breithaupt (2007), *Aja*, New York: Bloomsbury Academic, p. 71.
[31] Dwyer, *Back to the Fifties*, pp. 81–4.
[32] *WKRP in Cincinnati* (1978–1982), USA: CBS/MTM Enterprises; UK: ITV.
[33] See, for example, an anecdote about comparative American and British studio practices in James Hogg and Robert Sellers (2013), *Hello, Darlings! The Authorized Biography of Kenny Everett*, London: Bantam, pp. 96–7.
[34] Michael B. Kassel (1993), *America's Favourite Radio Station: WKRP in Cincinnati*, Madison, WI: The University of Wisconsin Press, p. 2.

1985.[35] The novel was first translated into English in 1986, and was a Brazilian reaction to the formatting of radio determined by time. The station featured in the story was an actual broadcaster in Rio de Janeiro, which transmitted Brazil's national time signal every minute, playing short adverts and uplifting messages in between – twenty-four hours a day. The station was Rádio Relógio (literally, Radio Clock), which broadcast on medium and short wave, and began in 1951 with a 'breathtakingly simple' format.[36] In this original programming, it gave a slowly spoken time check followed by the time signal of three 'pips' up to the top of each and every minute. That meant that each item on the station was no longer than fifty seconds, and these varied from 'did you know' stories, to encouraging exhortations, to spoken advertisements. Each one had the persistent tick of a clock underneath: 'a constant ping like drops of falling rain', according to Lispector.[37] In a society not known for its ability for keeping appointments on time, it paradoxically became a form of radio which could be left on in the background. Lispector used the imagery of the station as a counterpoint to highlight the lack of both coherent time and direction in her lead character's life. Macabéa was a lonely young woman from the poor north who had moved to the city in search of a job (Rio de Janeiro in the novel; São Paulo in the movie version).[38] As her life spiralled downwards, she found fleeting solace in the certainty of the brief announcements on the radio station. One commentator observed, 'As Macabéa's source of information and communication, this radio station determine[d] her spatial and temporal (dis)orientation in an anonymous urban space.'[39] The radio was shown as a depressing soundtrack to isolation and loneliness.

British cultural reactions

The bleakness of the Brazilian film version of Lispector's novel was visualized with shots of the concrete brutality of parts of urban São Paulo, and there was a

---

[35] Clarice Lispector ([1986] 1992), *The Hour of the Star*, trans. Giovanni Pontiero, Manchester: Carcanet. *A Hora da Estrela* (1985), [Film] Dir. Suzana Amaral, Brazil: Kino International.
[36] Bryan McCann (2004), *Hello, Hello Brazil: Popular Music in the Making of Modern Brazil*, Durham, NC: Duke University Press, p. 230.
[37] Lispector, *The Hour of the Star*, p. 37.
[38] Italo Moriconi (2000), '*The Hour of the Star* or Clarice Lispector's Trash Hour', *Portuguese Literary & Cultural Studies*, No. 4/5, Dartmouth, MA: University of Massachusetts, pp. 213–21.
[39] Roland Walter (2001), 'Clarice Lispector's *A Hora da Estrela*: Remapping Culture and the Nation-Space', *Tinta*, Santa Barbara, CA: University of California, Santa Barbara, 5 (Fall): 119.

similar representation to be found in a British drama-documentary from 1975. *Dawnbreakers*, directed by Laurence Boulting, was a short thirty-minute film about late-night radio, a new concept in Britain with the recent opening of Capital Radio in 1973. It presented a montage of images of an unwashed city populated by drunks, drug users, victims of physical abuse, lonely people calling the radio station to talk about their own pitiful states, and a solitary young woman (Carol Drinkwater) who was finding comfort by listening to the voices on the radio. The drama-documentary featured London's new ILR station, and the viewer watched an overnight presenter Louis Alexander in the studio. The cinema camera observed him as he broadcast at the microphone, and his producer and technical operator could be seen on the other side of the glass. The new format of all-night commercial radio was here an aural backdrop to the life on the streets in London; it was not a flattering juxtaposition. For all the polite conversation and gentle poetry readings in the Capital Radio studio, the (fictionalized) world outside as presented on screen was grim.

The lawless nature of metropolitan life in the 1970s was also highlighted in a TV crime drama, but this time through the medium of urban land-based pirate radio. A 1974 episode of a Thames TV crime drama series *Special Branch* (1969–74) called 'Sounds Sinister' had anti-terrorist police going undercover at a clandestine radio station which was broadcasting incriminating facts about key public figures.[40] In a confusing screenplay, the transmissions were illustrated with victims listening to a portable black-and-white television set, even though the station announced itself as 'Polestar – the Free Radio Network'. To add to the confusion, in one later scene a character called it 'a pirate TV station', even though it broadcast only audio.

The detectives used converted television licence detector vans to track the transmitter (Figure 6) which suggested to the audience that this was illegal *listening*, as well as pirate broadcasting. It was an example of radio breaking the law, with the message that criminals who used such technology would be caught and defeated by the Establishment. Indeed, the use of pirate radio in such contexts became a visual shorthand for law-breaking in TV dramas and comedies in subsequent decades, and examples are discussed in the chapters which follow.[41]

---

[40] Joseph Oldham (2017), *Paranoid Visions: Spies, Conspiracies and the Secret State in British Television Drama*, Manchester: Manchester University Press, pp. 50–8.

[41] For a discussion of land-based illegal stations in the 1970s and 1980s, albeit biased in their favour, see John Hind and Stephen Mosco (1985), *Rebel Radio: The Full Story of British Pirate Radio*, London: Pluto. See also Mike Baron (1975), *Independent Radio: The Story of Independent Radio in the United Kingdom*, Lavenham, Suffolk: Terence Dalton, pp. 70–1.

Figure 6 Investigators track a land-based pirate radio station. A communications expert (Richard Pescud, left) and detective chief inspector Alan Craven (George Sewell, right). *Special Branch* (1974), UK: Thames TV.

Elsewhere, the first few tentative British views of radio in the 1970s, as expressed in contemporary pop music, tended to be fiercely critical – particularly about music radio. 'Capital Radio', by The Clash (1977), was, after the theorist Stuart Hall, an example of 'articulation' where an ideological struggle was being played out in culture.[42] On the one hand, The Clash had a lucrative record deal with CBS Records, which represented a commercial transaction and offered international success for both the band and the record company, and on the other the group used its popularity to express here its disdain for contemporary music radio in London. The song, according to one biographer, 'bemoaned London's independent radio station, a conservative institution that Joe [Strummer] felt should be promoting punk rock and reggae', and included a mention of the station's head of music, and later programme controller, Aiden Day in less-than-flattering terms.[43] It ended with their guitar version of one of Capital Radio's

---

[42] Stuart Hall (1996), 'On Postmodernism and Articulation: An Interview with Stuart Hall, edited by Lawrence Grossberg', in David Morley and Kuan-Hsing Chen, eds, *Stuart Hall: Critical Dialogues in Cultural Studies*, London: Routledge, pp. 131–50. Stuart Hall offered the example of Rastafarian music as one such paradox where commercial records were used to criticize capitalist industries.

[43] Pat Gilbert (2004), *Passion Is a Fashion: The Real Story of The Clash*, London: Aurum Press, p. 151.

jingles, over which they suggested that the station was out of tune with current musical tastes. Four years later, the motif of radio was the subject of another track by the band, 'This Is Radio Clash' (1981); this time the topic was pirate radio. The song is discussed in the next chapter.

Before the British punk explosion at the end of the 1970s, a group from Newcastle had sung of the dangers of the music industry and the experience of hearing their own records on national radio. Lindisfarne released 'Taking Care of Business' as a single in 1974. It was a song complaining about unscrupulous managers and how Alan Hull, one of the founding members of the folk-rock band, felt he had been duped by signing a questionable contract. He suggested that control was out of the band's hands, in terms of both radio plays and monetary returns. Another musician, Elvis Costello, recorded two songs in successive years in 1977 and 1978; the first was 'Radio Sweetheart', the B-side of his debut single 'Less Than Zero', which was about teenagers in northern dance halls awkwardly seeking love and waiting to be asked to dance.[44] In contrast to the physical fumblings of actually finding boyfriends and girlfriends, Costello suggested in the chorus that his imaginary lover on the radio was much easier to deal with because she was physically apart from him. The year after, Costello released a savage critique of British broadcasting: 'Radio Radio' (1978). Like The Clash, it was an example of a commercially successful single becoming a pointed criticism of the very medium upon which it was promoted and had achieved popularity. The threat and anger were intensified by a persistent sibilant 'Listen, listen, listen' whispered under alternate lines of the chorus.

The Hitchhikers Guide to the Galaxy, which began in 1978 as a series on BBC Radio 4 and later came to be adapted for TV and film, had an incidental put-down of the radio industry in the book version. The hero of the story was Arthur Dent, who was described on the first page of the novel: 'He worked in local radio, which he always used to tell his friends was a lot more interesting than they probably thought. It was, too – most of his friends worked in advertising.'[45] With a throwaway reference, Douglas Adams, who had himself spent a short time working as a radio producer, managed to dismiss both professions. The implication was that provincial radio was an industry that lacked any artistic or creative merit and was looked down upon by workers in the advertising industry in London. In later episodes of the radio series, adapted after Adams's death,

---

[44] Elvis Costello (2015), *Unfaithful Music & Disappearing Ink*, London: Penguin, pp. 185–6.
[45] Douglas Adams (1979), *The Hitch Hiker's Guide to the Galaxy*, London: Pan, p. 9.

the Arthur Dent character became a 'BBC producer in Light Entertainment'.[46] Meanwhile, the original Radio 4 series was a 'richly textured comic-book style of [radio] production,'[47] and because of its success quickly became the object of satire by another BBC comedy show in the early 1980s, as explained in the next chapter.

Elsewhere, 'Transmission' by Joy Division (1979) was an impassioned post-punk performance by Ian Curtis and the band of a song which told of the de-humanizing effects of listening to mindless radio. 'On My Radio', by the Coventry-based ska-band The Selecter (1979), directly criticized British radio, which it felt played predictable music presented by unadventurous DJs. Yet again it paradoxically received substantial airplay on music radio stations. The lead singer, Pauline Black, sang of how she had given her boyfriend a red-coloured radio. However, their relationship failed to rekindle, and had subsequently ended. Here she was complaining that the radio was broadcasting a predictable mix of endlessly repeated banal pop songs, offering nothing of new interest to listeners, a broad sentiment already echoed by The Clash, Joy Division and Elvis Costello. These songs were amongst the first limited responses of the era by British writers and musicians to the medium. The decades that followed would see such criticism, satire and parody increase significantly.

This chapter has reflected upon American movies, music and TV sitcoms which circulated internationally in the 1970s. These presented the medium of radio variously as a crime-ridden, drug-addled, chaotic industry populated by curious characters who shrouded themselves in mystery by creating imaginary on-air personas. Yet through all this, American DJs were shown as energetic, entertaining and fiercely committed individuals. Their presence in British media would resurface briefly in the late 1980s and the 1990s, as described in Chapters 8 and 9. In contrast, British radio in the 1970s was seen by songwriters such as Joe Strummer and Elvis Costello as distant and out of tune with trends in popular culture. This critical trend was set to expand in the 1980s, as the next chapter explains.

---

[46] 'Fit the Twentieth' (2005), *The Hitchhiker's Guide to the Galaxy: Quandary Phase*, adapted and directed by Dirk Maggs, BBC Radio 4/Above the Title Productions, 10 May.

[47] David Hendy (2007), *Life on Air: A History of Radio Four*, Oxford: Oxford University Press, p. 194.

7

Video killed the radio star

Satire, politics and international listening, 1979 to 1984

Singing songs about the radio

From 1979 onwards, the amount of fault-finding by British writers, filmmakers and musicians began to increase significantly. This chapter explores the four years to 1983, and the somewhat belated cultural response to British radio. It was as if the creatives in the UK had waited before deciding to pass any judgement on what they heard from their radio sets, whereas American pop stars – as discussed in the previous chapter – had been singing about the radio for years. Using Michel de Certeau's heuristic, these 'strategies'/programmes produced by radio broadcasters in the 1970s were listened to by audiences who each reacted with 'tactics' to engage with what they heard.[1] Some tactics remained private and personal, whilst others eventually became public. Hence, it was that writers, musicians, filmmakers and TV scriptwriters turned their own tactics into fresh strategies when they commercially published their reactions to what they had heard on the radio. Audiences were at last able to listen to, and watch, professional creatives offering their own commentaries on radio media. Stuart Maconie, a writer and broadcaster, said:

> For most of the 1960s, pop music on the BBC meant the occasional oasis of beat music on the Light Programme . . . [introduced by] presenters who were authoritative and suave rather than zany or sensationalist. Consequently, the canon of American pop is full of heartfelt hymns and incidental references to

---

[1] Michel de Certeau (1984), *The Practice of Everyday Life*, trans. Steven Rendall, Berkeley, CA: University of California Press, pp. 35–7.

the joys of AM radio [. . .] whereas British pop songs about radio come much later, are fewer in number and often take a distinctly ambivalent or cynical view.[2]

What emerged at last in the late 1970s was a critical appraisal which was both deeply satirical and maintained a tinge of nostalgia towards radio's past. In between, this chapter traces the rise of radio's close involvement in the making and mending of relationships – through songs about romance and loneliness. Elsewhere, a growing politicization of journalism was represented in the film *The Ploughman's Lunch*, a movie that dealt with the conflict between professional ethics and personal ambition in the Margaret Thatcher years. By the beginning of the period considered in this chapter, the domestic radio industry had changed significantly and the reorganization of the national networks of the BBC was already more than ten years old. BBC Radio 1, launched in 1967, was now an established part of the national auditory landscape. Its first two breakfast presenters, Tony Blackburn followed by Noel Edmonds, had become household names. In the early 1980s, Dave Lee Travis and then Mike Read presented the show. BBC Local Radio, which also began in 1967, grew to twenty stations in 1979. Others followed including Radio Lincolnshire in 1980, and Radio York which gained a part-time licence to cover the Pope's visit in 1982 before beginning in earnest in 1983. By 1984, there were twenty-nine BBC stations, eventually extending to forty.[3]

Independent Local Radio (ILR), which, as mentioned in the previous chapter, started in 1973 with Capital Radio and LBC in London had expanded from nineteen stations in 1979 to fifty in 1984.[4] Radio had become a broadcast medium where local accents and opinions could be heard daily, for example on phone-in shows on BBC Local Radio and ILR stations. These stations also opened up the VHF radio band, which after 1984 would be denoted on-air by BBC stations as 'FM'. On medium wave Luxembourg continued, and Radio Caroline – off-air since its boat the MV *Mi Amigo* sank in heavy seas off the Kent coast in 1980 – returned to broadcasting between 1983 and 1991 from new studios on the MV

---

[2] Stuart Maconie ([2013] 2014), *The People's Songs: The Story of Modern Britain in 50 Songs*, London: Ebury Press, p. 280.
[3] For the first twenty years of BBC Local Radio see Matthew Linfoot (2011), 'A History of BBC Local Radio in England, c1960 – 1980', PhD diss., University of Westminster. Two memoirs recalled the 1980s and 90s in BBC Local Radio: Rony Robinson (2010), *Who's Been Talking?* Sheffield: ALD Print, and John Holmes (2020), *Celebrating 50 Years in Radio & Television: This Is the BBC Holmes Service*, Nottingham: self-published.
[4] Tony Stoller (2010), *Sounds of Your Life: The History of Independent Radio in the UK*, New Barnet, Hertfordshire: John Libbey, p. 358.

Ross Revenge anchored in the outer Thames estuary in international waters. The BBC's national services were broadcasting both on VHF (FM) and on medium wave (AM) by this time, although it would take until the end of the 1980s before Radio 1 had its own FM frequencies.

The eventual British responses to radio listening

The material in this period is dominated by radio comedy, and BBC shows that satirized the medium are discussed shortly. However, one significant British song of the age was 'Video Killed the Radio Star' by The Buggles (1979), which came to herald a new technological dawn. Interviewed in 2018, the duo behind the hit song recalled how it encapsulated their own nostalgia for the medium. The song lyrics began with the memory of listening as a child in 1952. Trevor Horn remembered his boyhood: 'When I was three or four, I'd lie in bed listening to Radio Luxembourg. When you're half asleep, it's like being stoned. I'd totally zone in.'[5] Paradoxically, it was the music video of this song which started MTV's 'visual onslaught of television' in 1981, initially in North America.[6] It was, according to Stuart Maconie, 'a song bemoaning but not resisting the coming of video and the end of the dominance of pop radio'.[7] In the subsequent decades it was music TV that became 'the wallpaper of modern life, left on inaudibly in hairdressers, hotel lobbies and office receptions'.[8] However, radio's demise had often been prematurely announced: for example, as preparations for the coronation of Queen Elizabeth II were underway in 1953, some were worried at the time that radio was under threat from new visual media. However, with hindsight, 'if television emerged from the coronation as the dominant medium, radio did not go gently into the good night of technological obsolescence'.[9] This was still the case at the dawn of the satellite TV age in Britain. Indeed, as the subsequent chapters explore, radio in Britain – from the 1980s onwards –

---

[5] Dave Simpson (2018), 'The Buggles: How We Made "Video Killed the Radio Star"', *The Guardian*, G2, 30 October: 11. Available online: https://www.theguardian.com/music/2018/oct/30/the-buggles-how-we-made-video-killed-the-radio-star (accessed 24 May 2021).
[6] Alasdair Pinkerton (2019), *Radio: Making Waves in Sound*, London: Reaktion Books, p. 206. *MTV Europe* began in 1987, and in Britain satellite TV began its growth from 1990 onwards. Prior to that Europe had the *Music Box* channel, on cable, from 1984 to 1987.
[7] Maconie, *The People's Songs*, p. 285.
[8] Maconie, *The People's Songs*, p. 285.
[9] Ian Whittington (2018), *Writing the Radio War: Literature, Politics and the BBC, 1939–1945*, Edinburgh: Edinburgh University Press, p. 186.

developed its own unique place in the media spectrum: 'Because radio is, for most, a secondary medium (in a double sense: as a source of entertainment and information, as a background to other activities) does not mean that it is basically "unimportant".'[10] It was therefore still deemed worthy of listening to, particularly during times of crisis such as annual floods, snowstorms and school closures and during the Covid-19 pandemic of 2020-1.

Radio became, towards the end of the twentieth century, part of the soundscape of modern life. The band The Members, for example, had already in 1982 declared that they preferred listening to the radio rather than their stereo record players. They explained in their song 'Radio' that the medium was much more exciting than other sources of music. It could heal broken hearts too. 'Pilot of the Airwaves' by Charlie Dore (1979) was a tribute to a favourite DJ, which assigned (perhaps) undue power to the voice at the microphone. It was about a lonely single woman tuning in at night for emotional comfort, again fitting into the contemporary trope of listening to the radio after dark. Alongside songwriting, Charlie Dore also worked as an actor, and took the female lead as a somewhat insouciant TV researcher in the film *The Ploughman's Lunch* (1983), discussed later in this chapter. Her movie role made a contrast to her sentimental lyrics in this song. Solitary listening also featured in 'Oh Yeah (On the Radio)' by Roxy Music (1980). It spoke of a song on the car radio which reminded the lead singer, Bryan Ferry, about his lost love. Again, listening to the radio brought twinges of nostalgia and wistful memories of a simpler time. This longing for human warmth was contrasted in the song 'On Your Radio' by Joe Jackson (1979). Jackson sang in the first person, reckoning that radio airplay was the pinnacle of success. Here was an artist at the start of his career but already cynical. He listed the former friends from his youth who he would never see again because he was now famous and had left those childish times behind. The Bay City Rollers, by now in 1979 calling themselves The Rollers, took their own cynical view of the pop industry in their song 'Turn on the Radio' that spoke of the dissolution and the excesses of the rock lifestyle. They were, it seemed, singing from personal experience.

The subject of relationships, but this time amongst staff who worked for the BBC, was central to the novel *Human Voices* by Penelope Fitzgerald. It was set at the beginning of the Second World War, but present-day staff recognized the

---

[10] Stephen Barnard (1989), *On the Radio: Music Radio in Britain*, Milton Keynes, Buckinghamshire: Open University Press, p. vii.

context of the story. Mark Damazer, a former controller of BBC Radio 4, wrote an introduction to a 2014 edition of the novel. He said Fitzgerald understood the Corporation's 'profound, fussy, sometimes vain but largely heroic and invaluable commitment to the truth – and expressed it in the form of a concise, witty and beautiful novel'.[11] *Human Voices* was about the challenges of being a woman working for the BBC in 1940, and Fitzgerald had herself been employed by the Corporation during this time. Hers was a darkly nostalgic book, about a sometimes overbearing and stifling organization that also allowed individual talent to experiment with radio forms, an institution run on military-style chains of command, yet nevertheless staffed by idiosyncratic people full of personality quirks, who were also fiercely creative. She described how 'The BBC loyally defended their own. As a cross between a civil service, a powerful moral force, and an amateur theatrical company that wasn't too sure where next week's money was coming from, they had several different kinds of language, and could guarantee to come out best from almost any discussion'.[12] Indeed, it had long been a view amongst media analysts

> that the people who worked for the BBC within its bureaucratic structure belonged to a self-enclosed world in which friends and colleagues became surrogates for the real audience, or consumer. This feature of being hermetically sealed had already been noted by [Tom] Burns (1977) in the title of his book: *The BBC: Public Institution and Private World*.[13]

Fitzgerald thus identified the BBC as a labyrinthine bureaucracy, where managers were known by their job title acronyms such as DPP (Director of Programme Planning) and RPD (Recorded Programmes Director).[14] Other writers have highlighted similar idiosyncratic titles, including CAMP (Current Affairs Magazine Programmes) and HOTS (Head of Office Training Section).[15] A former director general observed wryly that when he first joined the Corporation in 1999, he was 'GD, DDG, DGD' (Greg Dyke, Deputy Director

---

[11] Mark Damazer (1980), 'Introduction', in Penelope Fitzgerald ([1980] 2014), *Human Voices*, London: Fourth Estate, pp. xv.
[12] Fitzgerald, *Human Voices*, p. 43.
[13] Victoria Wegg-Prosser (1998), 'BBC Producer Choice and the Management of Organisational Change', PhD diss., Brunel University, pp. 11–12. Tom Burns (1977), *The BBC: Public Institution and Private World*, London: Macmillan.
[14] Fitzgerald, *Human Voices*, p. 25.
[15] Libby Purves (2002), *Radio: A True Love Story*, London: Hodder & Stoughton, p. 42; Jean Seaton ([2015] 2017), *'Pinkoes and Traitors': The BBC and the Nation, 1974–1987*, 2nd edn, London: Profile, p. 229. Matthew Linfoot's 2011 PhD thesis has a two-page list of BBC job title acronyms ('A History of BBC Local Radio in England', pp. v–vi).

General, Director General Designate).[16] Fitzgerald concluded that this tendency had a dehumanizing effect on employees, and the novel finished with three deaths each going largely unexplained to colleagues.[17] The suggestion from Fitzgerald was that the life of BBC staff could became worth less than the institution itself. In addition, in her novel employees could and did complain bitterly about their work, but paradoxically at the same time remained deeply proud both of the organization and the programmes they produced.[18] David Lloyd, a commercial radio DJ and ILR station manager who spent a short time in the late 2000s with the BBC, said, 'Every staff member spoke of the organisation as if speaking of an annoying errant brother they still loved unconditionally.'[19]

Meanwhile, relationships at a radio station – this time an imagined commercial one based in London – were satirized in the TV sitcom *Agony* (ITV, 1979–81). The comedy came from the personality of the lead character Jane Lucas (Maureen Lipman), who was a wisecracking magazine and radio agony aunt. She resembled Anna Raeburn, who actually devised and co-wrote the first six episodes.[20] Each show concentrated on Lucas's off-air life, and the scenes set inside the studio at 'Happening Radio 242' were short but did show the DJ (played by Peter Blake) as a cannabis-smoking lothario who was obsessed with his own self- image and looks. There was one intertextual reference in the final episode when one of the DJs declared that he was 'no Shoestring', a reference to the TV drama discussed later in this chapter.[21] For the last three decades of the twenty-first century, Raeburn was known as *the* radio agony aunt. She was herself a journalist who worked on-air alongside a professional when giving out advice. She made her name on her late-night *Anna and the Doc* show on London's Capital Radio in the 1970s and 1980s, then nationally in the afternoons on Talkradio in the 1990s and on LBC in the 2000s across London and in some regions on DAB. She was satirized in the BBC Radio 4 show *Radio Active* (discussed later in this chapter) as 'Anna Rabies', a forthright character who was intentionally rude to both radio colleagues and on-air callers. The portrayal of radio agony aunts/uncles will be returned to in Chapter 9, when the examples

---

[16] Greg Dyke (2004), *Inside Story*, London: HarperCollins, p. 151.
[17] Fitzgerald, *Human Voices*, pp. 199–200.
[18] Fitzgerald, *Human Voices*, p. 103.
[19] David Lloyd (2017), *Radio Moments: 50 Years of Radio - Life on the Inside*, London: Biteback, p. 265.
[20] Anna Raeburn (1984), *Talking to Myself*, London: Elm Tree, pp. 191–4, 197–202 and 204–5. Garry Whannel (1994), 'Boxed in: Television in the 1970s', in Bart Moore-Gilbert, ed., *The Arts In the 1970s: Cultural Closure?* London: Routledge, p. 189.
[21] 'Rings Off Their Fingers' (1981), *Agony*, ITV/LWT, series 3, episode 7, 1 March.

of the movie *Sleepless in Seattle*, the TV sitcom *Frasier* and an episode of the Scottish detective series *Taggart* will be considered.

Satire: Radio begins to eat itself

Poking fun at the BBC had already been an occasional response over the decades: from Will Hay impersonating John (Lord) Reith as a director general reluctant to meet either his staff or the public in the film comedy *Radio Parade of 1935* (Chapter 3), and Betty Jardine playing the overly officious music department secretary in Vera Lynn's *We'll Meet Again* (1943, Chapter 4), to Arthur Askey as a gullible TV make-up artist in *Make Mine a Million* (1959, Chapter 5). On radio, *The Goon Show* (BBC, 1951–60; see Chapter 5) typically began episodes with a joke about the Corporation, often prompted by the announcer's first words:

> Wallace Greenslade: This is the BBC Home Service. Will anybody start the bidding?
> Harry Secombe: Ten shillings there!
> Greenslade: Sold!
> Secombe: Good![22]

Now, from the early 1980s, the Corporation appeared to allow sustained ridicule from contemporary comedians. Much of their humour was a reaction to the growth during the 1970s of local radio, both BBC and ILR, and it was a trend which was set to continue into the 1990s.[23] For example, Chapter 8 discusses *Delve Special* (1984–8), *Radio Shuttleworth* (1988), *On the Hour* (1991–2) and *Knowing Me, Knowing You with Alan Partridge* (1992–3), each one commissioned and broadcast on BBC Radio 4, and each raised laughs at the expense of the medium. Before these shows, *The Burkiss Way* (1976–80) was a late-night BBC Radio 4 programme of puns, *double entendres* and absurdist humour.[24] It satirized popular radio and TV shows of the period including idiosyncratic continuity announcements in the style of Radio 4, and overenthusiastic radio promotions for imaginary forthcoming shows. A number of episodes of *The Burkiss Way* poked fun at *The Hitchhiker's Guide to the Galaxy* (see previous chapter) which had begun in 1978 and by its second series, a year later, was building a substantial and loyal radio audience particularly amongst the younger listeners to Radio 4.

---

[22] 'The International Christmas Pudding' (1955), *The Goon Show*, BBC Home Service, series 6, episode 9, 15 November.
[23] David Hendy (2007), *Life on Air: A History of Radio Four*, Oxford: Oxford University Press, p. 369.
[24] Hendy, *Life on Air*, p. 190.

It mocked its author Douglas Adams – who himself had contributed early sketches to *The Burkiss Way*. One episode began, 'But now the Scriptwriter's Guide to the Galaxy, by a man who would rather write *Doctor Who*', a reference to Adams's time as a scriptwriter for the popular TV series.[25] A year later, the character became 'Mister Different Adams', whose catchphrase began with, 'I see comedy as a kind of . . .', and was variously an 'isosceles triangle', 'cheese soufflé' and 'licence to print money'.[26] Each time the response from the rest of the cast was shouts of derision.

A satire of local radio appeared in the BBC Radio 4 series *Radio Active* (1980–7). This was harsher in its comedy in comparison to *The Burkiss Way*, relying more on causing offense through language rather than by using apparently innocent *double entendres*.[27] The characters' names were puns on radio and electrical equipment, so Anna Daptor (Helen Atkinson-Wood) said:

> This week's short story was a fascinating tale of murder and revenge read by Mike Channel. Unfortunately, he neglected to read it out loud, so I can't play you an extract from it.[28]

A running joke was the professional rivalry between the two DJs: Mike Flex (Geoffrey Perkins), a young ambitious presenter, and Mike Channel (Angus Deayton), a disillusioned elderly DJ. The show relied on 'laughing mercilessly at the amateurishness prevalent in some corners of broadcasting with its presentation of "Britain's first national local radio station"'.[29] The series was later developed for television as *KYTV* (BBC TV, 1989–93), using many of the same jokes, but in the context of a fictional satellite channel.

The journalist and satirist Richard Ingrams also pointed out in 1983 that the BBC had, in another spirit of openness and self-reflexivity, allowed itself to 'broadcast a two-part play about its founder John Reith just at the time when it was under attack from all quarters'.[30] That the BBC was being criticized from outside was nothing particularly new. Ingrams was reviewing a television drama by Roger Milner called *Reith*, which had been shown on BBC 1 television across

---

[25] 'Rise from the Grave the Burkiss Way' (1979), *The Burkiss Way*, BBC Radio 4, series 5, episode 2, 9 April.
[26] *The Burkiss Way* (1980), BBC Radio 4, series 6, episodes 1, 2 and 3; 11, 18 and 25 October respectively.
[27] Simon Elmes ([2012] 2013), *Hello Again . . . Nine Decades of Radio Voices*, London: Arrow, pp. 315–16.
[28] 'Pick of the Week' (1982), *Radio Active*, BBC Radio 4, series 2, episode 6, 20 September.
[29] Hendy, *Life on Air*, p. 372.
[30] Richard Ingrams (1983), 'Television: Meddlesome', *The Spectator*, 19 November, p. 46. *Reith* (1983), Roger Milner, BBC 1 TV, 14 and 15 November.

two nights in the peak slot after the mid-evening news. Ingrams concluded, sarcastically, that had Reith looked at the BBC in the 1980s, he might have reflected 'that his life's work had all been in vain'. Such antipathy towards the BBC elsewhere, including from newspapers owned by Rupert Murdoch, would be maintained for the next forty years.[31] In addition, well into the first two decades of the twenty-first century, it was the *Daily Mail* that joined in the chorus of disapproval, a paper that in contrast had in the early 1920s vigorously promoted itself, the wireless manufacturers and the BBC, through the new medium of radio as described in Chapter 1.[32] By the early 1980s, mainstream opinion had changed. However, to its credit, the BBC had always appeared suitably robust and self-aware to be able to take any such satire and criticism in its stride both in the 1980s, and in the 2010s with programmes like *W1A* that ridiculed the overly bureaucratic culture of such a large organization (see Chapter 10).

Stand-up comedy also poked fun at the absurdity of aspects of the radio industry. Jasper Carrott, an actor and TV presenter, began his career as a comedian and musician. One of his routines in the late 1970s was a ten-minute monologue about ILR, in which he shared anecdotes about BRMB (the station for the West Midlands), Capital Radio – which elicited a mixture of boos and cheers from the audience of the Theatre Royal, Drury Lane in London where the performance was recorded, and Piccadilly Radio, the station serving Manchester.[33] He talked about what was still at that time the relatively new experience of listening to all-night radio from a domestic broadcaster, and the idiosyncrasies of James Stannage, an abrasive phone-in host on Piccadilly Radio, as well as Tony Butler, who presented the sports show and football phone-ins on BRMB in the 1970s and 1980s.[34] In another, earlier, sketch, Carrott talked about his time working for BBC Radio Birmingham on its monthly folk programme.

---

[31] Alasdair Milne ([1988] 1989), *DG: The Memoirs of a British Broadcaster*, London: Coronet, pp. 157–72; also, Georgina Born (2004), *Uncertain Vision: Birt, Dyke and the Reinvention of the BBC*, London: Secker & Warburg, pp. 48–9; Julian Petley (2020), 'Foxification: Just What a Divided Country Doesn't Need', in John Mair, ed., *The BBC: A Winter of Discontent?* Goring, Oxfordshire: Bite-Sized Books, pp. 119–20.

[32] Asa Briggs (1961), *The History of Broadcasting in the United Kingdom, Volume I, The Birth of Broadcasting*, Oxford: Oxford University Press, pp. 46–8. Patrick Barwise and Peter York (2020), *The War Against the BBC*, London: Penguin, pp. 85–101. See also, Simon Dawes (2017), *British Broadcasting and the Public-Private Dichotomy: Neoliberalism, Citizenship and the Public Sphere*, Cham, Switzerland: Palgrave Macmillan, pp. 10–16 and 91–106.

[33] Jasper Carrott (1979), *The Unrecorded Jasper Carrott* (DJM Records) was a vinyl LP of some of his live routines, many of which appeared in a series of six programmes for London Weekend Television (1978–1981).

[34] D. P. Allen (2011), 'Independent Local Radio (ILR) in the West Midlands, 1972–1984: A Comparative Study of BRMB Radio and Beacon Radio', PhD diss, University of Worcester, pp. 101 and 176.

He characterized the station as a chaotic, badly organized, place and raised a laugh from his audience when he declared, 'The aim of local radio is to fill in time between the news in the cheapest way possible, which is why you always used to get hundreds of those phone-in programmes.'[35] The suggestion was that the output was low quality and boring to listen to, a stereotype that persisted, as discussed in Chapter 10. He went on to recount how the station failed to keep track of its schedules and repeatedly forgot which week the folk show – of which he was a contributor – should have been broadcast each month.

Radio was the subject of other comic narratives, this time in the long-running television series *Are You Being Served?* (BBC, 1972–85). This was a sitcom based in a department store, and was popular for its *double entendres*, stereotyped characters and easy laughs. In one episode, the staff had an opportunity to perform a show on the radio to advertise the shop.[36] One of the characters (John Inman as Mr Humphries) rather implausibly brought his battery-operated CB radio into work. The staff rehearsal was accidently broadcast on the radio equipment, and the whole of London heard the risqué and inappropriate material. The narrative suggested that radio broadcasts could attract complaints and threats of censorship, but at the same time there was an excitement and illicit joy in breaking such taboos of taste and decency.

The international turn: Radio crossing political borders

From the humour of the 1970s, and 1980s television sitcoms, this chapter now turns to international radio broadcasting. Since before the Second World War the BBC, like many national broadcasters across the world, realized the importance of short-wave transmissions as a way to spread information: as soft power promoting a country's image and as a way to keep expatriates in touch with their home country. One musician who had an appreciation of the BBC World Service was Joe Strummer, the lead singer of The Clash. His father worked for the British Foreign Office and until the age of ten, when he was sent to boarding school in England, Strummer followed his parents on their various foreign postings from

---

[35] Jasper Carrott (1975), *Rabbitts on and on and on* . . . (DJM Records). It was recorded live in Birmingham and Coventry. For local radio in the Birmingham region, see Allen, 'Independent Local Radio (ILR) in the West Midlands'. For BBC phone-ins, see Linfoot, 'A History of BBC Local Radio', pp. 279–81.
[36] 'Calling All Customers' (1983) *Are You Being Served?* BBC 1 TV, series 9, episode 4, 13 May.

Turkey (where he was born), to Egypt, Mexico and West Germany.[37] The title of The Clash song 'London Calling' (1979) was reminiscent of the top-of-every-hour opening announcement from the BBC World Service, 'This is London'. It was also some of the first words heard on the BBC in 1922 (see Chapter 1). Later, in the 1990s Strummer hosted a regular half-hour music show for the BBC World Service called *London Calling*. Excerpts from his radio programmes were included in a documentary about his life directed by Julien Temple, *Joe Strummer: The Future is Unwritten* (2007). In a similar radio-related vein, the song 'This Is Radio Clash' (1981) maintained the band's political awareness and appreciation of international events during the Cold War. The song was 'based on the conceit of a pirate radio broadcast'.[38]

An American response, also about cross-border international broadcasting, came from R.E.M. and their first single, released in 1981, called 'Radio Free Europe'. Any close reading of the lyrics was made difficult because, as singer Michael Stipe explained, his vocals on the track were 'complete babbling'.[39] Indeed, it was difficult to hear any coherent phrases apart from the title of the song itself in the tag of the chorus. The effect, if indeed any were intended, was to recreate the sibilant inconsistencies of short-wave radio transmissions. Just as James Joyce observed in the 1930s (see Chapter 4), such broadcasts could distort, interrupt, and cut short sentences and conversations. Radio Free Europe and sister stations including Voice of America and Radio Liberty had their heyday in the Cold War era. Along with the BBC World Service, they had provided regular broadcasts on short wave aimed at the Communist bloc from the end of the Second World War until the early 1990s and beyond.[40]

Radio has had a long history of transmitting beyond national borders, from Radio Luxembourg and the offshore pirates to the Cold War transmissions by government-backed broadcasters. Indeed, Hamid Ismailov's novel *The Railway*,

---

[37] Pat Gilbert (2004), *Passion Is a Fashion: The Real Story of The Clash*, London: Aurum Press, pp. 6–8. In the 1970s and early 1980s, the BBC World Service was not generally available to listeners in the UK apart from on a medium-wave frequency to a small part of South Eastern England. It began overnight rebroadcasting on BBC Local Radio frequencies in 1992. In 1995, it launched as a domestic DAB channel.

[38] Gilbert, *Passion Is a Fashion*, pp. 291–2.

[39] Richard Buskin (2009), 'REM "Radio Free Europe": Classic Tracks', November. Available online: https://www.soundonsound.com/people/rem-radio-free-europe-classic-tracks (accessed 24 May 2021).

[40] Asa Briggs (1995), *The History of Broadcasting in the United Kingdom, Volume V, Competition*, Oxford: Oxford University Press, pp. 679–717. Guy Starkey (2007), *Balance and Bias in Journalism: Representation, Regulation and Democracy*, Basingstoke, Hampshire: Palgrave Macmillan, pp. 119–21.

published in Russian in 1997 and in English translation in 2006, had one of the characters living in a small town in Uzbekistan. On the bedroom windowsill, there sat 'His Arrow wireless, with its two knobs and a needle that enabled him to drift across the world, encountering first a Chinaman who seemed to be casting raindrops on water, then an Indian whose sharp voice cut into Zangi-Bobo's soul, and then the thundering prayers of an Arab'.[41] The old man, Zangi-Bobo, was listening to broadcasts on short wave at night-time until the voices lulled him to sleep.[42] The author, Ismailov, was born in Kyrgyzstan and worked as a journalist in Uzbekistan before he moved to live in Britain in the early 1990s, where he worked for the BBC World Service until 2019.

Just as The Clash had referred to the announcement at the top of the hour on the BBC World Service, it was the British novelist Anthony Burgess, who used the closing words after each five-minute news summary as the title of his 1982 novel, *The End of the World News*.

The story was written as if it were a found manuscript after Burgess's death. The title was added by a fictional literary executor (Burgess under his own name of John Wilson) who wrote a forward from the south of France whilst listening to late-night bulletins from the BBC:

> Every hour, on the hour, I hear the bulletin of actualities, which sometimes finishes with the formula: 'This is the end of the World News.' This evocation of the formula in the title I have given to this book by my old friend will, I hope, not displease his shade. He too was an insomniac exile listening to the voice of Britain, much distorted as always by the jamming of the Russians and the Albanians in their efforts to stifle the air's truth. He served the truth through a lying medium. He sleeps well now. Would to God that I did.[43]

The novel was one continuous text with no chapter divisions and presented a science-fiction story weaving invented versions of events involving Leon Trotsky, Sigmund Freud and the evacuation of planet Earth as it faced destruction from a comet collision. Burgess used the BBC World Service to denote the physical separation of the character from his homeland. He was, in calling writing a 'lying medium' in this context, perhaps belittling the work done both by authors and by international broadcasters during the Cold War, whilst at the same time

---

[41] Hamid Ismailov (2006), *The Railway*, trans. Robert Chandler, London: Harvill Secker, p. 208.
[42] Ismailov, *The Railway*, p. 209.
[43] Anthony Burgess (1982), *The End of the World News: An Entertainment*, Harmondsworth, Middlesex: Penguin, p. x. Burgess himself lived in Monaco and the south of France from the mid-1970s until his death in 1993.

suggesting that creative fiction could itself bring into being new ways of looking at reality and history. Elsewhere, Burgess was known for his unfavourable views about presenters on pop music stations. He once wrote scathingly of pop DJs: 'They are the Hollow Men. They are electronic lice. They are already punished by being what they are.'[44] Which perhaps echoed the thoughts of Morrissey in 1986 when he said that he wanted to 'Hang the DJ' (see Chapter 8).

British politics and radio broadcasting: The late 1970s and early 1980s

By the end of the 1970s, portrayals of radio broadcasting had entered the political arena: from writers and singers mentioning Cold War stations, to films and TV series that reflected periods in Britain of recession, the continuing 'troubles' in Northern Ireland, social dislocation and the era of Margaret Thatcher's premiership. The issues of representations of the truth and of the rise of a culture of determined self-interest were manifest in two movies and a TV crime series. Firstly, *Radio On* (1979) was a black-and-white arthouse production, of which one critic said, 'the film offers a mythic and quietly compelling vision of late 1970s England stricken by economic decline and stalled between failed hopes of cultural and social change and the imminent upheavals of Thatcherism.'[45] The central character was a radio DJ called Robert B (David Beames) driving from London to the Bristol area and beyond with music and news bulletins providing the audio backdrop. The director, Chris Petit, explained:

> At its simplest, *Radio On* is about what we wore and how we looked and what we listened to, and, in terms of the electronic reality (as quoted by Kraftwerk at the beginning the film), it was also about technology. In 1979, compared to West Germany, which had a more comprehensive building programme, the UK was still very colourless, hence the monochrome of *Radio On*.[46]

The film opened with the credits typed, as if on a teleprinter, across the black cinema screen, placing the movie in the era of radio newsrooms that had such

---

[44] Anthony Burgess (1967), 'The Antis: The Weasels of Pop', *Punch*, 20 September, p. 431.
[45] Jason Wood (2008), '*Radio On* and the British Cinematic Landscape', DVD film booklet, London: BFI, pp. 1–3.
[46] Adam Scovell (2019), 'Chris Petit on Radio On: "In a world dedicated to waste, the act of driving becomes a moral choice"', 22 August. Available online: https://www.bfi.org.uk/news-opinion/news-bfi/interviews/chris-petit-radio-on-interview (accessed 24 May 2021).

equipment to receive news scripts. This cross-faded to the sound of a medium-wave radio receiver being tuned across stations playing music and talk. The 'radio' of the movie's title was seen in the opening scenes to be coming from both a transistor portable in the bathroom of a flat and a car radio. The movie had no defined plot but instead was a journey by car, a process made significant by the musical soundtrack where 'The car radio/cassette provides the necessary diegesis for the music; the ability to employ it as an editorial device which is controlled by the main protagonist, the enigmatic Robert B'.[47] Later, a news summary was heard on the radio, and Robert was seen making an announcement on a factory radio station, filmed in the United Biscuits Network studios at Osterley in West London.[48] His attitude towards his audience was patronizing: he dismissed messages and dedications sent in to him from night-shift co-workers by saying in a bored voice, 'You asked for "Help Me Make It Through the Night". Here's something better', as he played 'Sweet Gene Vincent' by Ian Drury. The radio during the first part of the movie repeatedly featured news bulletins mentioning a police raid in the West Country on an organized crime gang. In the absence of any sustained dialogue from the actors, this device helped to provide a narrative framework and also to contextualize the era with mentions of violence in Northern Ireland.

Later in the film, at Weston-super-Mare, Robert attempted to tune a transistor radio (Figure 7) and failing, threw it into a shoulder bag in half-hearted frustration. It was a gesture that summed up this character who 'seem[ed] to be overcome by ennui'.[49] One critic and academic later described the film as 'a soulless picaresque search though a drab English landscape'.[50]

The insertion of radio into representations of social life of Britain was highlighted by a TV detective series, which further reflected the way in which the medium was embedded in the contemporary media landscape. With law and order on the political agenda, the series *Shoestring* (BBC 1, 1979-1980)

---

[47] Sue Harper and Justin Smith (2012), 'Cross-Over', in Sue Harper and Justin Smith, eds, *British Film Culture in the 1970s: The Boundaries of Pleasure*, Edinburgh: Edinburgh University Press, p. 206.
[48] Many radio DJs from UBN, which broadcast to the company's factories via closed-circuit transmission between 1970 and 1979, went on to work in ILR commercial radio. See Lloyd, *Radio Moments*, p. 55. See also: Allen, 'Independent Local Radio(ILR) in the West Midlands', pp. 106–7; and Marek Korczynski, Michael Pickering and Emma Robertson (2013), *Rhythms of Labour: Music at Work in Britain*, Cambridge: Cambridge University Press, pp. 229, 237–9.
[49] John Patterson ([2004] 2008), 'A Film without a Cinema', originally published in the *Guardian*, 2 October 2004, reprinted in *Radio On* (2008), DVD film booklet, London: BFI, pp. 15–18.
[50] Andrew Higson (1994), 'A diversity of film practices: Renewing British Cinema in the 1970s', in Bart Moore-Gilbert, ed., *The Arts in the 1970s: Cultural Closure?* London: Routledge, p. 230.

Figure 7 Robert B (David Beames) sits on the seafront at Weston-super-Mare and tries to tune a transistor radio. *Radio On* (1979), Dir. Chris Petit, UK/Germany: The British Film Institute/Road Movies Filmproduktion.

reflected the public's interest in such debates.[51] The drama was set in Bristol, coincidentally linking it geographically to Chris Petit's, *Radio On*. The main character, Eddie Shoestring (Trevor Eve), bore some resemblance to a Chandleresque style of hardboiled, shabbily dressed, private detective.[52] He was depicted as an obsessive loner who was recovering from a nervous breakdown. The radio station interiors were filmed in locations kitted out as BBC-style radio studios, with red-and-green lights over a large clock next to a window to a control room. The presenters were seen to be operating the mixing desk themselves – signifying local radio, but again mostly failing to wear headphones when broadcasting.

The fictional Radio West on 329 metres medium wave was ambivalently portrayed: it could have been read as either an energetic free-wheeling commercial radio station or a portrayal of a BBC Local Radio station with fiercely

---

[51] Whannel, 'Boxed In', pp. 184–7.
[52] Whannel, 'Boxed In', p. 186. See also Seaton, *'Pinkoes and Traitors'*, p. 268.

independent-minded hands-on management.[53] In any event, its placing on the AM band acknowledged that mass listening to FM had not, by the end of the 1970s, yet fully happened. A year after *Shoestring* finished, Bristol's independent local radio station opened, coincidentally using the name Radio West. However, to re-emphasize the medium's 1970s modernity, Eddie Shoestring was taken to task in episode 1 for calling it 'the wireless', and in episode 2 a pair of fraudsters dealing in antiques disdainfully dismissed a valve radio receiver, which only played country bluegrass music, as being of no resale value.[54] In a further episode, radio became a reflexive narrative device, as the eponymous detective investigated a series of bogus ham radio broadcasts in order to track down a runaway husband.[55] The discovery turned upon the fact that the radio signals were found 'to be coming from the wrong direction' by an expert amateur radio operator listening in her spare bedroom. In a recognition of the tension between the radio newsroom and the general broadcast output, another episode had a hard-bitten, fiercely competitive news editor (Peter Rayburn, played by Derek Seaton) attempting to steal exclusives from Shoestrings's confidential telephone messages before the detective could investigate them and get them to air.[56]

Such a portrayal of aggressive radio journalism was also evident in the British film *The Ploughman's Lunch* (1983). This image of a tough, macho profession was a persistent one, often created by insiders for public consumption, and other examples by writers including James Long, Mark Tavener and Peter Hanington are discussed in Chapters 8 and 10. The creation of a mystique surrounding Corporation employees was – to an extent – ingrained in reality where, if not necessarily ruggedly masculine, the staff were definitely out of the ordinary. Libby Purves, who joined the BBC as a trainee in the early 1970s, later to become a presenter on Radio 4, recalled being told that 'A traditional BBC man is basically a civil servant with a secret spangled tutu worn under his suit'.[57] In other words, determined, dignified and serious but with a soft

---

[53] For details of such BBC Local Radio management styles during this period, see Liam McCarthy (2019), 'Connecting with New Asian Communities: BBC Local Radio 1967–1990', PhD diss, University of Leicester, pp. 86–8; and Linfoot, 'A History of BBC Local Radio', pp. 269–74.

[54] 'Private Ear' (1979), *Shoestring*, BBC 1 TV, series 1, episode 1, 30 September; and 'Knock for Knock' (1979), *Shoestring*, BBC 1 TV, series 1, episode 2, 7 October.

[55] 'The Link-Up' (1979), *Shoestring*, BBC 1 TV, series 1, episode 7, 11 November.

[56] 'I'm a Believer' (1979), *Shoestring*, BBC 1 TV, series 1, episode 11, 16 December.

[57] Purves, *Radio: A True Love Story*, p. 35. Ben Elton, a writer and comedian, was less flattering. He had a character in one of his novels set in the mid-1990s say that the BBC was 'A family in which almost every member was a jolly uncle or an aunt. A family of fat boozy old time-servers who earned little and drank much. Men and women who went through their entire lives without once wearing a stylish garment or having a fashionable haircut.' (*Inconceivable* (1999), London: Bantam, pp. 84–5) The novel is discussed further in Chapter 9.

creative streak inside. John Simpson, a BBC foreign correspondent and world affairs editor, recalled how – when he first joined the Corporation in the mid-1960s – staff seemed to be 'Slightly older versions of myself: tweedy, brief-cased, polite, earnest, conscientious, middle-class, slightly arty, non-conformist yet distinctly conformist as well'.[58] And the Broadcasting House newsroom had 'a preponderance of grey hair and cardigans, and a distinct scarcity of women'.[59] In comparison, the movie, *The Ploughman's Lunch*, recreated this atmosphere but emphasized the competitive and selfish streak in the Corporation's staff. The film's script was the first screenplay written by Ian McEwan, who was 'perhaps Britain's most distinguished novelist of the last quarter-century'.[60] It was an overtly political film, a 'state-of-the-nation piece', which raised the issue of 'the falsification of the past through established historical discourse'.[61] The title hinted at a pub lunch of cheese, bread and pickle, which was dismissed by one of the film's characters as a fictitious creation, supposedly of a rural worker's midday meal, to be served to busy metropolitan types. The film mixed fiction with scenes shot in front of real events: a radio journalist attempting to write a book about a controversial moment in the BBC's history, whilst working in Broadcasting House and attending the actual 1982 Conservative Party conference in Brighton.[62]

Like *Radio On*, *The Ploughman's Lunch* opened with the sound of a teleprinter typing the latest stories out on the newsroom machine to be processed by the journalists and subeditors, who were then seen dictating their radio versions of the stories to copy typists. James Penfield's (Jonathan Pryce) first words were to answer the telephone somewhat aggressively, only to fail to know the name of a staff journalist being asked for by the caller, who turned out to be a colleague who had left to join the commercial rival Independent Radio News (IRN). This emphasized the size and anonymity of the Corporation and its London newsroom. Ian McEwan had given the Penfield character a surname that was reminiscent of Evelyn Waugh's Pinfold from 1957 (see Chapter 5) who himself had delusional and psychological problems with the BBC. In *The Ploughman's*

---

[58] John Simpson ([1998] 1999), *Strange Places, Questionable People*, London: Pan Macmillan, p. 17.
[59] Simpson, *Strange Places*, p. 22.
[60] Brian McFarlane (2009), 'The More Things Change... British Cinema in the 90s', in Robert Murphy, ed., *The British Cinema Book*, 3rd edn, London: British Film Institute, p. 368. See also Chapter 4, where I discuss radio in Ian McEwan's 2007 novel *On Chesil Beach*.
[61] McFarlane, 'The More Things Change', p. 368; Sarah Street (2009), *British National Cinema*, 2nd edn, London: Routledge, p. 119.
[62] For a historical context of broadcasting in this era see Seaton, 'Pinkoes and Traitors', pp. 166–90.

Lunch, Penfield was an accomplished fabricator of the truth. He was embarrassed by his lower middle-class roots and chose to lie to colleagues that his parents were dead, whilst at the same time arrogantly claiming to being highly skilled at what he did as a network journalist. Yet his ambitions lay elsewhere, and his goals in the film were to attract the attentions of a girl he desired and write a book on the history of the Suez Crisis. The events surrounding the nationalization by Egypt of the Suez Canal in 1956, together with the 1926 British General Strike, were key moments for the BBC, when its impartiality and independence from government were questioned.[63] Other editorial dramas for the Corporation – including the 2003 Iraq War dossier, the Cliff Richard search of 2014 and the Princess Diana interview inquiry of 2021 – had not been directly fictionalized. The Jimmy Savile revelations are mentioned in Chapters 8 and 10.

In *The Ploughman's Lunch*, Susan (Suzy) Barrington (Charlie Dore, mentioned earlier in this chapter) was an upper-class single woman who worked as a researcher for London Weekend Television. When he failed to persuade her to spend the night with him, he pleaded:

Penfield: You don't trust me?
Barrington: I don't trust anyone. That's what comes of working in television.
Penfield: Oh no, in radio we're different.

Which again, was an untruth as his character's behaviour demonstrated. The viewers saw him willing to compromise to his publisher's intentions for a simpler version of his book, and to lie and use people to further his own interests. The overall tone of the movie reflected the period when many felt a general helplessness at world and national events.[64] It was also a time when the BBC was examining how it managed its own news output. David Hendy, an academic and former BBC producer, said, 'What threw BBC Radio's inadequacy in news coverage into particularly stark relief was the example being set by overseas broadcasters.

---

[63] Mélanie Dupéré (2021), 'BBC Independence and Impartiality: The Case of the 1956 Suez Crisis', *Revue Française de Civilisation Britannique* [Online], XXVI-I 2021. Available online: http://journals.openedition.org/rfcb/6992 (accessed 24 May 2021). See also Briggs (1961), *The History of Broadcasting, Vol I*, pp. 360–84 (on the events of 1926), and Briggs (1995), *The History of Broadcasting, Vol V*, pp. 75–137 (on the Suez Crisis); Tom Mills ([2016] 2020), *The BBC: Myth of a Public Service*, London: Verso, pp. 83–7.

[64] Amy Sargeant (2005), *British Cinema: A Critical History*, London: British Film Institute, p. 314 and 318.

During 1980 and 1981, several foreign reconnoitres were undertaken.'[65] American rolling news formats were listened to, French examples of how to mix news, music and speech were considered, as well as case studies of formats from Canada, Sweden and West Germany. In the film, the discussion of the news agenda took place at the morning editorial meeting. This had the air of a university seminar, with the duty news editor seemingly acting as a type of professor holding court in a room packed with his (almost exclusively male) acolytes. In a brief discussion of the Greenham Common women protestors, Penfield – who had previously met them by accident and had felt repulsed by their honest dedication to a cause – duplicitously dismissed them as 'cranks', in order not to reveal that he knew them and to avoid getting involved again. He added, 'It's a local radio story, if that', suggesting that BBC local journalism was of little relevance to the national news agenda. This reinforced the view that in the Broadcasting House newsroom 'journalistic standards [were] exacting but unadventurous'.[66] Instead, the BBC national news agenda was shown to be weighted towards Westminster politics, metropolitan stories and world events. The film also spoke to the rising tide of individual ambitiousness and the yuppie culture of the 1980s. As if to reinforce the message that London media organizations were creating self-serving radio and television output, the movie later showed the recording of a TV commercial. It added to the sense that the media – radio news, TV journalism and the production of commercials – was a world of artifice (reminiscent of the 'ploughman's lunch' of the movie's title) staffed by shallow individuals. This critical issue is further discussed in the next chapter where the image of the radio presenter and DJ is explored. For some, he (again a gendered profession) was a tortured soul; for others, he was a rebel who set the airwaves alight with excitement.

---

[65] Hendy, *Life on Air*, p. 260.
[66] Hendy, *Life on Air*, p. 22. Professional antagonism towards local radio is discussed further in Chapter 10.

8

Hang the DJ

Critiquing the present, remembering the past, 1984 to 1993

British commercial radio: From public service to profit-seeking

From its inception in 1973, Independent Local Radio (ILR) had been regulated along the lines of early commercial television, with a strong remit to public service broadcasting.[1] However, the Peacock Committee report into the future of broadcasting in 1986, whilst concluding that the licence fee should be retained as the means for financing the BBC, recommended that commercial radio should face less regulation.[2] It meant that by the beginning of the 1990s ILR had begun its transformation into what by the 2020s had become, in effect, a series of commercial networks. In the process, ILR stations were being released from their public service obligations. Many stopped broadcasting Sunday morning shows that reflected local religious events, and reduced their output of specialist music programmes in the evenings such as classical, jazz and folk as well as magazine programmes for ethnic minorities.[3] The effect was eventually to transform the stations from broadcasters with a public service remit into radio operations dominated by a profit motive.[4] By 1987 Capital Radio in London had introduced

---

[1] D. P. Allen (2011), 'Independent Local Radio (ILR) in the West Midlands, 1972–1984: A Comparative Study of BRMB Radio and Beacon Radio', PhD diss, University of Worcester, pp. 6–7.
[2] Tony Stoller (2010), *Sounds of Your Life: The History of Independent Radio in the UK*, New Barnet, Hertfordshire: John Libbey, pp. 163–4.
[3] Liam McCarthy (2019), 'Connecting with New Asian Communities: BBC Local Radio 1967–1990', PhD diss, University of Leicester, p. 148. However, regulatory changes also led to a number of former illegal ethic radio stations gaining broadcast licences from the 1990s onwards.
[4] Stoller, *Sounds of Your Life*, p. 144, and pp. 164–5. Simon Dawes (2017), *British Broadcasting and the Public-Private Dichotomy: Neoliberalism, Citizenship and the Public Sphere*, Cham, Switzerland: Palgrave Macmillan, pp. 121–5.

a 'contemporary hits radio' format, playing a well-researched but limited playlist of songs known to be popular with audiences that advertisers wanted to reach.[5] Such programming had long been used by American commercial radio stations. Between 1984 and 1993, creators of literature, music, TV and film continued to satirize contemporary British radio, from both within and outside the BBC. At the same time, the growing tendency to think nostalgically about radio was in evidence in both pop songs and novels. What had started in the early 1970s was now becoming an enduring trend.

Critiques of radio presentation: 'Hang the blessed DJ'

By the mid-1980s contemporary radio was losing some of its appeal, judging from the reactions of artists who criticized what they heard coming from their transistor radios. Morrissey's 1986 'Panic' was a stark warning from a critical listener. With his group The Smiths he sang about the banality of contemporary radio which seemed to have no connection with the world around him. The band's guitarist Johnny Marr explained:

> 'Panic' came about at the time of Chernobyl [in April 1986]. Morrissey and myself were listening to a [BBC Radio 1] Newsbeat radio report about it. The story about this shocking disaster comes to an end then *immediately*, we're off into Wham!'s 'I'm Your Man'. I remember actually saying 'what the f*** has this got to do with peoples' lives?' We hear about Chernobyl, then, seconds later, we're expected to be jumping around to 'I'm Your Man'[6]

For Marr and Morrissey, BBC Radio 1 was intent only on promoting inane music and mindless presenter chat. Meanwhile, the irony of The Smiths later being played on the radio was not lost. Music journalist and critic Paul Du Noyer observed at the time, 'Hard is the heart, for another thing, which cannot warm to a hit like "Panic", whose success obliged the daytime Radio One personnel to play a disc with the jauntily singalong chorus, "Hang the DJ, hang the DJ".'[7] It was, like 'Capital Radio' by The Clash (1977; see Chapter 6), an example of articulation where a commercially successful band criticized the industry it was

---

[5] Stoller, *Sounds of Your Life*, pp. 162–4.
[6] Danny Kelly (1987), 'Marr, interviewed by Danny Kelly, "Exile on Mainstream"', *New Musical Express*, London, 14 February, p. 44. Emphasis in original.
[7] Paul Du Noyer (1987), 'Morrissey Interview', August. Available online: https://www.pauldunoyer.com/morrissey-interview-1987/ (accessed 24 May 2021).

part of. The implication was that the BBC presenters, and by extension their programme producers who playlisted the tracks in each show, were out of tune with the sensibilities and concerns of young people. The daytime line-up by mid-1986 was Mike Smith on breakfast, followed by Simon Bates, Gary Davies, Steve Wright and Bruno Brookes.[8] From 1993, the newly appointed controller of the station, Matthew Bannister, began changing both its music policy and its roster of ageing 'personality' DJs. The aim was to attract a new, younger audience.[9] Meanwhile, the former Beatle George Harrison expressed similar sentiments to Morrissey in voicing his dislike of aspects of radio broadcasting. A track from his 1987 LP, *Cloud Nine*, called 'Devil's Radio' made it clear that he held radio presenters responsible for spreading lies and gossip. It was a song full of musical aggression and conveyed Harrison's mistrust of half-truths and inaccuracies that he felt were broadcast by stations which seemed more interested in chasing ratings than sharing what he regarded as the truth.

The image of the duplicitous, lying, DJ was seen in *The Kit Curran Radio Show* (Thames TV, 1984). It was created by writer Andy Hamilton and depicted ILR staff as scheming and selfish, who were content to distort the truth both on and off the air. Hamilton scripted the first six episodes himself and co-wrote series two with Guy Jenkin, simply titled *Kit Curran* (Thames TV, 1986).

Both later wrote a Channel 4 sitcom, *Drop the Dead Donkey* (1990–8), which satirized TV news journalism.[10] The Kit Curran character was a mid-morning DJ on an invented ILR station called 'Radio Newtown, broadcasting on 98.9 FM'. The station's newsreader, Damien Appleby (Clive Merrison), was seen arriving late and out of breath for his bulletin and then, once on air, making offensive hand gestures as he read items about Margaret Thatcher and the *Daily Express*. The television audience was able to see that this ILR journalist had significant political bias. In reality, British local radio stations were the opposite of this portrayal. The overwhelming majority broadcast inoffensively within the rules set by the BBC and the commercial regulators the Independent Broadcasting Authority (until 1990) and the Radio Authority (from 1991). To emphasize his

---

[8] See 'Listings, BBC Radio 1' (1986). *Radio Times*, issue 3258, 5 May, p. 40. Available online: https://genome.ch.bbc.co.uk/schedules/radio1/england/1986-05-05 (accessed 24 May 2021).

[9] David Hendy (2000), *Radio in the Global Age*, Cambridge: Polity, pp. 229–32. Also see Georgina Born (2004), *Uncertain Vision: Birt, Dyke and the Reinvention of the BBC*, London: Secker & Warburg, pp. 260–5.

[10] The final episode (1998) of *Drop the Dead Donkey* included a scene where the senior news anchor had an on-air argument when he appeared as a guest on a show fronted by a fictional version of TV and radio presenter Chris Evans. After the acrimonious live encounter, he was offered a job as a radio phone-in host on 'Radio Gab'.

Figure 8 Denis Lawson as a flamboyant commercial radio DJ. *The Kit Curran Radio Show* (1984), UK: ITV/Thames TV.

careless attitude, the opening episode showed Kit Curran (Denis Lawson, Figure 8) hosting a phone-in whilst reading a newspaper rather than paying attention to his callers. His arrogance and devious nature provided opportunities for the narrative to set up comic situations reflecting personality clashes with other characters.

The first series concerned Curran's continuing battles with the new station boss, Roland Simpson (Brian Wilde), who was described as ex-BBC. The characterization had him as a stickler for efficiency and accuracy who wore a grey three-piece suit and black tie, whilst the other staff dressed in casual clothes. Each episode involved their attempts to improve the listening figures.

These included clashes with the regulator over matters of taste and decency, fabricated political opinion polls, questionable by-election coverage and a dubious scheme to raise money from keep-fit classes. Even so, BBC Radio 1 was seen as the pinnacle of a DJ's career, and the final episode of series one concentrated on Curran's attempts to get a job with the Corporation. In the event, the BBC interview panel concluded that he was too flamboyant and individualistic to fit into such a large bureaucratic Establishment organization. In series two, the characters lost their jobs as the station went bankrupt and stopped broadcasting. In response they banded together and opened a pirate radio station in Brentford, West London, called 'Radio Kit', which transmitted on a frequency that interfered with emergency service communications. The radio station operation took second place in the narrative as Curran continued his life of deception by variously trying to get a loan from a bank, selling fabricated stories to the national press, promoting dubious alternative health cures, offering cheap replacement double glazing to homeowners affected by youth riots, and running an overpriced dating service for lonely people.

A top-thirty hit in Britain from an American band addressed this problem of unprofessional disc jockeys. R.E.M.'s 'Radio Song' (1991) was a critique of all that they considered bad about contemporary radio, and the endless repeats of songs. Their 'Radio Free Europe' was mentioned in the previous chapter. They were regarded as an 'intellectual' band, so lead singer Michael Stipe's comments and opinions carried critical weight.[11] Here the strident lyrical observations of 'Radio Song' were counterpointed by the lush audio production, complete with repetitive jangly guitars and a string section motif at the end of every verse. It was the banality of radio that Stipe was concerned with, particularly music radio formats where songs were picked by computer from a tight playlist.

Indeed, critics and researchers had long observed that daytime shows were dominated by easily recognizable chart music: 'Radio programmers tend[ed] to favour the safe and the familiar, and banish more demanding records, creating something of a "middlebrow" mainstream. The phenomenon resonates through history.'[12]

From criticism of the content of radio programmes, to a racialized satire of the receiver technology: the James Bond film *The Living Daylights* (1987) had a ghetto blaster refashioned by 'Q' to be a shoulder rocket launcher as 'Something we're making for the Americans'. The joke was that the large stereo radio cassette player was iconic of the music genres from the United States of hip-hop and rap.[13] The movie suggested that the British, with their typical reserve, would never walk around with a large transistor radio on their shoulder listening to urban dance music. LL Cool J started a trend with a track on his 1985 LP *Radio*, which declared, 'I Can't Live Without My Radio'.[14] He was sampled on Run

---

[11] Lucy Bennett (2013), 'Discourses of Order and Rationality: Drooling R.E.M. Fans as "matter out of place"', *Continuum: Journal of Media & Cultural Studies*, 27 (2): 214.
[12] Hendy, *Radio in the Global Age*, p. 225.
[13] Alasdair Pinkerton (2019), *Radio: Making Waves in Sound*, London: Reaktion Books, p. 171.
[14] The JVC 'ghetto-blaster', featured on the cover of his LP, *Radio* (1985), was a portable radio cassette player known as the JVC RC-M90.

DMC's 1988 song 'Radio Station', which recognized the power and immediacy of radio as a public space for the band to promote itself. This contrasted with the West Coast rap artist Ice Cube, who urged fans to "Turn off the Radio' (1989). The latter was a muscular polemic against radio stations in the United States which at the time were not, according to Ice Cube, playing his music. The irony, not lost, was that this track would never be played on the radio because of its offensive lyrics.

In 1992, the London-based Anglo-American duo Shakespears [sic] Sister released 'Hello (Turn Your Radio On)', which was an indictment of all that they saw as wrong with the media industry. It reflected on a society where people could be made to feel alienated and lonely by the overbearing scale of the mass media. They regarded radio, television and newspapers guilty of depersonalizing the effects of war, terrorist alerts and financial crises. The era had seen the rise of satellite TV, available in Britain from 1989 with the round-the-clock news channels of CNN from Atlanta, Georgia and Sky News from London. The BBC launched its own twenty-four-hour TV news channel in 1997. On radio, the Corporation experimented with a rolling news service on Radio 4's FM frequencies during early 1991 in order to provide continuing coverage of the First Gulf War.

This became the eventual basis for BBC Radio 5 Live, launched in 1994 as a news and sport station on AM and, later, on DAB and online.

Criticizing the BBC: Views of the Corporation from within

Rolling news formats were fertile ground for comedy on both BBC radio and television. Chris Morris and Armando Iannucci's creation *On the Hour* ran for two series on BBC Radio 4 (1991–2) and satirized this move towards twenty-four-hour news coverage.[15] The show featured bizarre introductions and headlines such as 'Wake up and smell the news', 'Dinosaurs died out on a Tuesday, claim experts' and 'A large jug of organic water is on display in Frettenham by the town clock. Visitors are requested to enter by the side'.[16] It also included direct criticism of intrusive journalism: 'Excuse me. You're critically injured

---

[15] Tim Crook (1999), *Radio Drama: Theory and Practice*, London: Routledge, pp. 125–9.
[16] *On the Hour*, BBC Radio 4. The first quote was from (1992), series 2, episode 4, 14 May; the other two from (1991), series 1, episode 4, 6 September.

with a shattered pelvis, pneumothorax and a partially torn off face. How do you feel?'[17] In addition, it poked fun at the overly serious continuity announcements of national BBC radio: '*On the Hour* continues on this frequency. If you wish to hear Radio 4's normal programmes, here's a packet of sand and a piece of old skin.'[18] Morris's acerbic humour translated easily to TV as *The Day Today*, which ran for six episodes on BBC 2 in 1994, and the controversial *Brass Eye* on Channel 4 (1997–2001). Alan Partridge, a character played by Steve Coogan, presented the sports news on both *On the Hour* and *The Day Today* – the conceit being that he knew next to nothing about sport:

> Once again, Oxford and Cambridge, the undisputed grand masters of racing boats on the Thames, are in the lead as they come under the bridge there; the famed bridge that, er, has cars on it. But where are the others! Where are the others? The other universities? They're nowhere to be seen![19]

Coogan launched a solo career, first with a BBC Radio 4 series *Knowing Me Knowing You with Alan Partridge*, which ran from 1991 to 1993, and then transferred to BBC television. A film, *Alan Partridge: Alpha Papa* (2013), is discussed in Chapter 10. The character had a distinct lack of empathy: the exact opposite of a successful radio presenter who should have been able to use direct address – to say 'good morning how are you' in such a way as to establish a one-to-one relationship with the listener and to be able to create that successfully at a distance between the radio studio and the audience.[20] He addressed one celebrity guest with the words: 'I read a bit in your book that was highlighted in yellow by a researcher for me.'[21] It was an unfeeling comment destined to cause offence. The character was based on a generic local radio presenter, and again took up the theme of the mindless banality of DJs in British radio in this period.

A contrasting view of broadcasters, specifically in the area of news, was seen in a novel by a former BBC journalist, James Long, which also provided a somewhat questionable image of the contemporary daily newsgathering operation of the Corporation. *Hard News* (1992) portrayed BBC journalists – in both radio and television – as macho, hard-drinking men who were determined to get to the

---

[17] *On the Hour* (1991), BBC Radio 4, series 1, episode 1, 9 August.
[18] *On the Hour* (1991), BBC Radio 4, series 1, episode 3, 23 August.
[19] *On the Hour* (1992), BBC Radio 4, series 2, episode 2, 30 April.
[20] Andrew Tolson (2006), *Media Talk: Spoken Discourse on TV and Radio*, Edinburgh: Edinburgh University Press, pp. 115–16.
[21] *Knowing Me, Knowing You* (1992), BBC Radio 4, series 1, episode 1, 1 December.

truth of a story.[22] Long used the opportunity to offer, at the beginning of the novel, his own criticism of the Corporation's bureaucracy around the time of the arrival of John (later Lord) Birt:

> Changes at the top of the BBC had filtered down through the News Division, stressing a new, intellectual approach to news, which to most of the experienced hands was pure anathema. Every day, it seemed, there were more people calling the shots who believed you could get the right perspective on a story by sitting in White City reading old newspaper cuttings rather than going out to see for yourself what was happening on the ground.[23]

Ultimately responsible for the working practices that James Long identified, Birt joined the BBC in 1987 as deputy director general and director of news and current affairs, and served as director general from 1992 to 2000. His time was marked out as the period when the BBC moved towards a more commercially driven organization, both internally and in the growing number of independent programme makers it commissioned.[24] James Long's novel had a fictional radio journalist, Steve Ross, quickly promoted to television news, where he watched in horror one day as his cameraman was murdered in the street during a riot in central London and the camera was stolen. The narrative then suggested that BBC producers were impervious to Ross's trauma as they insisted that he be interviewed live in the studio about the events of that day. James Long portrayed television journalism as a superior career for a broadcaster, more exciting and dangerous than radio. However, he included occasional brief mentions which passed comment on internal operations such as the General News Service (GNS) that served BBC newsrooms: how, he said – with a touch of litotes, it always spotted important stories first and was apparently meticulous at obeying the rules of English grammar in its scripts.[25] The novel ended with a dramatic chase to capture a team of terrorists who had stolen the video camera for their own murderous purposes. The overall suggestion was that, despite their obvious faults as drinkers and womanizers,

---

[22] James Long (1992), *Hard News*, Ringwood, Victoria, Australia: Claremont, pp. 150–9, 289.
[23] Long, *Hard News*, p. 19.
[24] Born, *Uncertain Vision*, pp. 57–60. David Hendy (2007), *Life on Air: A History of Radio Four*, Oxford: Oxford University Press, pp. 284–93. Victoria Wegg-Prosser (1998), 'BBC Producer Choice and the Management of Organisational Change', PhD diss., Brunel University. John Birt (2002), *The Harder Path: The Autobiography*, London: Time Warner, pp. 248–66.
[25] Long, *Hard News*, pp. 77, 200–1. The BBC's GNS, which supplied raw material for local, regional and national radio and TV services, moved in 2020 from London to Salford, near Manchester, and was renamed Central News Service (CNS).

BBC journalists were action figures that always solved the mystery and hence saved the day. A similar tough image, but in the form of a black comedy, was heard in the radio series *In the Red* (1995).[26] It featured a BBC crime reporter George Cragge (Michael Williams), who exasperated his Radio 4 editors, faced repeated disciplinary actions on account of his insubordination, but always managed to solve the murder mysteries and bring the exclusives to air. In a sequence of four linked radio series, Cragge investigated murders variously of bank managers, politicians, dentists and journalists.[27] The comic character bore some similarity with the more serious William Carver in Peter Hanington's novels discussed in Chapter 10.

An alternative portrayal of Corporation journalists was given in an episode of *Yes, Prime Minister* (1986–8), a BBC TV comedy which satirized the political climate and culture of the age. In one episode, 'The Tangled Web', BBC newsroom staff were cast as being in the thrall to the political establishment.[28] The cabinet private secretary Sir Humphrey Appleby (Nigel Hawthorne) did not realize his off-the-record disparaging comments about the unemployed were being recorded during a radio interview with Ludovic Kennedy (as himself). However, any hope that radio may have been able to speak truth to power was, for the viewer, dashed when it was revealed that the BBC producer had given the prime minister, Jim Hacker (Paul Eddington), the original copy of the audio tape of the offending interview. Whilst the narrative was perhaps an exaggeration of reality, and material would not in practice be handed over in such a manner, recent archival research has indicated that the BBC as an institution has, for almost all of its existence, had a tendency to follow the Establishment's views and bidding.[29] In effect, the portrayal in this episode of *Yes Prime Minister* served to reinforce that conclusion.

BBC Radio 4 continued to broadcast satires about itself, and before *On the Hour* there had been the gently observational comedy of *Delve Special* (1984–8) written by Tony Sarchet. It starred Stephen Fry as David Lander, an incredulous and somewhat inept investigative reporter parodying the

---

[26] *In the Red* (1995), Mark Tavener and Peter Baynham, BBC Radio 4, 5 January–16 February. The series was based on Tavener's novel of the same name (1990), London: Hutchinson. It was later adapted for television by Malcolm Bradbury (1998), BBC 2, 26 May–9 June.
[27] The other Radio 4 series were, *In the Balance* (1997, 6 February–13 March), *In the Chair* (1998, 5 June–10 July), and *In the End* (1999, 18 November–23 December). All were written by Mark Tavener alone.
[28] 'The Tangled Web' (1988), *Yes, Prime Minister*, BBC 2 TV, series 2 episode 8, 28 January.
[29] Tom Mills ([2016] 2020), *The BBC: Myth of a Public Service*, London: Verso, pp. 6 and 220. See also Patrick Barwise and Peter York (2020), *The War Against the BBC*, London: Penguin, pp. 297–320.

Checkpoint programmes (1973–85) presented by Roger Cook in which listeners could hear him confronting wrongdoers and often receiving a sharp physical response whilst his tape recorder still rolled.[30] One episode of *Delve Special* began with an imaginary government minister comically suggesting that one way to reduce the European grain mountain was to support the expansion of the corn dolly industry. The episode satirized the seriousness with which contemporary journalists reported on the strains and effects for British farmers of what was known at the time as the the European Economic (EEC) and its agricultural policy.[31] Each half-hour show was constructed in a documentary style, there was no audience, and Fry presented his links with an earnest voice to create a plausible simile of *Checkpoint*. Distinguishing it from its object of satire would, for a listener who had tuned in halfway through, have been somewhat difficult.

BBC Radio 4 was not the only object of ridicule in these years. Two characters on a BBC TV sketch series poked fun at Radio 1's ageing DJs. Smashie and Nicey were comic exaggerations of brainless pop DJs from the 1970s and 1980s. They were created by Paul Whitehouse and Harry Enfield in the latter's BBC television shows broadcast during the 1990s.[32] Their catchphrases included 'quite lidderally' and 'poptastic'.[33] The duo were a comic representation of the type of presenter Morrissey and The Smiths had been complaining about: ageing out-of-touch presenters wearing garish polyester bomber jackets, an exaggerated version of Steve Coogan's Alan Partridge. The popularity of the Smashie and Nicey stereotypes reportedly further encouraged Radio 1 to update its image. However, the characters created by Whitehouse and Enfield lost some of their humour with the revelations in the 2010s of decades of sexual abuse by the deceased BBC DJ Jimmy Savile.

---

[30] Hendy, *Life on Air*, pp. 239–42. Simon Elmes ([2012] 2013), *Hello Again . . . Nine Decades of Radio Voices*, London: Arrow, pp. 316–7. Stephen Fry also appeared in the Mark Tavener series *In the Red* and some of the associated spin-offs, mentioned earlier, where he played a nefarious controller of Radio 2.

[31] 'Bitter Harvest' (1987), *Delve Special*, BBC Radio 4, series 4, episode 2, 4 September. Incompetent interviewers were also satirized in *People Like Us* (1995-97), BBC Radio 4. This latter was written by John Morton who developed *W1A* mentioned in Chapter 10.

[32] *Harry Enfield's Television Programme* (1990–1997), BBC 2. Later episodes were known as *Harry Enfield & Chums* and shown on BBC 1. See David Lloyd (2017), *Radio Moments: 50 Years of Radio – Life On the Inside*, London: Biteback Publishing, pp. 125–6. Paul Whitehouse later co-wrote *Down the Line* (2006-13), BBC Radio 4, a satire of inane phone-ins.

[33] The latter word was reappropriated by Tony Blackburn for the title of his 2007 autobiography, *Poptastic: My Life in Radio*, London: Cassell Illustrated.

Still looking to the United States: Searching for the art of the DJ

American movies of this period showed the radio DJ to be variously an offensive phone-in host, a problematic individual who could enrage and provoke listeners with fatal consequences, and a loose cannon who defied management and institutional norms. Each representation fell far from the British experience even as they touched on the American reality.

Talk Radio (1988) starred Eric Bogosian as Barry Champlain, a character based on Alan Berg, a DJ who was killed by right-wing extremists in Denver in 1984. The dramatization had originally appeared as a stage play, co-written by Bogosian. The film version, directed by Oliver Stone, began with the camera relentlessly sweeping from place to place in the radio station. It took three and a half minutes before the audience saw the face of Champlain. He was revealed in a head-and-shoulders shot, addressing the microphone with headphones on and looking just beyond and above the camera. It was an aggressive and alienating view. The phone-in callers were not shown on screen, and this use of the *acousmêtre* technique (discussed in detail in the next chapter), with an unsettling off-screen audio presence, signified there was no empathy between Champlain and his audience who, for him, were disembodied voices that acted merely as fodder for his ego.[34] The narrative later revealed that it was this unseen audience who were a threat to the broadcaster.

The movie *The Fisher King* (1991) also featured murder connected with radio listening, whilst at the same time offering a form of redemption to the negativity of American shock jocks. It was the story of a fictional New York presenter Jack Lucas (played by Jeff Bridges in a characterization reminiscent of Howard Stern) whose on-air comments prompted a mass shooting at a bar. Yet again, the first sight of the character was of his lips close to the microphone. The narrative of the film was underlaid with religious references to a holy grail and quests to seek forgiveness from former sins. It was directed by Terry Gilliam, a former member of the Monty Python comedy team, who took dual US-British citizenship in the late 1960s. The story followed Lucas as he disappeared into a strange underworld and attempted to rebuild his life and career to become a milder and more socially acceptable broadcaster. The shock-jock phenomenon made money for some

---

[34] Crook, *Radio Drama*, p. 126. Michel Chion (1999), *The Voice in Cinema*, trans. Claudia Gorbman, New York: Columbia University Press.

American radio stations and networks, in particular when regulations, known as the fairness doctrine, were relaxed after 1987.

The only female representation of this sphere of the industry was Dolly Parton's portrayal of an innocent who moved to the city and accidently became a radio station's agony aunt. The movie *Straight Talk* (1992) suggested that such a character could end up on-air and dispense down-home Southern advice. Viewers had to suspend their belief at this narrative point, and the movie was neither a critical nor a box office success. British audiences would have been forgiven for thinking American DJs were either cheekily off-beat, anti-authoritarian or downright obnoxious. Indeed, the UK had always been more reserved when it came to radio presenters. This was partly through the regulation of the broadcasting industry and also through social custom and practice.[35] Kenny Everett was surreal and manically comic but usually managed to offend his BBC (and ILR) bosses more than his audiences. On LBC, from 1976 to 1990, Britain had Brian Hayes, who began his career in Australia.[36] There was also James Whale, who from 1982 onwards appeared on Radio Aire in Leeds, simulcast on ITV on Friday evenings, before later moving first to Talksport, then to LBC and Talkradio. Both were acerbic, but – with occasional rare exceptions – hardly ever offensive. In general, British radio presenters adhered to a civility of turn-sharing and 'processing' their callers in a polite, business-like and bureaucratic way.[37] They tended to give the listener a certain amount of respect:

> Talk radio [...] involves the input, in an absolutely essential way, of lay members of society whose substantive moral, political, intellectual convictions are treated, by professional broadcasters, as the basis for discussions, in the 'presence' of overhearers, of 'issues' defined as significant by callers themselves.[38]

Listeners' views were therefore held to be valid and not something to immediately ridicule. In Britain, the proliferation of phone-ins on ILR, national stations and BBC Local Radio had been 'a cheap way of providing public service radio [and had] allowed a much greater range of voices, opinions and topics than was the case before the late 1960s'.[39] It was a view that echoed Jasper Carrott's comments

---

[35] Guy Starkey (2011), *Local Radio, Going Global*, Basingstoke, Hampshire: Palgrave Macmillan, p. 121.
[36] Elmes, *Hello Again*, pp. 271–2.
[37] Ian Hutchby (1991), 'The Organization of Talk on Talk Radio', in Paddy Scannell, ed., *Broadcast Talk*, London: Sage, p. 129.
[38] Hutchby, 'The Organization of Talk', p. 135.
[39] Richard Rudin (2011), *Broadcasting in the 21st Century*, Basingstoke, Hampshire: Palgrave Macmillan, p. 120. See also, D. P. Allen, 'Independent Local Radio', p. 98.

in the previous chapter. The majority of such local phone-in programmes were polite affairs, where opinions were listened to carefully and gentle humour was the order of the day. Even so,

> Britain, though, has had an ameliorated version of the US 'shock jock' phenomenon. Most of the best-known phone-in hosts come from print journalism rather than, as in the United States, from a music presentation background.[40]

They tended to be brusque rather than ill-mannered, well-argued instead of aggressively confrontational. Examples included Derek Jameson a former Fleet Street editor who became a BBC Radio 2 presenter from 1985 to 2000, and from 2001 onwards Nick Ferrari, formerly a national newspaper reporter who moved to LBC.[41]

British nostalgia of the late 1980s

Commercial radio was changing in other ways in the late 1980s. A number of ILR stations were allowed and encouraged to run separate services on their AM (medium wave) and their FM transmitters. The emerging trend was for stations to continue contemporary music broadcasting on FM and to launch a 'gold' format station playing oldies from the 1960s and beyond on medium wave. Music radio was, itself, becoming a form of nostalgia that reflected the favourite songs enjoyed by an older audience.[42] In addition, musicians born at the end of the Second World War continued to write songs about romanticized notions of radio listening that offered a contrast to the complexities and problems of the present day. Van Morrison evoked the late 1950s of his youth, of tuning into foreign stations. He remembered how they seemed to be a world away from his teenage home in Belfast. A 1990 duet with Paul Durcan, 'In the Days Before Rock 'n' Roll', appeared on Morrison's album *Enlightenment*. The piece had a simple open chord structure, played with piano, acoustic bass and drums. Durcan began by declaiming his poem in a halting single-syllable style as a string section gently took up the melody. He listed the names of stations

---

[40] Rudin, *Broadcasting in the 21ˢᵗ Century*, p. 120.
[41] Lloyd, *Radio Moments*, pp. 218–220.
[42] Simon Reynolds (2011), *Retromania: Pop Culture's Addiction To Its Own Past*, London: Faber and Faber, p. xxix. See also McCarthy, 'Connecting with New Asian Communities', pp. 144–5.

printed on the dial of an old valve radio including Luxembourg, Hilversum, Budapest and Athlone. The poem evolved into the chorus, sung by Morrison, and evoked the simplicity of youth in the late 1950s: being able to listen to American artists such as Elvis, Fats Domino, Muddy Waters and Ray Charles on these foreign stations long before they were broadcast by the likes of the more conservative BBC.[43] The Hammond organ was played by Georgie Fame, and he used it intermittently to create the sound of Morse code interference, whilst Morrison imitated the noise of radio static – familiar to those of this generation who had spent their evenings searching across the medium, long and short waves for foreign stations playing their favourite music. The effect was to recall the writing of James Joyce in *Finnegans Wake* (see Chapter 4). Meanwhile, an episode in 1985 of the BBC radio comedy series, *Radio Active* (also discussed in Chapter 7), opened with a comic reference to poor-quality reception:

> And now a choice of listening. On VHF we have another in our series of cultural exchanges with BBC Radio 4. Listeners on medium wave can hear the same thing but with an altogether more muffled sound and a lot of sibilant esses. While listeners on short wave can hear a great deal of interference with bits of Morse code and the occasional police message. Here on long wave, there's an unexpected Dutch station cutting in.[44]

Elsewhere, Radio Luxembourg, which began in 1933, with a pause during the Second World War, finally closed its English language broadcasts on 208 metres in 1991. It had relied on the propagation effects of medium-wave transmissions after dark to target the UK, whilst using the wavelength during the daytime for French and German programming.[45] The last record it played was 'In the Days Before Rock 'n' Roll'.

Another song with nostalgic traces was 'Radio Ga Ga' by Queen (1984). Written by the drummer Roger Taylor, the lyrics referenced key moments in British radio history. This was a tune (like The Buggles in Chapter 7) that spoke about the memories of listening alone in a bedroom, and about being enveloped by the sounds coming from a transistor portable. The song tapped into a generation of radio listeners who 'grew up with radio [and] still pine[d]

---

[43] Brian Hinton (2000), *Celtic Crossroads: The Art of Van Morrison*, 2nd edn, London: Sanctuary Publishing, pp. 294–5.
[44] 'Wimbledon Special' (1985), *Radio Active*, BBC Radio 4, series 5, episode, 1, 5 July.
[45] Starkey, *Local Radio*, p. 13.

for the old radio days, for their intimate relationship with the box in their living room or bedroom, for a culture without television'.[46] It was the imagined past also evoked by Morrison and Durcan: when listening to the radio meant being engrossed in a programme and actively listening – instead of using the radio as a form of background noise with no personal interaction. Taylor referenced Orson Welles's American radio version of 'The War of the Worlds', mentioned in Chapter 3 and, in another couplet, the wartime 'finest hour' speeches of Winston Churchill. Queen were surveying current music radio output and finding it lacking even as other media were rising up to compete for audiences' attentions. What had taken the place of creative, compelling, broadcasts, was format radio designed to be unchallenging and inoffensive – and of course the television. As the academic Susan Douglas observed, many people missed 'The mental activity, the engagement, the do-it-yourself nature of radio listening'.[47] Another commentator, Stephen Barnard, identified 'Radio Ga Ga' as 'one of the most truly subversive records ever to find its way on to the airwaves'.[48] He said that it 'Undermined the jolly neutrality of daytime radio fare' and 'It questioned the very function of contemporary radio'.[49] In this respect it mirrored sentiments expressed by artists such as The Clash, The Smiths and R.E.M. Barnard added that he had heard normally calm DJs becoming defensive of their profession after playing the Queen track which, he said, confirmed the critique that Taylor had put forward.[50]

A novel of this period offered a reflection of the past, tinged with a sense of the Establishment's cultural rectitude of the 1950s. A. S. Byatt's *Still Life* (1985) featured intertextual references to T. S. Eliot, D. H. Lawrence, the Leavises and the novel *Lucky Jim* by Kingsley Amis. She harked back to the legacy of John Reith and to the pre-war years where she described the BBC staff, like its buildings, as being, 'a mixture of the austerely utilitarian and the civilized'.[51] The novel centred on the literary lives of individuals who circulated between Cambridge and London, as well as the south of France and a newly built university in North Yorkshire. One character was Alexander Wedderburn,

---

[46] Susan Douglas ([1999] 2004), *Listening In: Radio and the American Imagination*, Minneapolis, MN: University of Minnesota Press, p. 4.
[47] Douglas, *Listening In*, p. 4.
[48] Stephen Barnard (1989), *On the Radio: Music Radio in Britain*, Milton Keynes, Buckinghamshire: Open University Press, p. vi.
[49] Barnard, *On the Radio*, p. vi.
[50] Barnard, *On the Radio*, p. vi.
[51] A. S. Byatt (1985), *Still Life*, London: Penguin, p. 176.

in his mid-thirties, working for the BBC whilst trying to finish writing his play. Continuing her literary cross-referencing, Byatt created an individual who was reminiscent of the poet, dramatist and radio producer Louis MacNeice (see Chapters 3 and 4).[52] She described Wedderburn's garret office at the BBC, where he went to escape the noise of crying babies, as a suitably artistic retreat being 'on the top floor of Broadcasting House, lit by a sloping skylight, under which his desk fitted'.[53] In line with the novel's narrative of intertwined relationships, Wedderburn indulged in adultery and clandestine encounters.[54] Byatt's evocation of the life of this Broadcasting House employee bore similarities to Penelope Fitzgerald's tense creative atmosphere described in her 1980 novel, *Human Voices* (see Chapter 7).

A 1991 television adaptation of Agatha Christie's 'The Affair at the Victory Ball' made some major changes to the original short story which was published in 1923. It added radio into the narrative, in order to provide a setting for Hercule Poirot's solving of two deaths: a murder and a drug overdose.[55] He did so by hosting his own show, announced with the words, 'In a change to our published schedule', on the BBC's National Programme. Poirot gathered all the murder suspects together in the studio, reconstructed the crimes and identified the guilty person. Large ribbon microphones with the BBC logo added a visual nostalgic touch and offered a sentimental image of the 'golden age' of British broadcasting. After the programme, the detective and a BBC producer James Ackerley (Andrew Burt) were congratulating each other when a Broadcasting House receptionist (Sarah Crowden) rushed up to them:

> Mr. Ackerley! They've been trying to find you. The switchboard's been flooded with callers complaining about the dreadful accent, lowering the standard of spoken English, all that sort of thing. Sir John Reith's waiting to see you in his office.

To which Poirot, Belgian by birth, assumed she was referring to one of the other contributors. Which suggested that even a nostalgic view of the interwar years had to conform to established cultural and racial stereotypes.

---

[52] Byatt, *Still Life*, p. 308.
[53] Byatt, *Still Life*, pp. 178 and 244.
[54] Byatt, *Still Life*, pp. 159–75.
[55] *Agatha Christie's Poirot* (ITV) ran from 1989 to 2013 and starred David Suchet. 'The Affair at the Victory Ball' was episode 10 of series 3, first broadcast in 1991.

American nostalgia of the late 1980s

The reminiscing by British writers was reflected in American media creations during these years. *Good Morning, Vietnam* (1987) starred Robin Williams and was set in 1965. He played a fictionalized version of Adrian Cronauer, an actual Armed Forces Radio Saigon disc jockey of the era. The film opened with shots of nameless presenters reading announcements very badly. It gave an idea of how boring such radio could be and acted as an aural counterpoint to Williams's iconoclastic style. Later, with his face in close shot filling the screen, the microphone slightly to his left and headphones firmly on his ears, he let rip with his trademark 'Gooood Mornin' Vietnam'.

This, like both *Talk Radio* and *The Fisher King*, was another film to use the close-up as a framing device to introduce the lead DJ character. It created for the viewer a link between the mouth and the voice: the aurality detached from the rest of the human body, just as radio itself presented to the listener the pure sound without the full physical presence of the broadcast voice. *Good Morning, Vietnam* showed him to be excitable, disrespectful, unpredictable and therefore dangerous, but hugely popular with his audience of GIs. After his greeting, he added, 'Hey, this is not a test. This is rock 'n' roll!' He played what the military hierarchy considered to be transgressive music: The Beach Boys, Martha Reeves and the Vandellas, and James Brown instead of the likes of Ray Conniff. What was clear was that the director Barry Levinson understood what others had described as the role of the DJ in 'building a relationship with an audience', and that engaging music radio had a liveliness, a spontaneity and a performance element that adapted to 'accommodate perceived reactions' from the audience.[56] Indeed, the whole aim of the narrative was to foreground how much of a rebel and a live wire the fictional Adrian Cronauer was, and so to set up the story of his fall from grace. A giggling Williams declared into the microphone:

> The requests will be taken pretty soon! Where am I gonna take requests? Where can you call from? 'Yeah, I'm in a phone booth out in the DMZ [De-Militarized Zone]. I'm trying to call you right now!'

The intercutting of hand-held, shaky, camera shots gave the radio studio sequences an urgency and vitality. It emphasized how captivating live broadcasting was, and how the spoken word could create an image which confronted the authority

---

[56] Tolson, *Media Talk*, pp. 6 and 9–14.

of the military command. The listener, and by extension the cinema viewer, was attracted to this type of broadcast because of the very real danger of transgression.

Radio Days (1987), written and directed by Woody Allen, was a series of vignettes of life in a poor Jewish neighbourhood of New York in the 1940s. It was clearly autobiographical, and Allen provided the voice-over without appearing on screen. His boyhood persona was played by a child actor who exhibited mannerisms identifiable with the adult Woody Allen. He said at the beginning, and repeated at the end, that the film celebrated radio's non-permanence. All that was left of the radio shows was his memories, and 'I've never forgotten [...] any of those voices we used to hear on the radio, although the truth is with the passing of each New Year's Eve those voices do seem to grow dimmer and dimmer'. Allen confessed in the movie to being an avid and nostalgic listener.

One of the ripostes to the sentimentality of Woody Allen's memories was Garrison Keillor's novel, *Radio Romance* (1991), published in the United States with the title *WLT: A Radio Romance*. It was the story – initially at least – of a fictional radio station in Minneapolis. Just as Allen foregrounded his Jewish New Yorker heritage, so Keillor relied on the Scandinavian links of many families settled in the Mid-West. For British audiences, the regional stereotypes of the United States were not necessarily cultural reference points. As such, Allen's Jewish cultural references and jokes would be more recognizable than Keillor's references to Nordic stoicism and quietness. Keillor himself had been the host of a nostalgic radio variety show, *A Prairie Home Companion*, which aired in the United States between 1974 and 2016, and much later in Britain.[57] *Radio Romance* was a story which spanned the 1920s to the 1950s, and listening in those years was apparently 'more like a warm thing that hums and reminds you of your mother'.[58] It was a description that evoked Ed Ruscha's 1976 artwork mentioned in Chapter 6. Keillor also remarked: 'Radio, it's right in the home. You turn it on and everybody else has to shut up. A movie is just a picture, but people think that radio is real.'[59] In fact, radio was, according to the novelist, capable of illusion through its very ability to create images in the listener's mind. The finale of the book described how a leading character, who had led a controversial life, never had his biography published. Instead, the public's memory of his troubled

---

[57] Keillor's American programmes were rebroadcast in Britain on BBC 7 (later BBC Radio 4 Extra) from 2003 to 2016 as *Garrison Keillor's Radio Show*. See also Seán Street (2009), *The A to Z of British Radio*, Lanham, MD: The Scarecrow Press, pp. 156–7. A film version of *A Prairie Home Companion* was released in 2006.
[58] Garrison Keillor (1991), *Radio Romance*, London: Viking Penguin/Faber and Faber, p. 231.
[59] Keillor, *Radio Romance*, p. 75.

life and work began to fade of its own accord. Keillor's implication, in line with Woody Allen's nostalgia, was that media forms such as radio were transitory and made to be forgotten.

Younger creatives also joined in this continued wave of nostalgia. An American country hit of 1990 by Lionel Cartwright called 'I Watched It All (On My Radio)' remembered listening to a transistor radio, to music and the sports commentaries, after bedtime in the dark. Again, the motif of solitary teenage listening was presented, joining the memories of Woody Allen and Van Morrison, and the manner in which the radio had affected and touched them as boys growing up in the post-war era. Chapter 10 discusses further reminiscences from other writers and filmmakers in the first two decades of the twenty-first century. Next, Chapter 9 looks at the period from 1993 to 2006, when the focus shifted from the DJs and on-air personalities to the listeners themselves. *Sleepless in Seattle* (1993) revealed the consequences when the personal lives of two would-be lovers were transposed into the public sphere by the radio phone-in. Meanwhile, war films that featured radio – from the 1943 movie *We'll Meet Again* in Chapter 4 to *Good Morning, Vietnam* – had so far taken a broadly comedic approach to the subject of broadcasting. At the other emotional extreme, the effect of listening during times of armed conflict was underlined by the grim reality of radio's part in genocide – which became the subject of films that fictionalized events in Rwanda in the 1990s.

9

Death and psychology
Radio, genocide and loneliness, 1993 to 2006

The growth of local and community radio

This chapter examines the period at the end of the century, marked in Britain variously by the resurgence of the Labour party under Tony Blair, the notion of a 'cool Britannia' and the collective grief over the death of Princess Diana. It was a time of war in Europe in Kosovo, of genocide in Rwanda and of international terrorism after 9/11 in New York. Multichannel television had arrived in Britain, and media choice was increasing as access to the internet and the World Wide Web expanded. Digital (DAB) radio began in 1995 led by the BBC, with both its national services and local stations available, alongside their existing analogue frequencies on AM and FM. Meanwhile, Independent Local Radio (ILR) stations were consolidated into groups, often owned by institutional investors; networked shows became the norm, and remote switching meant that one studio could control separate transmitters with specific jingles to create the illusion of a local commercial station for the listener.[1] The Radio Authority handed regulatory duties of ILR to Ofcom in 2003 which, from then on, took responsibility for all commercial broadcast and telecoms regulation in Britain.[2] Before and during this period, there were experiments with licences for small-scale 'access radio' stations. These grew to become, by the mid-2010s, a sector of more than 300 low-powered

---

[1] Tony Stoller (2010), *Sounds of Your Life: The History of Independent Radio in the UK*, New Barnet, Hertfordshire: John Libbey, pp. 251–7.
[2] In addition, from 2017 Ofcom formally took over the regulation of all BBC domestic public service content. See: John Mair, ed (2021), *What's the Point of Ofcom?* Goring, Oxfordshire: Bite-Sized Books.

community stations run by an estimated 20,000 volunteers.[3] Each offered some form of social input into their area, both on- and off-air, for example media training or specialist programmes not available elsewhere. A number of community stations served faiths, including Christian, Sikh, Hindu and Muslim populations in towns and cities in Great Britain.

Meanwhile, artists, songwriters and filmmakers continued to examine and criticize radio, both in its comical and frivolous contexts and in the real horror of the genocide in Rwanda when it was used as a means to incite Hutus to kill Tutsis, some details of which are still disputed over a quarter of a century on. This chapter argues that film directors told these stories by each consistently employing a similar cinematic technique. In these examples, the radio became invisible, as part of the audio soundtrack of the film, and the viewer had to understand that the sounds were being listened to both by them and by the characters on screen. It was an unsettling experience.

The satirizing of British radio continues

But first, the recurring tendency of critiquing British radio by writers and musicians continued to gather pace. In Chapter 6, we saw how initial reaction in the mid- to late 1970s was somewhat tentative and limited to just a few artists. Twenty years on, creatives were publishing a sustained output that reflected their opinions about radio broadcasting. Some were nostalgic and sentimental, whilst others were directly critical of radio output. Nostalgia was evident in a track by Pink Floyd, who opened their LP *The Division Bell* (1994) with an instrumental 'Cluster One' written by David Gilmour and Richard Wright (both born in the mid-1940s). It began with one minute of atmospheric interference mixed over a recording of a dawn chorus. These sounds briefly suggested the long struggle of radio listeners with medium- and short-wave crackles caused by lightning strikes and other natural causes. It was a reminder of the challenges of listening to analogue radio, reminiscent of descriptions by James Joyce (Chapter 4), Michael Stipe and R.E.M. (Chapter 7) and BBC Radio 4's comedy *Radio Active* (Chapter 8). A gentle nostalgic pastiche of wartime

---

[3] Josephine Coleman (2021), *Digital Innovations and the Production of Local Content in Community Radio: Changing Practices in the UK*, Abingdon, Oxfordshire: Routledge, pp. 22–32 and 36. In comparison, Coleman estimated (p. 36) that the professional UK radio industry employed 13,000 people.

radio was evoked in a scene in the feature-length cartoon movie *Chicken Run* (2000) produced by the British company Aardman in conjunction with DreamWorks of the United States, and the French studio Pathé. Mel Gibson voiced an American rooster who encouraged the chickens to relax and listen to dance music on a wireless set. The chicken coop was made to look like a Second World War prison camp, and the music playing was in the boogie-woogie style of that period. The suggestion was that 1940s camaraderie was being created by communal radio listening.

Meanwhile, the English art of self-deprecation was manifested in *Radio Shuttleworth* (BBC Radio 4, 1998–2000). The episodes were created by Graham Fellows who played the character John Shuttleworth, a type of faintly ridiculous individual similar but lighter in tone to those in *Radio Active* and *Alan Partridge* discussed variously in Chapters 7 and 8. The conceit of *Radio Shuttleworth* was that it was ultra-local radio, based at home in Shuttleworth's lounge and, as one of its jingles sang, 'Serving the Sheffield region and a little bit further, even'. Celebrity guests would drop by to talk about nothing in particular. One episode had the TV presenter Richard Whiteley drinking too much sherry and attempting to sing a tuneless duet with Shuttleworth.[4] It was absurd, quirky, quaint and a parody of some of the inconsequential speech items on local radio in England. Another BBC Radio 4 comedy series that satirized radio was *Ed Reardon's Week* (2005–20), which featured a grumpy, middle-aged, struggling writer played by Christopher Douglas. In one episode, he was a guest on SAGA Radio Digital, a dismal fictionalized station with an inane presenter playing songs from Val Doonican and Matt Monro.[5] In another episode, Reardon came up with a scheme to pay off his debts: he wrote a radio drama for the invented local station Hemel Sound and included product placements for his newsagent, the kebab shop and his plumber.[6] It failed comically because his play, 'The South Tring Bubble', was set in the eighteenth century – well before such things existed. A satire of BBC working conditions came with one of Reardon's girlfriends, an alcoholic Radio 4 producer, who told him she was so lonely and overworked that she felt like 'the bride of Auntie'.[7]

---

[4] *Radio Shuttleworth* (2000), BBC Radio 4, series 2, episode 2.
[5] 'Pulp Non-Fiction' (2005), *Ed Reardon's Week*, BBC Radio 4, series 1, episode 2, 14 January. The real Saga Radio launched on DAB in several regions of the UK in 2001, aimed at the over 1950s. It finally closed in 2007 and became Smooth Radio.
[6] 'Name-Check, The' (2006), *Ed Reardon's Week*, BBC Radio 4, series 3, episode 1,15 December.
[7] 'Bride of Auntie, The' (2013), *Ed Reardon's Week*, BBC Radio 4, series 9, episode 6, 16 December.

Comment on employment conditions at BBC network radio and television also appeared in the novel *Inconceivable* (1999), by Ben Elton, which was set in the mid-1990s. The story revolved, in part, around the dilemmas of 'new men' who were confused about their roles both in society and in the home as gender equality became the norm. It was about a childless couple in their mid-thirties attempting to conceive and was written in the form of two diaries, one from each of the characters. The husband, Sam Bell, described himself as 'one of the BBC's most senior and experienced lunch eaters', as he entertained two emerging comics in his role as a commissioning editor of TV comedy; a job he found to be a 'pathetically unfulfilling way [. . .] to earn a living'.[8] Elton took the opportunity to find fault with the BBC's Producer Choice initiative introduced under the leadership of John Birt in the early 1990s. Like James Long (Chapter 8), who criticized the change in newsgathering priorities, Ben Elton regarded the notion of BBC departments having to invoice one another for collaborative work and to make sure that independent production houses could compete for commissions, to be a nonsense: 'The only difference being that some bloke with a ponytail in Soho takes a thirty-grand-an-episode production fee and gets to stick his company logo on the end of the programme.'[9] After a series of blunders at work, Sam Bell was demoted to radio, in a 'sideways shunt', to take up the post of 'Chief Light Entertainment Commissioning Editor, Radio' and moved to Broadcasting House from Television Centre.[10] The narrative of *Inconceivable* embodied the culture and social mores of the era, elsewhere reflected in the romantic comedies made by the contemporary filmmaker Richard Curtis (his movie *The Boat That Rocked* is considered in Chapter 10). Ben Elton's novel was adapted into a film, *Maybe Baby* (2000), which was poorly received both by critics and at the box office. Sam was played by Hugh Laurie, who in one scene was called away from editing a recorded comedy. He asked his deputy George (Adrian Lester) to finish the work, and after making sure that Sam has left the edit suite and was out of earshot, George declared, 'Just cut three minutes off the end! Let's go for a drink.' The implication was that BBC television producers were lackadaisical, and

---

[8] Ben Elton (1999), *Inconceivable*, London: Bantam, pp. 25 and 32.
[9] Elton, *Inconceivable*, p. 77. The Producer Choice internal market system at the BBC was dismantled in 2006. See Oonagh McDonald (1995), 'Producer Choice in the BBC', *Public Money & Management*, 15 (1): 47–51. Also, Victoria Wegg-Prosser (1998), 'BBC Producer Choice and the Management of Organisational Change', PhD diss, Brunel University; and Georgina Born (2004), *Uncertain Vision: Birt, Dyke and the Reinvention of the BBC*, London: Secker & Warburg, pp. 213–15.
[10] Elton, *Inconceivable*, pp. 190–2. The move from television to radio, denoted as a demotion, was also a plot line in the final episode of the TV sitcom *Drop the Dead Donkey* (Channel 4, 1990–1998). See Chapter 8.

more interested in drinking and socializing than in completing finely crafted television programmes.

The corporate shortcomings of the BBC in the 1990s also featured in Chris Paling's novel *The Silent Sentry* (1999). Paling was a BBC Radio 4 producer, and his lead character, Maurice Reid, worked for an identical large broadcast corporation that was in the midst of being reorganized by a senior management team. It again repeated some of the concerns by Corporation staff of changes introduced in the 1990s.

> One of the worst days of Maurice's career came when he, along with a hundred or so colleagues, was invited to attend a day of 'focus groups' in a conference centre. The idea, it seemed, was to come up with a consensus view of the values the Corporation was supposed to embody. Within a few minutes it was clear that the only ones who were unclear about those values were the consultants who had been brought in to 'facilitate' the focus groups.[11]

Such comments were echoed by Greg Dyke, who was the BBC's director general from 2000 to 2004 after many years in British commercial television. Reflecting on his first week at the Corporation, he recalled in his autobiography, 'I couldn't believe how bureaucratic and paper-driven the whole place was.'[12] Many of Paling's BBC characters were, like Penelope Fitzgerald's in her novel *Human Voices* (1980, Chapter 7), highly creative but cursed with a depressive and self-critical streak. The imperfections and lack of contemporary meaning in radio at the turn of the millennium were, perhaps unintentionally, reflected in two pop songs by Robbie Williams, 'Rock DJ' (2000) and 'Radio' (2004), both of which were lyrically lightweight and products of the hedonistic era of club and dance culture. Each added little in the way of sustained critique about the medium. On the other hand, examples from the United States in this period offered a scathing response to the perceived drop in the quality of radio programmes. The singer-songwriter Tom Petty was clear in his criticism of contemporary American music radio in the title track of his 2002 LP with the Heartbreakers, *The Last DJ*. The television series *The Simpsons* also lampooned the heavily formatted American radio industry in a 1994 episode where Bart won an elephant in a radio competition.[13] The DJs initially refused to deliver the prize but were

---

[11] Chris Paling (1999), *The Silent Sentry*, London: Vintage, pp. 207-8.
[12] Greg Dyke (2004), *Inside Story*, London: Harper Collins, p. 155.
[13] 'Bart Gets an Elephant' (1994), *The Simpsons*, USA: Gracie Films/20th Television, series 5, episode 17, 31 March (USA); later broadcast in Britain on Sky 1 (1 May 1994, subscription only) and BBC 2 on 23 December 1998.

threatened with being replaced with computerized equipment if they failed to do so. The joke being that the presenters were so lacking in intelligence that they were deeply impressed by the dismal automated system.

Radio also found itself represented as a sonic backdrop to the British-developed *Grand Theft Auto* series of video games, particularly from series III to V (2001–13) with virtual radio stations in the game such as Emotion 98.3, which played adult-orientated tracks including 'Tempted' by Squeeze, as well as 'stations' playing grime, funk, R&B and country music, with spoof DJ links voiced by actors. The audio soundtrack had the effect of linking radio listening to criminal activity. Players could select a station once they were 'in' their stolen car. Elsewhere, Barry Manilow suggested that radio listening itself was an escape from the daily grind of reality in his 2001 song, 'Turn the Radio Up', which was a typical Manilow creation that combined catchy melody and lyrics. It was, he thought, a medium that could lift the spirits, and which played music that could relieve worries and fears.

Pirate radio: Making fun of English land-based illegal broadcasters

The activities of land-based illegal broadcasters continued throughout the 1980s and 1990s. Many were small-scale collectives who wanted to broadcast their favourite music to people in their area, mostly in urban spaces. The regulators continued to regard them as unglamorous operators who were often, 'revelling more in their illegality than in any sense of service'.[14] The pirate stations in the bigger cities often broadcast drum'n'bass and gansta rap on FM and were satirized by Pulp in the song 'Sorted for Es and Wizz' (1995). It told of stations offering delivery services of illegal drugs and giving details of unlicenced raves and dance events. But the songwriter and bandleader Jarvis Cocker added a note of caution at the end of the song when he wondered what happened to the casualties of substance abuse, effectively taking the glamour out of both drug-taking and pirate radio.

---

[14] The comments were made by Tony Stoller, chief executive of the Radio Authority from 1995 to 2003. See Stoller, *Sounds of Your Life*, p. 313. See also John Hind and Stephen Mosco (1985), *Rebel Radio: The Full Story of British Pirate Radio*, London: Pluto; Mike Baron (1975), *Independent Radio: The Story of Independent Radio in the United Kingdom*, Lavenham, Suffolk: Terence Dalton, pp. 70–1.

Chapter 6 had mentioned a 1974 episode of *Special Branch* (ITV), which included the security services going undercover at a land-based pirate radio station. Now, the TV comedy drama series *Minder* (ITV/Euston Films, 1979–1994) also gave recognition to pirate radio in one of the final episodes of the last of the original series when Arthur Daley (George Cole) took a cheap advert spot for his car lot, only to hear the station being raided by the authorities the moment his commercial went to air.[15] Elsewhere, the punk band the UK Subs released the album track 'Rebel Radio' (1997), which with a duration of 1'43" was a rallying cry to illegal FM land-based broadcasters. It celebrated that they often played songs which only featured on the mainstream stations weeks or even months later. The theme of unlicensed broadcasting will be returned to in Chapter 10. The UK Subs continued their opposition to radio with a 2011 track, 'Radio Unfriendly', which presented a critical overview of the airwaves. It listed the genres that singer and bandleader Charlie Harper detested: the sounds of girl and boy bands, middle-of-the-road songs, news and talk radio, and stations which repeated tracks from a limited playlist. However, with such a comprehensive list, Harper thought it was probably just his age that was making him grumpy and reactionary. His solution was to suggest 'DIY radio', in other words using a mp3 digital device to listen to personal favourites.

Radio on-screen: The movie soundtrack and the *acousmêtre*

A significant representation of radio came in three films during this period, each about events in Rwanda: *Hotel Rwanda* (2004), *Shooting Dogs* (2005) and *Sometimes in April* (2005). They employed a cinematic method that placed the radio away from the screen and on to the audio soundtrack. Using a heuristic suggested by the French film critic Michel Chion, this tactic rendered the radio as a form of all-knowing and all-powerful *acousmêtre*. This technique has been mentioned in passing in previous chapters, but here it comes into particular prominence in these films and their narrative treatment of radio.

Radio in the early 1990s had a special place in Rwandan society: cheap and portable hand-held transistor sets proliferated, meaning that broadcasts could be shared with neighbours. In a country where literacy rates were low, the radio was an important means to keep in touch locally via the FM stations, and on

---

[15] 'On the Autofront' (1994), *Minder*, ITV/Central/Euston Films, series 10, episode 8, 24 February.

short wave for national and international information. Messages could be sent and received instantly, information could be shared with hundreds of thousands; it was a mass medium that penetrated the home, the village square, the street and the backyard. Significantly, what was said on the radio was trusted by listeners. So, when stations such as RTLM in Kigali began broadcasting hate messages and incitements to murder, people listened.[16] Some estimates suggested that radio directly contributed to 50,000 deaths during the genocide of 1994.[17]

What follows is a consideration of how subsequent fictionalizations have dealt with depicting sound broadcasting in a time of genocide. In the previous chapter, Robin Williams was seen, in *Good Morning, Vietnam*, broadcasting into a microphone in the radio studio whilst the camera lingered on his facial gestures as he delivered his comic lines. Since the movie was about a wayward DJ, the emphasis was on Robin Williams. The camera occasionally cut to shots of American soldiers (his audience) dancing, smiling, swaying and reacting physically to the music on the radio. The viewer was not offered any more audience reaction than this: there was no opportunity, for example, to hear the soldiers talk about their listening. Even cutting away briefly to see them listening had the effect of interrupting the flow of Williams's comedy. In this visualization, the filmmaker had to make a choice depending on whether the narrative was primarily about the radio or about the audience, and in this respect the story itself determined the visual form of 'the radio' on screen. The challenge for filmmakers turning events in Rwanda into movie stories was how to capture and represent the cumulative effects of the crude, provocative, threatening and hateful moods of the original radio broadcasts in 1994. Michel Chion, a contributor to *Cahiers do Cinéma*, used the term *acousmêtre* to refer to something that existed only on a movie's soundtrack. It was, he said, 'a special being, a kind of talking and acting shadow', one that might be seen at any moment on screen.[18] He went on to suggest that the *acousmêtre* brought a malevolent and possessive power to the narrative, enthralling the viewer and making them want to know, and see,

---

[16] Christine L. Kellow and H. Leslie Steeves (1998), 'The Role of Radio in the Rwandan Genocide', *Journal of Communication*, 48 (3): 125. See also, David Hendy (2000), *Radio in the Global Age*, Cambridge: Polity, pp. 202–5. For a historical analysis of the way radio had previously been used during the build-up to armed conflict, particularly in 1930's Germany, see Suzanne Lommers (2012), *Europe – On Air: Interwar Projects for Radio Broadcasting*, Amsterdam: Amsterdam University Press, pp. 179–234.
[17] Alasdair Pinkerton (2019), *Radio: Making Waves in Sound*, London: Reaktion Books, p. 152.
[18] Michel Chion (1999), *The Voice in Cinema*, trans. Claudia Gorbman, New York: Columbia University Press, p. 21.

what was going on.[19] Films which used this effect included Alfred Hitchcock's *Psycho* (1960), where Norman (Anthony Perkins) had an argument with his off-screen – and dead – mother, and Stanley Kubrick's *2001: A Space Odyssey* (1968), where HAL the computer became an all-knowing voice capable of sensing the unspoken feelings of the astronauts.

The effect for the viewer was that they assumed that the unseen voice had power of both omniscience and omnipotence. It was this that added the narrative tension and created a threat. In a similar way, *Hotel Rwanda* had the radio of RTLM as a soundtrack at the beginning of each scene, sometimes in local languages and at other moments in English with a Rwandan accent, to bring a moment of suspense and maintain a constant physical threat to the narrative.[20] The film, based on real events, was nominated for three Oscars. It told the story of a resort manager, Paul Rusesabagina (Don Cheadle), trying to save the hundreds of refugees who came to his hotel seeking safety. Also playing on the movie's soundtrack was the BBC World Service and other foreign radio news bulletins to give international context. The film opened in blackness, with an initial cacophony of a radio being tuned, complete with interference and static redolent of Pink Floyd's 'Cluster One'. This compelled the viewer to concentrate on the words of the radio announcers that followed. Later, music was used to add to the tension with unsettling flute sounds to create a sense of foreboding.[21] The Hutu-supporting radio station RTLM's 'discourse was purposefully provocative and crude', as its presenters repeatedly used the racist term 'cockroaches' to describe their Tutsi opponents.[22] Its listeners thought it to be the voice of the government and therefore to be trusted as an authoritative voice.[23] RTLM, which opened in 1993, was exceptionally popular, and the presenters' incitement to hatred was often in a local language, 'whereas broadcasts in other languages – English, French and Kiswahili – were more innocuous'.[24] The discourse of hate was framed in a 'kill or be killed' form and often used a reversal technique by describing invented Tutsi atrocities.[25] The intention was for the Hutu listeners

---

[19] Chion, *The Voice in Cinema*, p. 141.
[20] Maurice Taonezvi Vambe and Urther Rwafa (2011), 'Exploring the Communicative Function of Light, Sound and Colour in Hotel Rwanda', *Journal of African Cinemas*, 3 (1): 43–9.
[21] Vambe and Rwafa, 'Exploring the Communicative Function', pp. 43–9.
[22] Jason McCoy (2009), 'Making Violence Ordinary: Radio, Music and the Rwandan Genocide', *African Music: Journal of the International Library of African Music*, 8 (3), p. 88. See also, Kellow and Steeves, 'The Role of Radio', p. 118.
[23] Kellow and Steeves (1998), 'The Role of Radio', p. 123.
[24] Kellow and Steeves (1998), 'The Role of Radio', p. 119.
[25] Kellow and Steeves (1998), 'The Role of Radio', p. 120.

to form their own outraged reaction to such unsubstantiated descriptions and to take revenge. This depiction of the radio in *Hotel Rwanda* drew it from a private listening to a form of public address system. In one scene, first hotel staff then crowds along a road were seen with transistor radios to their ears, whilst the audio of the radio transmission was also available to the viewers via the movie soundtrack; the inference was that all could hear. It was an example of a mediated sound having its proximity altered by cinema. What was received by an individual listener from a radio held close to the ear now had the effect of becoming a public address to all, announcing an ambush of the refugees trying to leave the sanctuary of the hotel.[26]

Hotel Rwanda never showed the RTLM broadcasters, their studio building, or how they conducted their programmes apart from a brief reference to a man in charge of importing machetes who had appeared on the radio station. The mention was so brief that the viewer did not connect this minor character with the persistent racial abuse heard on the movie soundtrack. The film's narrative was resolved by another use of Chion's heuristic: in a nod to Western audiences a BBC World Service-type voice said that refugees were heading to the Democratic Republic of the Congo, followed by the insertion on the soundtrack of children's voices singing as if the very air itself has been purified and made innocent in some way. The film showed scenes of the refugee camp and the movement of vast numbers of people. This transformation of the *acousmêtre* fitted with Michel Chion's analysis of how HAL, the *2001* computer, met his demise: his circuits were slowly deselected, and the viewer could see the electronic source of the voice as it deteriorated. HAL ended by singing hesitantly as it returned to its original state when first released from the factory.

A similar approach to the audio treatment of the radio was used in *Sometimes in April* (2005). However, this film showed the on-air RTLM studio for the briefest of scenes at the beginning in order to give narrative context. The movie was an HBO Films production, made for the English language TV market by the Haitian director Raoul Peck and starring the British actors Idris Elba and Oris Erhuero. The story centred on the relationship between brothers Honoré (Oris Erhuero), a broadcaster on RTLM who was standing trial for his part in the genocide, and Augustin (Idris Elba), who had witnessed many killings and attempts on his own life yet had managed to escape. It was a movie about a

---

[26] For a discussion of the dynamic effects of film sound production see: Arnt Maasø (2008), 'The Proxemics of the Mediated Voice', in Jay Beck and Tony Grajeda, eds, *Lowering the Boom: Critical Studies in Film Sound*, Urbana, IL: University of Illinois Press, pp. 36–50.

Figure 9 DJ Max (Charles Bwanika, left) introduces Honoré Butera (Oris Erhuero, right), who begins one of his 'historical reviews' on RTLM. *Sometimes in April* (2005), Dir. Raoul Peck, Rwanda/France/USA: HBO Films.

personal quest for truth and reconciliation. In a series of flashbacks, the film moved between the courtroom and the genocide ten years before. In order to establish the ubiquity of radio voices, and their importance to the story, the viewer first heard the *acousmêtre* effect with Honoré voicing a letter, offscreen, that he had sent to Augustin from prison in 2004.

Then in a flashback to 1994, he was seen in a series of rooms which were presented as the radio studios of RTLM: full of bustling people and extrovert characters. The camera tracked Honoré's smiling entrance and followed him into the studio where he delivered his comments, described by the DJ on air as 'historical reviews' (Figure 9). This, the film was suggesting, was always how radio was: remarkable sounds produced in unexceptional spaces and transmitted to credulous minds.[27] Honoré and the other presenters were handsome, full of physical presence as they addressed the microphones, with the lighting accentuating their facial features. These images intentionally contrasted with the incitement to murder and racist comments being made. The power of Michel

---

[27] Jeffrey Richards (2010), *Cinema and Radio in Britain and America, 1920–1960*, Manchester: Manchester University Press, p. 147.

Chion's *acousmêtre* lay in its unseen voice but, by letting the viewer see – if only for a short time at the beginning of the film – Honoré in the radio studio, the director Raoul Peck had humanized the off-screen threat and thereby made the later violence even more personal and tragic. It was no longer the work of a mysterious voice but of a murderous, prejudiced, human being.

From this scene in the radio studio, the film cut to an exterior, the sound of the radio now off-screen and emphasizing its panoptic presence, as young men were seen signing up to the militia and receiving weapons. The radio station sequence had lasted less than two minutes and during the rest of the film, in between flashbacks, Honoré was shown in the courtroom in 2004, where he was also surrounded by microphones, computer screens and lines of sight which allowed only his head to be seen. The rest of the film had radio as a key element of the soundtrack, using RTLM (in English) to highlight the fear and tension in an anonymized voice. At other moments, a BBC World Service-style bulletin gave a sense of international perspective, Radio France Internationale was heard introducing a soccer [sic] game in the Africa Cup, held in Tunisia in 1994, and for the benefit of Western cinema viewers a North American radio newsreader announced that Kurt Cobain has been found dead at his home in Seattle. The cinema viewer was effectively being treated as a radio listener, and heard a soundtrack which variously added emotion, brought historical context and carried the narrative.

Shooting Dogs (2005) (released as *Beyond the Gates* in the United States) was co-written and co-produced by David Belton who had worked as a BBC news producer in Rwanda at the time of the genocide. The movie presented events through the character of a young English teacher, Joe Connor (Hugh Dancy). The sound of the radio, and hence its presence – particularly that of RTLM – was again persistent in the soundtrack and was a constant murmur during scenes of tension. However, unlike *Hotel Rwanda*, clips from RTLM (some in English, others in local dialect) did not appear until twenty minutes into the movie, which had already featured UN military radio chatter and an extract from a BBC World Service correspondent's report. The effect for the viewer was to dilute the threatening power of domestic radio in the genocide. Instead, the film introduced the character of a BBC correspondent, Rachel (Nicola Walker), who was asked with her crew to help the staff and pupils at the Catholic school run by Father Christopher (John Hurt). The movie's subtext was about how Western journalism largely failed the Rwandan people at the time: photographers and film crews shot footage of bodies, knowing that they would never be broadcast on the nightly TV news programmes and that their editors at home would find other stories to fill their bulletins.[28] This storyline reflected that the Rwandan conflict was underreported at the time in 1994. However, as could be seen here, ten years later the genocide become the subject of numerous films, even as the International Criminal Tribunal for Rwanda set up by the United Nations Security Council carried on its hearings from 1994 to 2015.

A final example of the representation of radio's role in the Rwanda genocide was a multimedia theatre presentation, *Hate Radio* (2011), by Milo Rau which had been performed in Austria, Rwanda, Germany and Belgium. On stage was a recreation of the RTLM studios divided from the audience by Perspex screens. Inside the actors played the presenters laughing, joking and swapping racist comments using some of the original transcripts.

Meanwhile, on the wall were projected harrowing videos of victims' testimonies. The intention was to link the effect of the original broadcasts to the causes of the genocide. One reviewer described it as a difficult play to watch, 'The stark horror of their conversation was heightened by the calm and casualness of their behaviour.'[29] The theatre, because of its three-dimensional space, was able to offer such multimedia representations which cinema and TV were not able to do. The performance connected the voice to the individual, to the radio, to the crime and to the victim themselves. The theatre audience was a viewer of the broadcasters, a listener to the hatred and a witness to the subsequent horrific results. Yet again, in the midst of this, the radio studio on the stage was a mundane everyday space which in itself was utterly unremarkable yet gave rise to exceptional sounds.

Radio agony aunts and uncles: Stories from Seattle and Glasgow

Other ways to depict radio on the screen were seen in this period in the sitcom *Frasier* (NBC, 1993–2004; Channel 4, 1994–2004) and the movie *Sleepless in Seattle* (1993). Both were an emotional world away from the depictions of events

---

[28] See for example: Edgar Roskis (2007), 'A Genocide Without Images: White Film Noirs' in Allan Thompson, ed, *The Media and the Rwanda Genocide*, London: Pluto Press, pp. 238–41.

[29] Fergus Morgan (2019), 'Hate Radio: Review', *The Stage*, 1 March. Available online: https://www.thestage.co.uk/reviews/hate-radio-review-at-ntgent--disturbing-verbatim-play-about-rwandan-genocide (accessed 24 May 2021).

in Rwanda. However, they confirmed radio's representation in cinema and TV as either a visualization of the studio (with the unseen listeners off-screen) or – in the case of *Sleepless in Seattle* – with the radio DJ as an *acousmêtre* heard only in the soundtrack. The latter gave her authority, power and a tendency to belittle the grief and loneliness of a widower who had found himself live on the radio. Both productions were white American middle-class comedies, which between them had much in common: both were first published in 1993, and both were set in Seattle in the United States. Each had the radio embedded in their plot and narrative: the characters played by Meg Ryan and Tom Hanks would not have got together in *Sleepless in Seattle* unless his son had called a radio phone-in, and Frasier Crane's pomposity was built largely on his public status as a fictional radio host in that same city. Both will be discussed shortly in more detail.

The fascination with radio 'problem-line' phone-ins, featuring members of the public calling in to share their most intimate emotional problems with the unseen radio audience, was shared by British listeners. As mentioned in Chapter 7, Anna Raeburn had given her advice on London's Capital Radio in the 1970s and 1980s, and her work had become the basis for the TV sitcom *Agony* (ITV, 1979–81).[30] That programme was a comedy about the relationships between the agony aunt, her colleagues and her partner. Now *Frasier* and *Sleepless in Seattle* shifted the focus to depict the listeners and their engagement with the radio. Problem-line programmes were both voyeuristic and exhibitionist at the same time, depending on whether you were listening or phoning in. Other British media 'agony aunts' of this period included Claire Rayner, who, after training as a nurse and midwife, changed career and worked as a journalist appearing on television and writing newspaper advice columns.

Before her, Marjorie Proops had been a newspaper journalist and giver of advice for much of the 1950s to 1980s. The one qualified psychiatrist who regularly broadcast was Dr Anthony Clare. His BBC Radio 4 programme *In the Psychiatrist's Chair* ran for twenty years from the early 1980s and featured just one celebrity guest each episode who was probed for details of their private and emotional life.[31] It was a programme that both highlighted the psychiatrist's work and opened what was at times a somewhat uncomfortable aspect of a well-known person's life. Indeed, Claire Rayner wept openly when asked difficult

---

[30] Anna Raeburn (1984), *Talking to Myself*, London: Elm Tree Books, pp. 157–61.
[31] Simon Elmes ([2012] 2013), *Hello Again . . . Nine Decades of Radio Voices*, London: Arrow, pp. 327–9.

questions about her unhappy childhood.[32] Elsewhere on both BBC Local Radio and commercial stations, the weekly problem-line phone-in was a regular feature, and audiences became comfortable listening to others who chose to share their intimate problems, particularly in the hours after dark when the market for radio tended to be smaller and listeners were more likely to pay close attention to a detailed conversation.[33] Broadcasters themselves understood the dual nature of radio. For example, John Tusa, a journalist and arts administrator, who between 1986 and 1993 was managing director of the BBC World Service, said in 1991:

> Radio – international or domestic – is at once an act of public and private communication; it manages to be both general to its audience and particular to each member of it; it can sway millions, but it does so through millions of individual moments of listening; it is a gesture of human outreach which can go straight to the heart.[34]

Anna Raeburn agreed: 'Radio provides a remarkable mixture of intimacy and anonymity.'[35] The idea of personal problems being aired in such a public forum was used in a Scottish crime drama series *Taggart*, in an episode called 'Wavelength' (ITV, 2000). It concerned the story of a womanizing radio phone-in therapist (Aden Gillett) at a fictional Edinburgh station, Caledonia FM, who went home to find his wife had been murdered. Two more women died before the case was finally solved. The narrative suggested that there were dangers in any public discussion of intimate personal problems. The presenter was portrayed as a somewhat self-obsessed character who deceived his listeners. His show *Warm Words* belied the fact that he was seen by the television audience not to be attentive or concentrating on his callers' problems when they were on-air talking to him in the studio.

There were similarities in this negative television portrayal of radio therapists with the two examples from the United States which follow. Indeed, British viewers were able to understand the conceits of both *Frasier* and *Sleepless in Seattle*, and to engage with the 'interfacing of the "private" and the "public"' on

---

[32] David Hendy (2007), *Life on Air: A History of Radio Four*, Oxford: Oxford University Press, pp. 236–8.
[33] David Hendy (2010), 'Listening in the Dark', *Media History*, 16 (2): 215–32.
[34] John Tusa (1992), *A World in Your Ear: Reflections on Changes*, London: Broadside Books, p. 24. The quotation was originally delivered in a speech by Tusa to the Radio Academy in 1991.
[35] Raeburn, *Talking to Myself*, p. 161.

display.[36] Here were radio shows presented by fictional trained individuals who could, publicly, discuss the intimate problems of the callers to create a form of prurient entertainment. *Frasier* was one of the most successful sitcoms of this period, running in Britain on Channel 4 from 1994 to 2004 and still showing on repeat on British TV almost two decades later.[37] Frasier Crane (Kelsey Grammar) was a qualified psychiatrist who was a snobbish pedant. The story in each episode revolved around his relationships with his brother, his father and the latter's live-in home-help. At work, on his three-hour daily show at KACL-780 AM, it was the personality clash with his producer Roz (Peri Gilpin) which provided the comedy. Frasier had no complex technical controls on view in the studio in front of him. Indeed, his microphone was on a short table stand so as not to interfere with the framing of the TV shot, whilst he pressed a button on a panel in front of him to denote getting the next caller on air. This acted as a physical punctuation mark signifying to the television viewer that a voice with telephone-line quality would be heard next. In addition, instead of headphone talkback with his producer in the next-door studio, Frasier talked live to Roz on air. Hence, the introduction of a new caller became, 'And who do we have next Roz?', to which she opened her microphone in her studio, named and introduced them. It was technically inaccurate, but a mise-en-scène arrangement for the television viewer to show that Roz was the character in control of the radio production: she sat at a complex mixing desk, answered the phones and verbally directed Frasier in all he did. The narrative irony was that Roz, despite being in charge of things on-air, had little control over her chaotic love life. Each episode included short scenes of Frasier in the radio studio, often at the beginning of the programme or during a pause in the main narrative to act as a humorous counterpoint. For example, when he corrected one phone-in guest's poor grammar, Frasier was told by the caller that he was an 'intellectual pinhead with a superiority complex'.[38] In another episode, a thirteen-year-old, who called to say he was being bullied at school, rejected Frasier's patronizing

---

[36] Ian Hutchby (1991), 'The Organization of Talk on Talk Radio', in Paddy Scannell, ed., *Broadcast Talk*, London: Sage, p. 119.

[37] The series, together with *Friends* and *Sex and the City*, was one of three American import successes for *Channel 4 in* the UK during the 1990s and 2000s. Stephen Pile (2004), 'The last laugh?', *The Daily Telegraph*, 24 January. Available online: https://www.telegraph.co.uk/culture/tvandradio/3610803/The-last-laugh.html (accessed 24 May 2021).

[38] 'Here's Looking at You' (1993) *Frasier*, series 1, episode 5. The year in this and all other references was the original US transmission date by NBC.

on-air advice and retorted, 'The real surprise here is they pay you to dole out this balloon juice.'[39]

Frasier's brother Niles (David Hyde Pierce), also a psychiatrist, repeatedly belittled him. When they wanted to make a reservation at a popular new restaurant, Frasier said reassuringly, 'Niles, you're forgetting the cachet my name carries in this town.' To which he answered, 'Actually I'm not. If the *maître d'* happens to be a housewife we're in.' Insinuating that his brother's radio audience comprised lower-class middle-aged women.[40] In another episode a second psychiatrist was hired because Frasier's show was so popular. He said, 'They could hardly ask me to do another three hours. Imagine how exhausting that would be.' To which Niles replied, sarcastically, 'And for you as well.'[41] Frasier habitually offered an 'invitation to speak' to his caller: 'Hello, this is Dr Frasier Crane. I'm listening.'[42] However, the comedy was built upon his aloofness, and when one caller went on at length about his problems, Frasier started to mess around silently in his studio making his producer next door (and the television audience) laugh. The caller had apparently no idea that he was being patronized.[43] It was a comic version of the scene in *Taggart*, described earlier.

In contrast to *Frasier*, where the radio audience were part of the soundtrack, the viewer of *Sleepless in Seattle* (1993) was offered selected members of a radio audience but no sight of the host of the phone-in show, who remained an unseen disembodied voice.

Sleepless in Seattle was about a long-distance audio relationship: between a widower Sam Baldwin (Tom Hanks) and a single woman Annie Reed (Meg Ryan). The cinema viewer heard the radio under pictures of the unfolding action, but was shown neither the faces of the broadcasters, their studio, nor buildings they were transmitting from, suggesting that the 'radio' was a media form that was somehow everywhere and nowhere. The film itself was a critical and financial success. Sam Baldwin moved to Seattle with his eight-year-old son after the death of his wife. As he continued to grieve, his son Jonah (Ross Malinger) called a late- night phone-in. Listening hundreds of miles away in her car, Annie heard: 'Welcome back to *You and Your Emotions* with Dr Marcia Fieldstone broadcasting live, networked across America, from Chicago.' The

---

[39] 'Guess Who's Coming to Breakfast?' (1994) *Frasier*, series 1, episode 13.
[40] 'Dinner at Eight' (1993), *Frasier*, series 1, episode 3, 30 September. David Hyde Pierce also appeared in *Sleepless in Seattle* as Annie's elder brother.
[41] 'Dr. Nora' (1999), *Frasier*, series 6, episode 20, 29 April.
[42] Hutchby, 'The Organization of Talk on Talk Radio', p. 120.
[43] 'Guess Who's Coming to Breakfast?' (1994) *Frasier*, series 1, episode 13, 6 January.

camera stayed on Annie's face as she drove and listened, whilst the off-screen audio continued:

Jonah: Hello this is Jonah.
Dr Marcia: How old are you?
Jonah: I'm eight.

To this the radio host's only response was a non-judgemental 'You're up late'. The film revolved around the boy's attempts to find a woman to keep his father happy, and after speaking to the phone-in host, he passed the handset to his father who, instead of being upset at any infringement of his privacy, began to publicly express his grief. The film had already made significant assumptions about professional radio: that it allowed minors to take part in an 'agony aunt' broadcast late at night, that the parent was not consulted, that no consent was given and that the station could have later given out Sam's private address to any women who may have wanted to write to him.

The whole transaction left Annie transfixed and weeping in her car, whilst the film's narrative implied that the radio programme was a performance rather than a therapy session. Dr Fieldstone (Caroline Aaron) said, 'We'll resume right after these messages. Sam, Jonah, don't go away. I'm talking to "Sleepless in Seattle".' Evidently, commercial imperatives were more important than the mental health of the listeners who phoned in. Dr Fieldstone's character was another example of the *acousmêtre* effect, where the unseen voice became all-knowing and powerful. The effect for the viewer was to be able to witness how this off-screen voice could control the emotions and actions of the on-screen characters. Indeed, at one point she said to Sam somewhat threateningly, 'You can tell a lot from someone's voice.' She had also demonstrated off-screen power by renaming him 'Sleepless in Seattle', thereby removing his own name. The film highlighted how radio agony aunts translated intimate, private conversation into the public realm: Annie Reed pulled up at a truck stop, only to find the waitresses similarly enthralled by the voice of Sam Baldwin on the radio. The radio conversation was curtailed abruptly when, even though Tom Hanks's character was in full emotional flow sharing his sadness at the passing of his young wife, Dr Fieldstone cut across him and said brusquely, 'Well folks, it's time to wrap it up . . .', and so closed the programme. Later in the movie, the commodification of the phone-in callers was confirmed when cinema viewers heard a 'best-of' compilation of Dr Fieldstone's show where she gave each caller an alliterative name: 'Marooned in Miami' and 'Desperate in Denver', to add to 'Sleepless in Seattle'. The effect of this *acousmêtre* was to belittle the personal problems of these callers and to reduce them to subjects for public entertainment. The final scenes of the film used the previous physical distance of the Ryan and Hanks characters to add suspense as the two attempted to establish a rendezvous in New York before the Empire State Building observation deck closed for the evening, and so provide the eight-year-old boy with a family again.

This has been another chapter that has focused on the act of listening. It has discussed a range of soundtrack arrangements and mises-en-scène of radio used by movies and television series in the 1990s and early 2000s. Radio was a 'conversation' – especially when there was a phone-in going on. In a conventional narrative with two actors in the same room, the camera could cut between the faces and could also show reverse shots that revealed the emotions of a character as they listened. This arrangement was not possible for radio on film, where the listener and broadcaster were physically separate. The solution for directors was to present either the radio studio, the act of broadcast, or to show the listener attending to the programme. The other part of the communication was then in the soundtrack. It might have been the noise of the radio creating tension and fear, as in *Hotel Rwanda*, or a phone-in caller's comment allowing the presenter to pull a face of disdain, for example in *Frasier*, which granted the viewing audience a privileged vantage point. Or it could have been an unseen presenter turning a listener's private problems into public entertainment. In such depictions, and despite what might have been regarded as its incomplete representation on film and television, the viewing audience was able to decode the visual and acoustic signs offered by directors who chose to represent radio from either point of view.

10

Listening back and looking forward
Nostalgia and new technology, 2006 to 2022

Hearing, not listening

This chapter draws to a close this review of 100 years of radio broadcasting in Britain by examining how the decade and a half to 2022 has been reflected in cultural output. The previous chapter considered the radio audience as 'listeners'; now the focus shifts to regard them as 'producers' too. This was also a period when the established notions of 'broadcasting' and of real-time linear radio, that were produced and listened to at the time of transmission, were breaking down. But first, this chapter begins with a consideration of the only sculpture to be included in this study, and one which encapsulated an aspect of radio's essence in its past and its present forms.

In 2008, the Tate Modern gallery in London unveiled a work by the Brazilian conceptual artist Cildo Meireles called *Babel*. It presented the visitor with a large-scale audio\visual installation: it was a tower of radio receivers, the oldest and largest at the bottom and the newest and smallest towards the top.[1] *Babel* represented the act of hearing radio, but in a hushed almost reverential immersive museum space, with yellow and red lights visible in the low light of the room (Figure 10).

The artist said inspiration for many of his installations came from Orson Welles's radio play 'The War of the Worlds' (see Chapter 3), broadcast in the United States ten years before Meireles's birth. He said the 1938 drama represented a work of art in itself because it broke down the barriers between fiction and reality, and because it provoked an audience reaction.[2] He also explained the biblical

---

[1] Guy Brett, ed. (2008), *Cildo Meireles* (exhibition catalogue), London: Tate Publishing, p. 168.
[2] Cildo Meireles and Frederico Morais (2008), 'Material Language', trans. Stephen Berg, *Tate Etc.*, Issue 14, Autumn, pp. 103–4.

Figure 10 *Babel* (2001–6), Cildo Meireles, born 1948; metallic structure, radio sets; (h) 450 centimetres (w) 260 centimetres; Tate. © Cildo Meireles; Photo © Tate.

link of this particular piece: 'From the start, the reference was Babel, in the sense that, by accumulation, it would become a tower of incomprehension, more than comprehension [. . .] because each radio was tuned to a different station, broadcasting different sounds.'[3] Even so, the story in the Bible had God destroy the tower because it was built by a people who were consumed by egotistical pride.[4] The radios were heard, during a visit by the author in January 2020,

---

[3] Brett, *Cildo Meireles*, p. 168.
[4] Genesis 11.1-9.

to play a news bulletin from BBC Radio London and a local community radio station host who welcomed a guest into his studio.[5] Overlaid was the sound of violins and stringed instruments being tuned. Visitors were observed to point their mobile phones instinctively at the installation and take a photo or short video of it without being prompted. Each person did not spend long in the room, perhaps just over one minute in front of the piece. This lack of attention suggested that Meireles had indeed represented radio as a medium of inattentiveness, a babble, rather than something to listen to and concentrate upon. In doing so, he had also depicted radio receivers as old museum pieces.

The Tate Modern had averaged over five million visitors each year between 2008 and 2019.[6] Meireles's sculpture had recontextualized the life and meaning of each radio and consigned the medium to the museum.

The return to nostalgia?

If the sculpture *Babel* played with the notion of radio's own function, there were several film and TV representations of radio in this period, each one of which told of its history.

Nostalgia, as discussed in Chapter 6, had always been a complex subject to pin down, even if it was – according to the speculations of academics from the 1970s onwards – a proactive expression of society's desire to look to the past in order to establish a version of the present.[7] From the late 1970s to the mid-2010s, some commentators had at times treated nostalgia with a certain amount of disdain.[8] This book has argued however, that since the release of *American Graffiti* (1973) onwards, radio nostalgia was less of a hollow pastiche and more of a critical comparison through a nuanced, if at times occasionally slightly exaggerated, memorializing of an imagined listening past.[9] Elsewhere,

---

[5] Personal observation, Tate Modern, London, 3 January 2020.
[6] 'Visits made in 2019 to visitor attractions in membership with ALVA' (2020), Association of Leading Visitor Attractions. Available online: https://www.alva.org.uk/details.cfm?p=423 (accessed 24 May 2021).
[7] Fred Davis (1979), *Yearning for Yesterday: A Sociology of Nostalgia*, New York: The Free Press, p. vii.
[8] See, for example, Fredric Jameson (1984), 'Postmodernism, or the Cultural Logic of Late Capitalism', *New Left Review*, no. 146, July–August, pp. 53–92. Available online: https://newleftreview.org/issues/i146/articles/fredric-jameson-postmodernism-or-the-cultural-logic-of-late-capitalism (accessed 24 May 2021). David Lowenthal (2015), *The Past Is a Foreign Country – Revisited*, Cambridge: Cambridge University Press, pp. 31–54.
[9] Lowenthal, *The Past Is a Foreign Country – Revisited*, pp. 304–5 and 315–24.

nostalgia was proving to be a persistent tendency. Academics and cultural commentators including Simon Reynolds, Michael Dwyer and Stephen Brown had during the 2010s thought about nostalgia's enduring presence in our lives. It was, each variously thought, a critical remaking of the present explained by factors including: demographic changes as the baby boomer generation aged; economic uncertainty which caused people to worry about their own future; technology that offered an easily available online archive of the past through Google, YouTube and others; and as a reaction to increasing divisions wrought by rises in populism, nationalism and worries about immigration. [10]

The following examples are arranged in the chronological order of their subject period. Together they provide a type of summary of how radio's history has been represented by media in the 2010s. For example, one episode of a television costume drama about the English landed gentry *Downton Abbey* (ITV, 2010–15) concerned itself with radio in the 1920s, and presumed that the wireless was a modern novelty which was admired enthusiastically by the younger characters in the stately home.[11] The drama presented a version of a familiar trope of modernity and technology in a struggle with tradition.[12] The episode was set in April 1924, and the earl of Grantham (Hugh Bonneville, who also appeared in *W1A* mentioned later) was initially reluctant to have a wireless set in the house. He finally agreed to rent one when he learnt that King George V (voiced by Jon Glover) was to broadcast a speech from the British Empire Exhibition. The boosters of the new technology, according to the show's creator and scriptwriter Julian (later Lord) Fellowes, were the female characters. The earl's daughter Rose MacClare (Lily James) said, 'I'm told they're far more efficient now, and much easier to tune.' Radio listening evidently crossed class boundaries, and one of the maids (Sophie McShera as Daisy Mason) said, 'I like the idea of the wireless: to hear people talking and singing in London and all sorts.' But his lordship voiced his disapproval:

---

[10] Simon Reynolds (2011), *Retromania: Pop Culture's Addiction to Its Own Past*, London: Faber and Faber, pp. 197–201; Michael D. Dwyer (2015), *Back to the Fifties: Nostalgia, Hollywood Film, and Popular Music of the Seventies and Eighties*, New York: Oxford University Press, pp. 8–10; Stephen Brown (2018), 'Retro Galore! Is There No End to Nostalgia?' *Journal of Customer Behaviour*, 17 (1–2): 9–29.

[11] *Downton Abbey* (2014), ITV/ITV Studios, series 5, episode 2, 28 September. For a discussion of the use of props in visually contextualizing period dramas including *Downton Abbey*, see Alex Bevan (2019), *The Aesthetics of Nostalgia TV: Production Design and the Boomer Era*, New York: Bloomsbury Academic, pp. 79–100.

[12] For a critical appreciation of *Downton Abbey*, see, Phil Harrison (2020), *The Age of Static: How TV Explains Modern Britain*, London: Melville House, pp. 171–6.

'That people should waste hours huddled around a wooden box, listening to someone talking at them, burbling inanities from somewhere else!' And he added, 'It's a fad. It won't last.' That ironic comment was intended as easy comedy for the twenty-first-century viewer. After the wireless arrived and was installed, the family and servants gathered to listen to the king's broadcast. Predictably, his lordship was impressed, and after all had listened in attentive silence, he declared, 'Well, I hope you've all taken something of value from it'.

A vision of what radio may have been like ten years later, in the 1930s, appeared in the film *The King's Speech* (2010), which offered representations of Britain-in-empire, the future King George VI and of radio production during the period.[13] It was the story of the relationship between the voice and the microphone. As the film opened, the viewer saw a large bullet-shaped grey metal microphone suspended in mid-air over a desk, both phallic and threatening. A contrast was established between the shots in the studio of the suave professional announcer in a dinner suit and bow tie, and the prince (Colin Firth) struggling to deliver a speech at Wembley Stadium to nation and Empire. The speech impediment for which he sought treatment was visualized by close camera work and fish-eye-type lenses to emphasize the physical and mental pressure of talking. The film followed the prince's unconventional friendship with his vocal coach and mentor, Lionel Logue (Geoffrey Rush), from 1934 to the coronation and to the onset of war. In a final scene, Logue and King George VI stood alone together in a curtain-lined room in Buckingham Palace for what was his September 1939 radio address at the outbreak of war. Logue encouraged him seconds before the microphone went live: 'Forget everything else and say it to me as a friend', which re-emphasized that radio broadcasters were trained to address the individual listener. The intimate address of the king to the microphone in front of him, and Logue, the other side of it in the same small room, was intercut with shots of people listening to the wireless in groups: in pubs, living rooms, factories and public squares. This underlined how the intimacy of radio talk was also attended to in public spheres by groups listening together.[14] After his

---

[13] King George VI 'held a deep antipathy for the microphone.' See Thomas Hajkowski (2010), *The BBC and National Identity in Britain, 1922–1953*, Manchester: Manchester University Press, p. 93. See also, Asa Briggs (1970), *The History of Broadcasting in the United Kingdom, Volume III, The War of Words*, Oxford: Oxford University Press, p. 96. A separate radio drama, also called 'A King's Speech' and written by Mark Burgess, was produced in 2009 for BBC Radio 4 a year before the David Seidler's script became the movie version.

[14] Kate Lacey (2013), *Listening Publics: The Politics and Experience of Listening in the Media Age*, Cambridge: Polity, p. 69 and 135–9. See Chapter 3 in this volume for a discussion of royal broadcasting and public listening in the interwar years.

broadcast, the BBC technicians inside the palace applauded the king, and the crowds cheered as he stepped on to the balcony to wave at his subjects below.

Similar to *The King's Speech*, the novel *London Rain* (2015) by Nicola Upson was set in 1937 during the coronation of George VI. The story had an amateur detective working out how a BBC reporter in a commentary box was shot just after finishing his description of the royal pageantry. Upson portrayed the BBC as a secretive organization, which wanted to keep the murder of one of its well-known staff members quiet and out of the daily papers.[15] It was a less-than-flattering image, and she described Broadcasting House as, 'an austere, modern building in a stripped classical style, which dwarfed its Georgian neighbours and seemed itself to be torn between past and future'.[16] The novel used real historical names from the BBC of the era such as Val Gielgud, John Snagge and Freddie Grisewood. So, to some extent it recalled both Gielgud's 1934 murder mystery novel (see Chapter 2) and Winifred Holtby's technique of mixing real people with invented characters (see Chapter 3).

A 2010 television version of an Agatha Christie novel opened with the sounds of radio in the 1950s. 'The Pale Horse' (ITV) had been adapted to include the character of Miss Marple (Julia McKenzie) into the narrative.[17] Neither the original book (1961), the previous TV version (ITV, 1996), nor the two BBC radio drama presentations (1993, 2018) had been a vehicle for this character, but nonetheless the story was chosen to be part of this Miss Marple television series.[18] From the start, she was seen listening to a play by Shakespeare on the radio. As the main titles rolled, the four-minute opening sequence of the feature-length drama created suspense and tension in order to tease the viewer into the narrative, which was a story of good against evil. Shots of damp, foggy, darkened streets, of footsteps and of a woman on her deathbed were intercut with Miss Marple switching on her wooden Art Deco wireless receiver to find *Macbeth* being performed. They were easy visual and audio tropes used by the director (Andy Hay) and the screenwriter (Russell Lewis) to establish a narrative of murder, religion and witchcraft.

---

[15] Nicola Upson (2015), *London Rain*, London: Faber & Faber, pp. 148 and 152–9. Another representation of the BBC in the 1920s and 1930s, intermixing real and fictional characters, appeared in a novel by Sarah-Jane Stratford (2016), *Radio Girls*, London: Allison & Busby.
[16] Upson, *London Rain*, p. 4.
[17] 'Pale Horse, The' (2010), *Agatha Christie's Marple*, ITV/Agatha Christie Ltd, series 5, episode 1, 3 August.
[18] *Agatha Christie's Marple* (2004–2013), ITV. Geraldine McEwan took the title role from 2004 to 2009, and Julia McKenzie took over from 2009 onwards.

One episode of the BBC drama series *Father Brown* (2013–present) addressed the topic of radio celebrity and fame.[19] The series itself was loosely based on short stories written between 1910 and the mid-1930s by GK Chesterton, with the TV version set later in the 1950s in the English Cotswolds. Father Brown (Mark Williams) was the parish priest who solved the mysteries in this postwar rural idyll. The episode was called 'The Theatre of the Invisible', and told how a fictional popular BBC Light Programme quiz *Up to You* came to town. The show was reminiscent of a long-running weekly programme presented by Wilfred Pickles called *Have a Go*.[20] In the *Father Brown* episode, the radio show's producer, given the slightly pretentious double-barrelled name Jeremy Mayhew-Bowman (Simon Bubb), killed both a landlady and the programme's announcer Richie Queenan (Arthur Bostrom). BBC stars and producers were portrayed as egotistical, petulant and temperamental. Police Inspector Mallory (Jack Deam) said, 'I'll be glad to see the back of these show-business types, They're not the same as the likes of us.' His sergeant agreed. It may have been a fiction, but radio of the era and those working in the industry – whilst having the outward trappings of show business – were collectively cast in a negative light.

In contrast, a wistful nostalgic view of radio in the 1960s was presented in the film *The Boat That Rocked* (2009) (released in North America as *Pirate Radio*). It was an ensemble comedy production about the exploits of individuals on board a radio ship in the North Sea and the struggles of enthusiastic male radio professionals against authority.[21] The gender stereotype reflected the culture of the period when this movie was set. Visually, the movie recreated the physical environment of the radio studio of this era, with gramophone decks, jingle cartridge players and reel to reel tape machines. The film began with sounds of a radio being tuned in to BBC broadcasts: a woman with a clipped voice saying, 'Are you sitting quite comfortably?' and announcements for the Home Service and a market report for farmers. This cut to a boy going to bed and secretly listening to a transistor radio in his darkened room. The cinema viewer was then

---

[19] 'Theatre of the Invisible, The' (2017), *Father Brown*, BBC 1/BBC Studios, series 5, episode 12, 16 January.
[20] *Have a Go* ran on the BBC's Light Programme from 1946 to 1967. Simon Elmes ([2012] 2013), *Hello Again ... Nine Decades of Radio Voices*, London: Arrow, pp. 148–52.
[21] For historical background to the era, see Robert Chapman (1992), *Selling the Sixties: The Pirates and Pop Music Radio*, London: Routledge. See also Asa Briggs (1995), *The History of Broadcasting in the United Kingdom, Volume V, Competition*, Oxford: Oxford University Press, pp. 502–15; Matt Mollgaard (2012), 'Pirate Stories: Rethinking the Radio Rebels', in Matt Mollgaard, ed., *Radio and Society: New Thinking for an Old Medium*, Newcastle upon Tyne: Cambridge Scholars Publishing, pp. 55–6.

shown shots of people listening and dancing as one of the lead characters, The Count (Philip Seymour Hoffman) introduced the Kinks's 'All Day and All of the Night'.[22] The message was that here was a DJ who was breaking the unwritten rules of Reithian restraint to the widespread enjoyment of the listening audience. The film was fictional, and 'Radio Rock on 203 metres medium wave' was a creative invention, as was the accidental sinking of the vessel at the end of the story. The movie also represented the listeners as dedicated fans when they arrived on a flotilla of boats to rescue the crew and DJs. It was a form of victory, even if the stations were eventually outlawed by act of parliament in 1967 which made it an offence to supply such a vessel. In fact, Radio Caroline continued to broadcast intermittently from sea until 1991, later legally establishing itself in South East England the 1990s as first a satellite and then an online radio station, with additional DAB and analogue services opening in the 2020s.[23]

An imagined view of 1960s British music culture was presented in David Mitchell's novel *Utopia Avenue* (2020), which followed the eponymous fictional band and its brush with fame. Throughout the novel, the BBC, hospital radio, American Armed Forces Network radio and pirate stations were an understated part of daily life: unexceptional and accepted by the characters. Mitchell used it as a device to introduce mentions of contemporary chart hits, in order to anchor the story in the era.[24] Radio thus became a nostalgic device that played Sandie Shaw in a coffee bar, the Tremeloes on a car radio and Scott McKenzie on an offshore radio station. To provide linkages both within the novel and to other works by Mitchell, a fictional DJ, Bat Segundo, was introduced who broadcast first on a British pirate station 'Radio Bluebeard one-nine-eight long wave, brought to you by Denta-dazzle gum'. and then later on a New York station 'Locomotive 97.8FM', where he interviewed members of the Utopia Avenue band during their North American tour.[25] Bat Segundo had previously appeared in Mitchell's 1999 novel *Ghostwritten*, where he was a late-night New York radio phone-in DJ talking to a sentient supercomputer moments before the impending apocalypse.[26]

---

[22] 'The Count' was based on the DJ Emperor Rosko, according to Nick Bailey (2019), *Across the Waves: From Radio Caroline to Classic FM*, n. p: Otherwise, p.70.
[23] For an account of the station in the 1980s and 1990s, see Steve Conway ([2009] 2014), *Shiprocked: Life on the Waves with Radio Caroline*, Dublin: Liberties Press.
[24] A technique also used by movies and TV period dramas. See Reynolds, *Retromania*, p. xix.
[25] David Mitchell (2020), *Utopia Avenue*, London: Sceptre/Hodder and Stoughton, pp. 150 and 147.
[26] David Mitchell (1999), *Ghostwritten*, London: Hodder and Stoughton, pp. 383–429.

Finally, a touch of nostalgia was evident during this period in a number of travelogue and first-person accounts of radio memories by authors including Simon Elmes, a BBC radio producer, Charlie Connelly, who wrote two radio-based travel books, and John Osborne, who was a long-standing fan of the medium.[27] Collectively, these books represented a form of fan writing: works by authors both from within the industry and without who often used a light touch of deprecating humour to write endearingly about radio in Britain.

Critique, comedy and satire

Whilst the dominant examples during this period from the mid-2000s onwards had been nostalgic creations, the thread which has woven itself through much of the past 100 years has been a desire to offer critiques: both of the medium itself and of those who make programmes. Bruce Springsteen's 'Radio Nowhere' (2007) used a biblical reference to speaking in tongues whilst asking if there was anyone actually listening to the automated contemporary music stations. This computerization was a trend that had established itself both in the United States and at British commercial stations.[28] Elsewhere a comedic antidote to such feelings came from the country singer Reba McEntire, who used double entendres in her 2010 song, 'Turn on the Radio', to tell of her revenge on a former lover. She refused to see him anymore but suggested that he could always hear her voice and her songs on the radio. She went on to imply that this would be the closest he would now get to 'turning her on'. A British television comedy series further established adult themes around the subject of commercial radio. *FM* (ITV 2, 2009) lasted for just six episodes and featured strong language and vulgar jokes; ironically, not themes allowed on radio stations.[29] The series was scheduled for late-night transmission on ITV 2, a channel aimed at under thirty-five-year-olds. The lead character Lindsay (Kevin O'Dowd, who also starred in

---

[27] Simon Elmes (2007), *And Now on Radio 4: A Celebration of the World's Best Radio Station*, London: Arrow Books. Charlie Connelly ([2004] 2005), *Attention All Shipping: A Journey Round the Shipping Forecast*, London: Abacus, and ([2019] 2020), *Last Train to Hilversum: A Journey in Search of the Magic of Radio*, London: Bloomsbury. John Osborne (2009), *Radio Head: Up and Down the Dial of British Radio*, London: Simon & Schuster.

[28] Tony Stoller (2010), *Sounds of Your Life: The History of Independent Radio in the UK*, New Barnet, Hertfordshire: John Libbey, pp. 256–7 and 331–5. See also, Guy Starkey (2011), *Local Radio, Going Global*, Basingstoke, Hampshire: Palgrave Macmillan, pp. 156–9.

[29] *Ofcom Guidance: Offensive Language on Radio* (2011), Ofcom. Available online: https://www.ofcom .org.uk/ data/assets/pdf_file/0014/40541/offensive-language.pdf (accessed 24 May 2021).

The Boat That Rocked) was portrayed as an incompetent and socially naïve DJ at the fictional 'Skin 86.5 FM'. He swapped jokes and insults on-air with his arrogant co-presenter Dom (Kevin Bishop). Their cynical producer Jane (Nina Sosanya) was shown in the control room behind the glass, but still heard on-air – in a similar mise-en-scène of the studio used in the series *Frasier*, mentioned in the previous chapter. The episodes of *FM* were intertextual, with cameo appearances from actual presenters including Jamie Theakston (BBC Radio 5Live, Radio 1, Heart), Richard Bacon (BBC Radio 5Live) and Tim Westwood (BBC Radio 1, 1Xtra, Capital Radio).

A portrayal of a confused sense of professional ability was shown in a mockumentary *W1A* (2014–17). It was one of three such comedies in this genre that were broadcast by BBC television in this period. The other two, *People Just do Nothing* and *Hospital People*, are discussed in the following text. In a moment of self-reflexivity, the BBC commissioned three series of *W1A* which satirized its own management structure and its bureaucracy.[30] Some critics thought that it was a little too revealing: 'As an example of the BBC's creative energy, *W1A* is a wonderful advocate for the corporation; as a view on its inner workings, it's hard not to see it as slightly self-sabotaging.'[31] The media commentator Raymond Snoddy added, 'The satire [of *W1A*] often failed to keep up with the toe-curling BBC reality.'[32] The main character Ian Fletcher (Hugh Bonneville, also seen in *Downton Abbey*) was given the nonsensical job title of Head of Values. In one episode he took a train from London to appear live on Radio 4's *Woman's Hour* and be interviewed by (Dame) Jenni Murray (played by herself).[33] In the railway carriage, Fletcher asked, 'Why is *Woman's Hour* from Manchester on Friday?' Tracey Pritchard (Monica Dolan), a BBC Senior Communications Officer, replied, 'OK, that's a good question, Ian. I'm not being funny or anything, but I'm not sure anyone knows that.' Which captured some of the idiosyncrasies of the Corporation, where custom and practice could be lost in the midst of time.[34]

---

[30] For historical context and a sociological account of the Corporation, see Tom Burns (1977), *The BBC: Public Institution and Private World*, London: Macmillan, pp. 45–6. Also: Georgina Born (2004), *Uncertain Vision: Birt, Dyke and the Reinvention of the BBC*, London: Secker & Warburg, pp. 239–41.

[31] Charlotte Higgins (2015), 'We Love W1A. But, Dear BBC, is it Wise to Lay Bare Your Foibles So Mercilessly?' *The Guardian*, 15 May. Available online: https://www.theguardian.com/commentisfree/2015/may/15/w1a-bbc-licence-fee-john-whittingdale (accessed 24 May 2021).

[32] Raymond Snoddy (2020), 'Letter to the Director General', in John Mair, ed., *The BBC: A Winter of Discontent?* Goring, Oxfordshire: Bite-Sized Books, p. 45.

[33] *W1A* (2014), BBC 2, series 1, episode 2, 26 March.

[34] In reality, *Woman's Hour* on Radio 4 had been broadcast a couple of days each week from Manchester/Salford for many years. Shortly after this episode of *W1A* was aired, *Woman's Hour* moved full-time to London. The two events were unconnected.

A novel that offered a magic reality telling of taking part in a radio programme was Michael Paraskos's *In Search of Sixpence* (2016). His narrative technique mixed autobiography and reality with a fictional version of those same things. Hence, the novel began as the author prepared for an imaginary radio interview with Mariella Frostrup at Broadcasting House, who between 2002 and 2020 was a presenter of Radio 4's *Open Book* (which he renamed *Book Choice*).[35] She observed, 'For example, I notice in canto seven of your book you have a fictionalised version of me ask you about this, as though you want your father to be seen as a kind of Don Quixote.'[36] This was disorientating because that was exactly what the reader was actually reading; it played with the idea of both time and fiction. Paraskos mixed reality, present events and fantasies of the future with past descriptions, to create a novel that explored an author's relationship with his work, his family and the public at large. In the process the book itself became another character within the narrative, whilst the BBC later morphed into an extreme political broadcast station, suggesting a separation, a gulf, between artist, radio and audience.

Lack of professional ability in local radio was also a theme in this period. An episode of the comedy drama series *Doc Martin* (ITV, 2004–19) called 'It's Good to Talk' featured an incompetent presenter at a fictional community station, Radio Portwenn.[37] She conducted a stilted interview with a tongue-tied character who tried – and failed – to explain why he was setting up sea-fishing trips for tourists. She then attempted to commentate as the doctor (Martin Clunes) performed an emergency tracheotomy in the radio studio on a fellow guest who had just collapsed. Doc Martin, in line with his character, repeatedly ignored her and then told her to 'Shut up!', all live on-air. A critique of unprofessional journalism appeared in *The Trouble with Maggie Cole* (2020, ITV), where the lead character (Dawn French) gave a drunken radio interview which was then played on a fictional West Country station, Coastland FM. The recording contained potentially libellous comments about many of the residents in the village, and the comedy drama played out as the characters each resolved the revelations about their personal lives. The scandal spread, reflecting the contemporary multimedia world, as the interview audio and personal revelations became repeated both on social media and in the national press. The question

---

[35] Michael Paraskos (2016), *In Search of Sixpence*, Mitcham, Surrey: Friction Fiction, p. 23.
[36] Paraskos, *In Search of Sixpence*, p. 26.
[37] 'It's Good to Talk' (2015), *Doc Martin*, ITV/ITV Studios, series 7, episode 3, 21 September.

for the viewer was why a radio journalist should act in such an unethical manner by getting a guest drunk in order to obtain an interview.

Local radio, both BBC and commercial, had historically been held in disdain by staff at national radio stations. A common criticism by Corporation headquarters staff was that local radio was 'parish pump' in both its outlook and professional quality.[38] One BBC comedy reinforced that view, specifically of the hospital radio sector. Britain has around 200 such stations run by volunteers broadcasting to in-patients often on closed-loop systems. *Hospital People* (BBC 1, 2016–17) was, like *W1A*, filmed as if a fly-on-the-wall documentary series. The comedian Tom Binns played multiple characters, including a DJ called Ivan Brackenbury ('the cheerful earful'). He incorporated many of the stereotypes of such volunteers, including a voice that was overly nasal and had a slight lisp. The presenter had a dramatic jingle which somewhat tastelessly announced, 'From maternity to the morgue, from cardiovascular to urogenital, this is hospital radio. Ivan Brackenbury!'[39] He reflected the 'parish pump' in-joke in the radio industry. Brackenbury played inappropriate songs for patients, for example: 'Maneater' by Daryl Hall and John Oates for one who had been diagnosed with MRSA (Methicillin-resistant Staphylococcus aureus); Free's 'All Right Now' for a man who had just had his left foot and left arm removed; and 'Holding Back the Years' by Simply Red for another having surgery to pin back his ears.[40]

Similar displays of broadcasting incompetence existed in the third BBC comedy in the mockumentary genre, *People Just Do Nothing*. It was first produced by a team of writers and performers on YouTube in 2010–11, before being commissioned by BBC 3 for five series between 2014 and 2018. The original style did not change much: the characters spoke straight to camera, and there was an occasional directorial voice asking questions off-camera. The series was set in West London on an estate of council-owned tower blocks where the young men ran a fictional pirate radio station.[41] It followed the tropes of low-level antisocial behaviour and recreational substance abuse in the representation

---

[38] Matthew Linfoot (2011), 'A History of BBC Local Radio in England c1960–1980', PhD dis., University of Westminster, London, pp. 316–7.
[39] *Hospital People* (2016), BBC 1/Roughcut TV, series 1, episode 1, 21 April. Some of Brackenbury's other jingles, which sung the days of the week, were similar to those from the offshore pirate station Radio London featured on the 1967 LP *The Who Sell Out*. See Chapter 5.
[40] *Hospital People* (2016–7), BBC 1/Roughcut TV, series 1, episodes 1, 3 and 5 (April to May), respectively.
[41] John Hind (2016), 'Making Airwaves', *i* [newspaper], 17 August, pp. 34–5.

of illegal broadcasters seen in Chapters 6 and 9.[42] The comedy came from the ineptitude of the characters:

> Grindah (Allan Mustafa): Kurupt FM in it! The rest are irrelevant.
> Beats (Hugo Chegwin): That's the slogan.
> Grindah: You don't need to tell them it's the slogan. Just let them realise when we say it all the time.
> Beats: We used to say 'Kurupt FM. Like it or Lump it' as well.
> Grindah: Better to have one that rhymes though. Rolls off the tongue better.
> Beats: Aerodynamic.[43]

In another scene, Steves [sic] (played by Steve Stamp) explained that he had appeared in court for running the pirate radio station in his flat and had received a community service order and an electronic tag, but 'They said it was such a low-level pirate radio operation that it wasn't worth me getting sent down for. [. . .] So, the judge said that technically we weren't even a radio station because the radius of the area was so small, he described it as kids messing around in a bedroom'.[44] The characters were endearing without being positive role models and followed in the tradition of British comic characters such as Steve Coogan's Alan Partridge (see Chapter 8), who was the subject of a 2013 movie *Alan Partridge: Alpha Papa*. It was produced by BBC Films and was an extended pastiche of local commercial radio. The movie began with the fictional North Norfolk Digital being taken over by an international multimedia company, reflecting the changes to British commercial radio in the 2010s. After fifteen minutes, the narrative turned into black humour when the late-night DJ Pat Farrell (Colm Meaney) held staff hostage at gunpoint in the studio building.

Crime and thriller: Radio in the here and now

A Scottish crime drama series had previously been used to depict local commercial radio (*Taggart*, 2000; see Chapter 9). This time *Rebus* (ITV, 2000–7),

---

[42] For a discussion of contemporary unlicenced stations in the London area playing grime music, see Alex de Lacey (2019), '"Let us know you're locked": Pirate Radio Broadcasts as Historical and Musical Artefact', *Popular Music History*, 12 (2): 194–214.
[43] 'Secret Location' (2014), *People Just Do Nothing*, BBC 3/Roughcut TV, series 1, episode 1, 20 July.
[44] 'Car Boot' (2018), *People Just Do Nothing*, BBC 3/Roughcut TV, series 5, episode 1, 12 November.

an adaptation of Ian Rankin's series of novels and short stories about an Edinburgh detective, included radio in the narrative of one episode. 'The First Stone' significantly expanded the original short story, added a fictional Edinburgh radio station Waverley FM and included intrigue amongst senior clergy of the Church of Scotland.[45] The episode opened with detective inspector John Rebus (Ken Stott) driving and listening to radio presenter Mike Walker (Ewan Stewart) talking about the Church of Scotland's forthcoming General Assembly. The DJ elicited listener responses via e-mail for ideas about what the collective noun for bishops and ministers might have been. The drama flattered neither the church, whose senior leaders were found dead one by one in compromising poses, nor the work of radio presenters, as Walker became a suspect to the murders.[46] The narrative used the public forum of the phone-in to allow the killer to advertise his forthcoming crimes but the presenter, speaking off-air after his programme, dismissed the calls saying,

> Oh, head-cases like an audience [to talk to], and it's that kind of show. I get them all. People who are of sound mind don't normally need to phone a radio show to have an argument. That's what marriage is for.

At a stroke, and with a quick throwaway barbed comment, the public who engage with radio stations were condemned and a patriarchal presentation of Scottish domestic life was reinforced.

Two other television crime drama series also included episodes with negative portrayals of radio. *New Tricks* (BBC 1, 2003–15) featured the work of a fictional Metropolitan Police unit that re-examined unsolved crimes. In 'A Face for Radio' (2008), a popular DJ, on an imaginary commercial greatest hits station Roxy Radio, died on-air during an arson attack on the studios.[47] The case had remained unsolved for ten years when the team of detectives decided to look again at the evidence. The story included an obsessive listener who had collected recordings of every show the DJ had broadcast. In addition, a fellow presenter faced claims of misogyny and of potential child abuse. It was a premonition of events after the death of Jimmy Savile in 2011, as hundreds of

---

[45] 'The First Stone' (2007), *Rebus*, STV, series 4, episode 2, 12 October.
[46] For a consideration of possible deep-rooted historical and ideological connections between Scottish religion and popular culture, including incidental similarities in the backgrounds of the 1930s documentary filmmaker John Grierson and the BBC's first director general John Reith, see John Caughie (1986), 'Broadcasting and Cinema: 1: Converging Histories', in Charles Barr, ed. (1986), *All Our Yesterdays: 90 Years of British Cinema*, London: BFI Publishing, pp. 189–205.
[47] 'A Face for Radio' (2008), *New Tricks*, BBC 1/Wall to Wall, series 5, episode 3, 21 July.

people came forward to say they had been abused by him during his decades in radio and television, as well as during his voluntary work in hospitals. Elsewhere, a long-running crime series *Midsomer Murders* (ITV, 1997– present) included a radio station in an episode called 'Till Death Do Us Part' (2020).[48] This featured three murders: of a DJ, a producer and a shareholder of a station confusingly called both Radio Midsomer and Midsomer FM during the programme. The narrative quickly established that radio station staff were belligerent and cynical: they were dismissive of the late-night phone-in callers, who off-air were called 'nutters' by one of the DJs. The viewer was led to think that everyone who worked in radio was a potential killer. In the end it turned out that the murders were a series of crimes of passion by the mother of an extended family linked to the victims.

Using the radio airwaves to announce a life-changing moment in a narrative featured in *Slow Horses* (2010), a novel by Mick Herron and the first instalment in his Jackson Lamb series of spy thrillers. It was set in contemporary London and had a character, Min Harper, who mistakenly left a computer disk of classified information on a tube train, and only knew of his error when he heard about it on the following morning's BBC Radio 4 *Today* programme.[49] Later in the novel, a gruesome threat to behead a hostage live on the internet was broken by Corporation journalists when news of it first appeared, 'on a BBC blog around 4 a.m.' before spreading to other media outlets in saturation coverage.[50] The flagship *Today* programme also appeared in the novel *A Dying Breed* (2017) by Peter Hanington, who used his direct experience of producing the programme to create a thriller involving a seasoned cynical BBC reporter who was teamed with a young radio producer to work on a foreign news assignment in Afghanistan. The reporter, William Carver, was portrayed as self-centred, unpredictable yet gifted. The novel quickly introduced the general reader to the mechanics of putting a breakfast current affairs programme on-air.[51] In this book, the first of a series by Hanington, BBC reporters were tough dedicated professionals, the fictional opposite of the traumas some foreign correspondents had experienced

---

[48] 'Till Death Do Us Part' (2020), *Midsomer Murders*, ITV/Bentley Productions, series 20, episode 5, 6 January.
[49] Mick Herron (2010), *Slow Horses*, London: John Murray, p. 61. For a factual description of the *Today* programme in this era, see David Hendy (2007), *Life on Air: A History of Radio Four*, Oxford: Oxford University Press, pp. 318–25.
[50] Herron, *Slow Horses*, pp. 104–5, 123.
[51] Peter Hanington (2016), *A Dying Breed*, London: Two Roads, pp. 27–52.

in these years.[52] It was also a counterpoint to the sarcasm of the BBC Radio 4 sitcom character Ed Reardon, who had once bemoaned contemporary news programmes and their presenters for what he regarded as their 'abandonment of radio journalism in favour of the reading out of asinine tweets'.[53] Carver's use of a satellite phone to get a link between the roof of the BBC office in Kabul and Broadcasting House in London was a description of late 1990s and early twenty-first-century technology, a nostalgic touch for BBC staff who worked with such equipment at the time.[54] The reporter established contact, and on his headphones heard a voice saying: 'Hello this is London. You're through to Broadcasting House Traffic. Who've I got?'[55] The next response confirmed the relationship between technicians and journalists in this department of newsgathering. Traffic was a twenty-four-hour operation for correspondents around the world who filed their reports back to BBC headquarters and offered themselves for live two-ways into news programmes and bulletins, '"Hello there Brenda." "Is that Billy Carver's voice I'm hearing?" "It is." "Lovely! Long time, no hear. So what can I do for you today? Are you going live?" "Yep. *Today* programme, seven o nine."'[56] She then went through a ritual of asking him to talk about his breakfast, to establish the audio level of his line connection.[57] It was a fictional exchange which in its everyday mundaneness reflected the technical organization of the Corporation's newsgathering. Just as the battered old journalist re-established his professional connections to the BBC, the young producer Patrick Reid had to earn his stripes through danger and adventure in the getting of the story. At the end, William and Patrick were already planning their next adventure.[58] That came in Hanington's 2019 novel, *A Single Source*, which in the course of its first fifty pages provided contemporary descriptions of BBC Radio 4 *Today*'s running orders – including style comments on packages, reporter two-ways, news bulletins, presenter cues and ad-libs – as well as mentions variously of Twitter feeds and the closure of the

---

[52] Jo Healey (2020), *Trauma Reporting: A Journalist's Guide to Covering Sensitive Stories*, Abingdon, Oxon: Routledge. See, for example, 'Fergal Keane: BBC Africa editor leaves role because of PTSD' (2020), BBC, 24 January. Available online: https://www.bbc.co.uk/news/entertainment-arts-51236199 (accessed 24 May 2021).

[53] 'The Fourth Sausage' (2016), *Ed Reardon's Week*, BBC Radio 4/BBC Studios, series 11, episode 6, 8 November.

[54] Hanington, *A Dying Breed*, pp. 341–4.

[55] Hanington, *A Dying Breed*, p. 343.

[56] Hanington, *A Dying Breed*, p. 343.

[57] 'What did you have for breakfast?' is the standard radio journalist's question to check recording equipment. See Humphrey Carpenter (1996), *The Envy of the World: Fifty Years of the BBC Third Programme and Radio 3 1946–1996*, London: Weidenfeld and Nicholson, p. 282.

[58] Hanington, *A Dying Breed*, p. 418.

BBC Caversham Park monitoring centre. Set during the events of the 2011 Arab Spring in Egypt, it evoked the mechanics and the ethics of contemporary radio newsgathering and made reference to the power of social media and how BBC journalists were by that stage learning about digital media, including new jargon such as 'linger time' on web pages.[59]

Radio and new ways of listening: The next generation

As Britain and much of the world moved into this digital age, dominated by the internet, social media, mobile phones, connectivity and instant information, there were commentators – often academics who had worked in the radio industry – speculating about where radio would go in the future. Andrew Dubber thought, 'It doesn't matter whether we call "radio" one thing or another – or even if radio exists at all in any recognisable form.' His point was that we shall still be communicating with one another.[60] The way listeners engaged with radio receiving equipment had also changed across the decades. Turning a tuning dial of a wireless set had become the push of a button of a car radio, a swipe of a touch screen, a 'like' on an 'app' on a mobile phone, or a verbal command to a smart speaker powered by artificial intelligence.[61] However, Richard Rudin identified a deeply enduring affection by the British public for radio and

> Radio's transformation, at least in industrial or post-industrial societies such as the UK, from being a foreground medium – something that demanded the fullest attention of the listener – to being a background medium, which accompanied other activities, has allowed it to integrate with other media in the online world, leading to renewed interest in the use of audio.[62]

Free-to-air, linear broadcasts had been joined by podcasting, streaming and on-demand services. A number of creative writers in the 2010s were thinking about radio in new ways, yet they still evoked fundamental, enduring truths about the medium. One example of this integration, or convergence, formed

---

[59] Peter Hanington (2019), *A Single Source*, London: Two Roads, p. 286.
[60] Andrew Dubber (2013), *Radio in the Digital Age*, Cambridge: Polity, p. 176.
[61] Angeliki Gazi and Tiziano Bonini (2018), '"Haptically Mediated" Radio Listening and its Commodification: The Remediation of Radio through Digital Mobile Devices', *Journal of Radio & Audio Media*, 25 (1): 109–25.
[62] Richard Rudin (2011), *Broadcasting in the 21st Century*, Basingstoke, Hampshire: Palgrave Macmillan, p. 61.

the narrative backdrop to Alice Oseman's novel, *Radio Silence* (2016). It was a story aimed at teenagers and, like the *Catcher in the Rye* by J. D. Salinger first published in 1951, there was a tone of address that intentionally excluded adults and directly targeted its age group. It concerned a teenager living in Britain aged seventeen, preoccupied with her A-level results and applying to university. True to the genre, it contained storylines about feelings of alienation, making friends and blended multicultural families. There were explorations of questions of gender, sexuality and the language used by a younger generation between themselves but not in front of their parents. Oseman's work included mentions of contemporary consumer products and TV shows from the start of the century, for example *The Office*, *Made in Chelsea*, Twitter, Facebook and Tumblr. The central concept was an audio podcast called 'Universe City', which was a 'show about a suit-wearing student detective looking for a way to escape a sci-fi, monster-infested university'.[63] Oseman played with the phrase 'Radio Silence', using it capitalized as the name of the character who produced and presented the podcast series. The heroine later realized that the boy she was with was 'Radio Silence' himself. It was the surprise of the moment when voice and visuals merged together: to realize that the face in front of her was the one who had enthralled with his podcasts all this time. The essential technical development, noted elsewhere by commentators, was the ability of the listener to message and contact a presenter directly, which marked out radio's passage into the twenty-first century:

> Listening habits are changing and listeners are increasingly used to both listen to radio and leave comments on social media, where their feelings and opinions are public, searchable, accessible and measurable.[64]

The theme of emotional connection was also reflected in a piece of music released by James Blake that same year, with the identical title. 'Radio Silence' (2016) evoked the heartache of humankind's own frailty when it came to relationships. Blake, a keyboard player and vocalist, worked with electronic music to create moments of intense reflection using a sparse musical style. Taken together, Alice Oseman's and James Blake's images of radio linked the medium to feelings of emotional fragility and to a struggle to connect with others.

---

[63] Alice Oseman (2016), *Radio Silence*, London: Harper Collins, p. 10.
[64] Tiziano Bonini (2015), 'Introduction. The Listener as Producer: The Rise of the Networked Listener', in Tiziano Bonini and Belén Monclús, eds, *Radio Audiences and Participation in the Age of Network Society*, New York: Routledge, pp. 2–3.

A graphic novel *The Last Broadcast*, created by two Brazilians, writer André Sirangelo and artist Gabriel Iumazark, featured a podcast also coincidentally called 'Radio Silence', which was used in off-frame speech bubbles to drive the narrative forward.[65] The book, written in English and released by an American publishing house, was aimed at teenagers. It was the story of a search across an apocalyptic subterranean world which was entered through a building at the base of a remote transmitter tower outside San Francisco. The story involved a 'last broadcast' transmitted in the 1930s which the characters managed to receive in the present (reminiscent of Ray Bradbury's 1968 Radio 3 play, mentioned in Chapter 6). There were passing references in its 200 pages to CB and ham radio, valve receivers, atmospheric interference, phone-ins, spiritism and Arthur Conan Doyle – which happened to link back to the earliest representations of radio, for example Rudyard Kipling's 1902 short story mentioned in Chapter 1 and the idea that radio transmission was somehow other-worldly.

A dark and troubling portrayal of podcast listening appeared in Olivia Sudjic's novel *Asylum Road* (2021). The narrator for much of the story was Anya, a young woman who had settled in London after a traumatic childhood in Sarajevo during the Bosnian War. Set in 2017 and by now an adult studying for her PhD, it related her crumbling relationship with Luke, both of whom were initially portrayed as comfortable upper-middle-class people. They spent much of their time together listening to true crime podcasts. However, Sudjic used this as a device to denote a growing imbalance in the relationship: throughout it was Luke, who controlled the selection and playing of podcast episodes, as 'he pressed resume', and later as she listened 'to the murder Luke put on'.[66] Indeed, she explained that 'Solving a murder was a better way for us to feel connected', and had begun her narration of the novel with the stark sentence 'Sometimes it felt like the murders kept us together'.[67] Radio in the second decade of the twenty-first century was evidently moving away from a physical instrument that received broadcasts to become a multiplatform audio form not dependent on a particular device.

---

[65] André Sirangelo and Gabriel Iumazark (2015), *The Last Broadcast: An Urban Exploration Adventure*, Los Angeles, CA: Archaia. For a summary of contemporary American podcasting, see the non-fiction graphic book Jessica Abel (2015), *Out on the Wire: The Storytelling Secrets of the New Masters of Radio*, New York: Broadway Books. Abel describes podcasting as 'narrative non-fiction', known by British radio professionals as a 'package' or 'short-form documentary'.
[66] Olivia Sudjic (2021), *Asylum Road*, London: Bloomsbury, pp. 30 and 62.
[67] Sudjic, *Asylum Road*, pp. 10 and 3.

If radio was no longer solely a medium requiring the technology of a discrete receiver, then one wonders why three episodes of the children's stop animation series, *Bob the Builder* (CBeebies, 1998–2011) had analogue radio as their subject matter. Plausibly, it was an example of children's TV made by adults and as such resembled Professor Branestawm (Chapter 2) for its comedic representation of the grown-up world of the radio. In one of these, Bob and his friends, and by inference the young viewers at home, were told, 'We're going to build a studio where you make radio shows.' They also constructed a transmitter tower 'to send the shows out to radios all over Sunflower Valley'.[68] The station, called Bob FM, was of a reassuringly old-fashioned technology. The machines had to choose themes for their own programmes. In an intertextual joke, one of them asked for help with an idea for his show from a Mr Bernard Bentley, the 'creative producer'. He was a character in a suit and tie with a moustache and goatee beard (see Figure 11), reminiscent of Val Gielgud mentioned in Chapter 2 (see Figure 2). 'Well, of course, I'm the producer', he said in a supercilious yet disarmingly honest tone, 'I don't actually have any ideas myself'.

Another animated series, *Hey Duggee* (CBeebies, 2014–present), featured the radio in an episode called 'The Radio Badge'. The seven-minute story, also aimed at preschool children, revealed that Duggee had previously operated a station called Clubhouse Radio, but had closed it down when Cheese Radio, a pirate vessel operated by the mice, became popular. The story offered a brief retelling of 1960s radio and a discussion of the effects of competition, the demise and the resurgence of radio.[69]

A more contemporary account was to be found in two novels, aimed at pre-teenagers, which took radio as their subject and offered it as a disruptive way of rapidly achieving young fame. The author Christian O'Connell created a comic narrative in his two books called *Radio Boy* that captured the desire by eleven-year-olds to fit in, and the sarcasm they often used to protect themselves from the ridicule of their peers. O'Connell had presented the Virgin Radio (later renamed Absolute Radio) breakfast show in the UK from 2006 to 2018.[70] He had subsequently moved to Australia to continue his radio presentation work.

---

[68] *Bob the Builder* (2008), 'Radio Bob', CBeebies/HiT Entertainment, series 16 [Project: Build It], episode 2, 6 August. The other two radio-related episodes were also first broadcast in August 2008: 'Spud the DJ', series 16, episode 4 and 'Silent Scoop', series 16, episode 5.
[69] 'The Radio Badge' (2020), *Hey Duggee*, CBeebies/Studio AKA, series 3, episode 11, 2 June.
[70] David Lloyd (2017), *Radio Moments: 50 Years of Radio – Life on the Inside*, London: Biteback Publishing, pp. 241–2.

Figure 11 Mr Bernard Bentley as the 'creative producer' at the new radio station in Sunflower Valley. 'Radio Bob' (2008), *Bob the Builder, Project: Build It*, UK: CBeebies/HiT Entertainment.

His two books featured a young boy who found emotional security and the acceptance of his peers by running an online radio station from his garden shed. The stories included knowing references to the British radio industry. For example, O'Connell characterized hospital radio as 'run, for the most part, by overly enthusiastic volunteers with bad breath and sandals'.[71] He satirized contemporary commercial stations for their repetitive playlists: 'Most stations only seem to have one CD actually, as they just play the same songs over and over.'[72] O'Connell also created a conceited professional, Howard Wright, as the fictional breakfast presenter of Kool FM, who had launched a talent contest which turned out to be more about burnishing his own credentials rather than about helping new DJs enter the industry.[73]

Overall, these children's books and animated shows offered an image of radio that was either stuck in the present or reliant on the past. Elsewhere, there were

---

[71] Christian O'Connell (2017), *Radio Boy*, London: HarperCollins Children's Books, p. 10.
[72] O'Connell, *Radio Boy*, p. 33.
[73] Christian O'Connell (2018), *Radio Boy and the Revenge of Grandad*, London: HarperCollins Children's Books.

enduring continuities evident as radio's centenary approached. For example, in a country-tinged contemporary Christian track, 'Jesus on the Radio' (2019), Jamie Kimmett began by lamenting the fast pace of his modern world and the spiritual dilemma he faced between listening to a news programme or to a religious station. In the UK, 2019 was the tenth anniversary of Christian stations UCB and Premier transmitting on national DAB. Both had set a new style of programming in Britain by broadcasting a mix of music and conversation to the converted and by being funded almost completely by listener donations.[74] It was also just over eighty years since a southern gospel singer, Albert E. Brumley, had written a song called 'Turn Your Radio On' (1937). His song about a spiritual radio station was a sideways reference to North America's AM 'border radio' stations which transmitted from Mexico from the 1930s onwards, also remembered as the 'home' of Wolfman Jack mentioned in Chapter 6.[75] The point being that the old analogue technologies continued doggedly to exist. Even at British broadcasting's centenary in 2022 there were, for instance, still millions of short-wave radio receivers in the world: indeed, where I write this I have at least five around me. Such radio technology may well have become antiquated – international broadcasting on short wave began in the 1930s and took on real significance during the Cold War between the 1950s and the 1980s – but its continued use meant that it still had worldwide audiences.[76] Even though some state broadcasters were by the end of the 2010s shifting to the web: Canada and the Netherlands had already switched their short-wave transmitters off in 2012; there were others including China, Voice of America and some Christian evangelical broadcasters still using the short-wave transmission system.[77] Just like Hamid Ismailov's character Zangi-Bobo, an old snuff-seller listening alone in his bedroom in a small town in Central Asia, mentioned in Chapter 7, it was a voice from the radio set which touched the soul. And that is how it has always been.

---

[74] Martin Cooper and Kirsty Macaulay (2015), 'Contemporary Christian Radio in Britain: A New Genre on the National Dial', *Radio Journal: International Studies in Broadcast & Audio Media*, 13 (1–2): 75–87.

[75] Gene Fowler and Bill Crawford (2002), *Border Radio: Quacks, Yodelers, Pitchmen, Psychics, and other Amazing Broadcasters of the American Airwaves*, Austin, TX: University of Texas Press. 'Turn Your Radio On' was covered by Ray Stevens in 1971. See Chapter 6.

[76] David Edgerton (2006), *The Shock of the Old: Technology and Global History Since 1900*, London: Profile, pp. 1–11.

[77] 'Short-wave radio: tuning out' (2012), *The Economist*, 7 July, p. 62.

Afterword

This book has investigated how writers, composers, musicians, film directors, poets, conceptual artists and TV scriptwriters have thought about the radio and have realized it in their creative works. It has been a story of the century of broadcasting over Britain: of the initials BBC, as well as about European stations, pirates at sea and on land, about independent commercial, community, hospital and online stations, and about podcasts and on-demand services. It has looked for themes, reactions, dialectics and tropes. Sometimes 'radio' has been connected to illegal and criminal activities. At others it has found humorous acceptance along with satire, and sometimes it has been ridiculed. Often, radio stars have been represented by the stereotype of social inadequates with hearts of gold who nonetheless are somehow able to reach out and touch people's lives, despite all their failings. Radio, with its lack of physical presence between the presenter and listener, can still carry just a small sense of wonder. The writers and creatives discussed in these pages have also had a tendency to reflect on an imagined past, when listening as a teenager seemed to have just that feeling of sublime awe.

However exhaustive this survey has been, it still represents a personal tribute to the radio industry in Britain and to its listeners. I have chosen examples widely and, I hope, without favour. If you think I have missed a film, song, novel, or TV show which addresses the subject of radio and listening, or if I have omitted a detail, then do please get in touch.[1] As the title suggests, this has been primarily a discussion of texts which have circulated in Britain over the past 100 years. Hence, examples from the United States and other countries have been included only when they have been popular in the UK, or in some cases have shown a peculiar reaction to the medium of radio. Once again, I am open to suggestions of other examples to include in any further editions of this book.

Finally, the first 100 years of creative works inspired by the radio – as evidenced in these pages – has to a large extent been dominated by material mostly created by, and featuring, white middle-class males. As radio enters its second century, your correspondent looks forward to an industry seen more and more to be run on equal gender, class and ethnicity lines that reaches out, reflects and engages with all sectors of the community at large. That will be radio's legacy.

---

[1] https://prefadelisten.com/contact/.

References

Primary sources (1): Printed, visual, musical, electronic and works of art

(Where a work is referred to in more than one chapter, it is referenced in the chapter in which it is first discussed.)

Chapter 1

(Sources previewed in the book summary section of this chapter are not included here.)

Caught by Wireless (1908), [Film] Dir. Wallace McCutcheon, USA: Biograph Company.

Kipling, Rudyard (1902), [Short story] 'Wireless', *Scribner's Magazine*, XXXII (2): 129–43.

Le Queux, William ([1922] 2019), [Novel] *The Voice from the Void: The Great Wireless Mystery*, CreateSpace/Amazon print-on-demand.

Le Queux, William ([1922] 2019), [Novel] *Tracked by Wireless*, Fairford, Gloucestershire: Echo Library.

Chapter 2

Novels, short stories and poetry

Allingham, Margery ([1931] 1950), *Look to the Lady*, London: Penguin (published in the United States as *The Gyrth Chalice Mystery*).

Auden, W. H. ([1932] 1986), 'The Orators: An English Study', in W. H. Auden (ed.), *The English Auden: Poems, Essays and Dramatic Writings 1927-1939*, ed. Edward Mendelson, London: Faber and Faber, pp. 59–110.

Christie, Agatha ([1926] 1964), 'Wireless', in Agatha Christie (ed.), *The Hound of Death*, Glasgow: Fontana/Collins, pp. 75–88.

Christie, Agatha ([1931] 1965), *The Sittaford Mystery*, London: Pan Books/Collins.

Gielgud, Val and Holt Marvell (1934), *Death at Broadcasting House*, London: Rich & Cowan.

Green, Henry ([1926] 2001), *Blindness*, Dallas, TX: Dalkey Archive Press.
Green, Henry ([1929] 1991), *Living*, London: Harvill/HarperCollins.
Greene, Graham ([1935] 1943), *England Made Me: A Novel*, Harmondsworth, Middlesex: Penguin.
Hesse, Herman ([1929] 1965), *Steppenwolf*, trans. Basil Creighton, Harmondsworth, Middlesex: Penguin.
Hunter, Norman ([1933] 1946), *The Incredible Adventures of Professor Branestawm*, Harmondsworth, Middlesex: Penguin.
Lawrence, D. H. ([1928] 2010), *Lady Chatterley's Lover*, London: Penguin.
Lawrence, D. H. ([1929] 2004), 'Broadcasting to the G. B. P.', in Seán Street (ed.), *Radio Waves: Poems Celebrating the Wireless*, London: Enitharmon Press, pp. 49–50.
Macaulay, Rose ([1926] 1938), *Crewe Train*, Harmondsworth, Middlesex: Penguin.
Macaulay, Rose ([1928] 1986), *Keeping Up Appearances*, London: Methuen.

Film and TV

BBC: The Voice of Britain (1935), Dir. Stuart Legg, UK: GPO Film Unit.
Big Ben Calling (1935), Dir. Ivar Campbell, UK: Sound City Production (also known as *Radio Pirates*).
Death at Broadcasting House (1934), Dir. Reginald Denham, UK: Phoenix Films.
London Calling! Behind the Scenes in an 'OB' ([c1925] 2014), UK: Pathé Pictorial, 13 April. Available online: https://youtu.be/vb6bwYqdbD4 (accessed 24 May 2021).
'Look to the Lady', *Campion* (1989), [TV] Screenplay: Alan Plater, BBC 1, 22 and 29 January.
Out of the Blue (1931), Dir. Gene Gerrard, UK: British International Pictures.
Radio Parade (1933), Dirs. Archie De Bear and Richard Beville, UK: British International Pictures (also known as *Hello Radio*).
Street Song (1935), Dir. Bernard Vorhaus, UK: Radio Pictures.

Music

'We Can't Let You Broadcast That' (1932), Norman Long, composers: H. M Burnaby and N. Long [78-rpm] (Columbia DB 1216).
'You Can't Make Love by Wireless' (1923), Words: P. G. Wodehouse and G. Grossmith Jnr, music: J. Kern, London: Chappell. From the Musical *The Beauty Prize* at the Winter Garden Theatre, Drury Lane, London.

Radio

Airy Nothings (1928–1931), Gordon McConnel, BBC 2LO (London) and 5XX (Daventry).

London Calling (1994), Jimmy Perry, BBC Radio 2, 19–22 September.
Saturday Playhouse: Death at Broadcasting House (1996), Val Gielgud and Holt Marvell, adapted by Sue Rodwell, BBC Radio 4, 2 March.

Chapter 3

Novels and poetry

Betjeman, John ([1937] 1983), 'Slough', in *John Betjeman's Collected Poems*, compiled by The Earl of Birkenhead, London: John Murray, pp. 22–4.
Heslop, Harold ([1935] 1984), *Last Cage Down*, London: Wishart.
Holtby, Winifred ([1936] 1954), *South Riding: An English Landscape*, Glasgow: Fontana.
Orwell, George ([1936] 1962), *Keep the Aspidistra Flying*, Harmondsworth, Middlesex: Penguin.
Warner, Rex ([1937] 1990), *The Wild Goose Chase*, London: Merlin Press.
Waugh, Evelyn ([1938] 1943), *Scoop: A Novel About Journalism*, Harmondsworth, Middlesex: Penguin.

Film

Command Performance (1937), Dir. Sinclair Hill, UK: Grosvenor Sound Films.
Feather Your Nest (1937), Dir. William Beaudine, UK: Associated Talking Pictures.
Head over Heels (1937), Dir. Sonnie Hale, UK: Gaumont-British Picture Corpn.
Music Hath Charms (1935), Supervising dir. Thomas Bentley, UK: Associated British Picture Corpn.
Radio Lover (1936), Dirs. Austin Melford and Paul Capon, UK: City Film Corporation.
Radio Parade of 1935 (1934), Dir. Arthur B. Woods, UK: British International Pictures (released in the United States as *Radio Follies*).
She Shall Have Music (1935), Dir. Leslie Hiscott, UK: Imperial Pictures.
Sing as You Swing (1937), Dir. Redd Davis, UK: British Independent Exhibitors' Distributors.

Theatre

Ascent of F6, The ([1938] 1958), W. H. Auden and Christopher Isherwood, London: Faber & Faber.
Listening In: A Musical Burlesque in Seventeen Radio Calls, (1922), D. Worton and W. Hay (book), B. Lee and R. P. Weston (lyrics), H. Darewski (lyrics and music), London: Apollo Theatre.

Out of the Picture: A Play in Two Acts (1937), Louis MacNeice, London: Faber and Faber.

Music

'We're Frightfully BBC' (1935), The Western Brothers, composers: K. Western and G. Western [78-rpm] (Columbia DX 685).

Radio

'Commander Sir Stephen King-Hall' (1961), *Desert Island Discs*, BBC Home Service, 18 September. Available online: https://www.bbc.co.uk/sounds/play/p009y6fy (accessed 24 May 2021).
'War of the Worlds, The' (1938), Dir. Orson Welles, *The Mercury Theatre on the Air*, USA: CBS, 30 October.

Chapter 4

Novels, short stories and poetry

Auden, W. H. ([1936] 1986), 'Letter to Lord Byron', [poetry] in W. H. Auden (ed.), *The English Auden: Poems, Essays and Dramatic Writings 1927–1939*, ed. Edward Mendelson, London: Faber and Faber, pp. 167–99.
Buchanan, George (1938), *Entanglement*, London: Constable.
Crompton, Richmal ([1945] 1989), *William and the Brains Trust*, London: Macmillan Children's Books.
Greene, Graham ([1938] 1971), *Brighton Rock*, London: Penguin.
Joyce, James ([1939] 2012), *Finnegans Wake*, Ware, Hertfordshire: Wordsworth Editions.
MacNeice, Louis ([1939] 1998), *Autumn Journal*, [Poetry] London: Faber and Faber.
Morton, J. B. (1944), *Captain Foulenough & Company*, London: Macmillan & Co.
Warner, Rex ([1938] 1986), *The Professor*, London: Lawrence & Wishart.

Film

Back-Room Boy (1942), Dir. Herbert Mason, UK: Gainsborough Pictures.
Band Waggon (1940), Dir. Marcel Varnel, UK: Gainsborough Pictures.
Brass Monkey (1948), Dir. Thornton Freeland, UK: United Artists (also known as *The Lucky Mascot*).

Freedom Radio (1941), Dir. Anthony Asquith, UK: Two Cities Production.
Happidrome (1943), Dir. Phil Brandon, UK: Aldwych Productions.
Helter Skelter (1949), Dir. Ralph Thomas, UK: Gainsborough Pictures.
Hi Gang (1941), Dir. Marcel Varnel, UK: Gainsborough Pictures.
In Which We Serve (1942), Dirs. Noël Coward and David Lean, UK: British Lion Film Corporation.
It's That Man Again (1943), Dir. Walter Forde, UK: Gainsborough Pictures.
Let's Be Famous (1939), Dir. Walter Forde, UK: Associated Talking Pictures.
Lilli Marlene (1950), Dir. Arthur Crabtree, UK: Monarch Film Corporation.
Millions Like Us (1943), Dirs. Sidney Gilliat and Frank Launder, UK: Gainsborough Pictures.
On Chesil Beach (2017), Dir. Dominic Cooke, UK: Lionsgate.
One of Our Aircraft is Missing (1942), Dirs. Michael Powell and Emeric, Pressburger UK: Anglo-Amalgamated Film Distributors.
This Happy Breed (1944), Dir. David Lean, UK: Two Cities Film.
True Story of Lili Marlene, The (1944), Dir. Humphrey Jennings, UK: Crown Film Unit.
Way Ahead, The (1944), Dir. Carol Reed, UK: Two Cities Films (released in the United States as *Immortal Battalion*).
We'll Meet Again (1943), Dir. Phil Brandon, UK: Columbia Pictures.

Theatre

On the Frontier ([1938] 1958), W. H. Auden and Christopher Isherwood, London: Faber & Faber.

Radio

How to Listen (1946), Stephen Potter, BBC Third Programme, 29 September.
'Last Goon Show of All, The' (1972), *The Goon Show*, BBC Radio 4 and simulcast on BBC 2, 5 October.

Chapter 5

Novels, poetry and magazines

Larkin, Philip ([1961] 1988), 'Broadcast', in *Collected Poems*, ed. Anthony Thwaite, London: The Marvell Press and Faber and Faber, p. 140.
Radio Fun (1938–1959), Amalgamated Press, (1959-1961), Fleetway Publications.
Waugh, Evelyn ([1952] 1964), *Men at Arms*, Harmondsworth, Middlesex: Penguin.

Waugh, Evelyn ([1957] 1998), *The Ordeal of Gilbert Pinfold: A Conversation Piece*, London: Penguin.

Wyndham, John ([1951] 1954), *The Day of the Triffids*, Harmondsworth, Middlesex: Penguin.

Film and TV

Armchair Detective, The (1951), Dir. Brendan J. Stafford, UK: Meridian Films.

Climb Up the Wall (1960), Dir. Michael Winner, UK: Border Film Productions.

Dateline Diamonds (1965), Dir. Jeremy Summers, UK: Viscount Films.

Day of the Triffids, The (1981), John Wyndham, adapted by Douglas Livingstone, BBC 1 TV, 10 September–15 October.

Day of the Triffids, The (2009), John Wyndham, adapted by Patrick Harbinson, BBC 1 TV, 28–29 December.

Down Among the Z Men (1952), Dir. Maclean Rogers, UK: E J Fancey Productions.

Green Man, The (1956), Dir. Robert Day, UK: Grenadier Films.

Hancock (1961), 'The Bowmans', BBC TV, series 7, episode 2, 2 June.

Hancock (1961), 'The Radio Ham', BBC TV, series 7, episode 3, 9 June.

Happy Family, The (1952), Dir. Muriel Box, UK: London Independent Producers.

Key Man, The (1957), Dir. Montgomery Tully, UK: Anglo Amalgamated (released in the United States as *Life at Stake*).

London Entertains (1951), Dir. E J Fancey, UK: E J Fancey Productions.

Make Mine a Million (1959), Dir. Lance Comfort, UK: British Lion/Elstree Independent Film Production.

'Not so Jolly Roger' (1966), *Danger Man*, ITV/ITC, series 3, episode 23, 7 April (known in the United States as *Secret Agent*).

This is the BBC (1959), Dir. Richard Cawston, UK: BBC.

Twenty Questions Murder Mystery, The (1950), Dir. Paul L Stein, UK: Pax Pendennis Production.

Vacances de Monsieur Hulot, Les (1953), Dir. Jacques Tati, France: Cady F.

Voice of Merrill, The (1952), Dir. John Gilling, UK: Tempean Film (released in the United States as *Murder Will Out*).

Where Eagles Dare (1968), Dir. Brian G. Hutton, UK: Metro-Goldwyn-Mayer.

Young Ones, The (1961), Dir. Sidney J Furie, UK: Associated British Picture Corporation.

Music

(All subsequent popular music catalogue numbers are UK single releases, unless otherwise stated.)

'Big Dee Jay, The' (1959), Paddy Roberts, composer: P. Roberts [10″: *Strictly For Grown-Ups*] (Decca LF 1322).
'B.J. the D.J.' ([1964] 1965), Stonewall Jackson, composer: H. Lewis [LP: *Greatest Hits*] (CBS BPG 62587).
'Brown Eyed Girl' (1967), Van Morrison, composer: V. Morrison (London HLZ 10150).
'Made in Japan' (1972), Buck Owens, composers: B. Morris and F. Morris (USA: Capitol ST 11273).
'Magic Transistor Radio' (1973), Beach Boys, composer: B. Wilson [LP: *Holland*] (Reprise K 454008).
'Roll Over Beethoven' (1956), Chuck Berry, composer: C. Berry (London HLU 8428).
'Tiny Blue Transistor Radio' (1965), Connie Smith, composer: B. Anderson [LP: *Connie Smith*] (RCA Victor LPM 3341).
'We Love the Pirates' (1966), The Roaring 60's, composers: G. Stephens, J. Carter and T. Kennedy (Marmalade 598001).
Who Sell Out, The (1967), The Who [LP] (Track 612-002).

Radio

Day of the Triffids, The (1957), John Wyndham, adapted by Giles Cooper, BBC Light Programme, 2 October–6 November. (re-recorded for BBC Radio 4, 20 June–25 July 1968).
Day of the Triffids, The (2001), John Wyndham, adapted by Lance Dann, BBC World Service, 18 and 22 September.
Ordeal of Gilbert Pinfold: A Conversation-Piece, The (1960), BBC Third Programme, 7 June.

Chapter 6

Novels

Adams, Douglas (1979), *The Hitch Hiker's Guide to the Galaxy*, London: Pan.
Lispector, Clarice ([1986] 1992), *The Hour of the Star*, trans. Giovanni Pontiero, Manchester: Carcanet.

Film and TV

American Graffiti (1973), Dir. George Lucas, USA: Universal Pictures.
Dawnbreakers (1975), Dir. Laurence Boulting, UK: Cassius Films Productions.
FM (1978), [Film] Dir. John A. Alonzo, USA: Universal Pictures.

'Honeymooners' Return, The' (1971), *For the Love of Ada*, Thames TV, series 3, episode 1, 15 March.
Hora da Estrela, A (1985), [Film] Dir. Suzana Amaral, Brazil: Kino International.
Last Waltz, The (1978), Dir. Martin Scorsese, USA: MGM/United Artists.
Play Misty for Me (1971), Dir. Clint Eastwood, USA: Universal Pictures.
'Sounds Sinister' (1974), *Special Branch*, Thames TV, series 4, episode 7, 28 March.
WKRP in Cincinnati (1978–1982), USA: CBS/MTM Enterprises; UK: ITV.

Music

'Capital Radio' (1977), The Clash, composers: J. Strummer and M. Jones (CBS CL 1).
'Car on a Hill' (1974), Joni Mitchell, composer: J. Mitchell [LP: *Court and Spark*] (Asylum SYLA 8756).
'Caravan' (1970), Van Morrison, composer: V. Morrison [LP: *Moondance*] (Warner Bros WS 1835).
'Clap for the Wolfman' (1974), The Guess Who, composer: K. Winter (USA: RCA Victor APB0-0324).
'Drug Store Truck Drivin' Man' (1969), The Byrds, composers: G. Parsons and R. McGuinn [LP: *Dr. Byrds & Mr. Hyde*] (CBS CS 9755).
'FM (No Static at All)' (1978), Steely Dan, composers: W. Becker and D. Fagen (MCA MCA 374).
'I'd Like to See Jesus on The Midnight Special' (1978), Tammy Wynette, composers: D. Smith and R. Seay (USA: Epic 8-50538).
'Mama Told Me Not to Come' (1970), Three Dog Night, composer: R. Newman (Stateside SS 8052).
'On My Radio' (1979), The Selecter, composer: N. Davies (Two-Tone CHS TT 4).
'Radar Love' (1973), Golden Earring, composers: G. Kooymans and B. Hay (Track 2094 116).
'Radio Radio' (1978), Elvis Costello, composer: E. Costello (Radar ADA 24).
'Radio Sweetheart' (1977), Elvis Costello, composer: E. Costello (Stiff BUY 11 [B-side]).
'Ramble on Rose' (1972), Grateful Dead, composers: J. Garcia and R. Hunter [LP: *Europe '72*] (Warner Bros. K 66019).
'Road Runner' (1979), Sex Pistols, composer: J. Richman [UK double LP: *The Great Rock 'n' Roll Swindle*] (Virgin VD 2510).
'Roadrunner' (1976), Jonathan Richman and the Modern Lovers, composer: J. Richman (Beserkley BSERK 1).
'Rock and Roll' (1970), The Velvet Underground, composer: The Velvet Underground [LP: *Loaded*] (Atlantic 2400 111).
'Taking Care of Business' (1974), Lindisfarne, composer: A. Hull (Charisma CB 228).

'This Flight Tonight' (1971), Joni Mitchell, composer: J. Mitchell [LP: *Blue*] (Reprise K 44128).
'Transmission' (1979), Joy Division, composer: Joy Division (Factory FAC 13).
'Turn Your Radio On' (1971), Ray Stevens, composer: A. E. Brumley (CBS S 7634).
'WASP, The' (Texas Radio and the Big Beat)' (1971), The Doors, composer: The Doors [LP: *L. A. Woman*] (Elektra EKS-75011).
'Wavelength' (1978), Van Morrison, composer V. Morrison (Warner Bros. K 17254).
'W.O.L.D.' (1974), Harry Chapin, composer: H. Chapin (Elektra K 12133).
'Wolfman Jack' (1972), Todd Rundgren, composer: T. Rundgren [LP: *Something / Anything?*] (Bearsville K65501).
'Yesterday Once More' (1973), Carpenters, composers: J. Bettis and R. Carpenter (A&M AMS 7073).
'You Turn Me On, I'm a Radio' (1972), Joni Mitchell, composer: J. Mitchell (Asylum AYM 511).

Radio

'Fit the Twentieth' (2005), *The Hitchhiker's Guide to the Galaxy: Quandary Phase*, adapted and directed by Dirk Maggs, BBC Radio 4/Above the Title Productions, 10 May.
Leviathan '99 (1968), Ray Bradbury, BBC Radio 3, 18 May.

Art

Smells Like Back of Old Hot Radio (1976), Ed Ruscha, Tate Modern, London.

Chapter 7

Novels

Burgess, Anthony (1982), *The End of the World News: An Entertainment*, Harmondsworth, Middlesex: Penguin.
Elton, Ben (1999), *Inconceivable*, London: Bantam.
Fitzgerald, Penelope ([1980] 2014), *Human Voices*, London: Fourth Estate.
Ismailov, Hamid (2006), *The Railway*, trans. Robert Chandler, London: Harvill Secker.

Film and TV

'Calling All Customers' (1983), *Are You Being Served?* BBC 1 TV, series 9, episode 4, 13 May.

Joe Strummer: The Future is Unwritten (2007), Dir. Julien Temple, UK: Vertigo Films.
Ploughman's Lunch, The (1983), Dir. Richard Eyre, UK: Goldcrest Films.
Radio On (1979), Dir. Chris Petit, UK /Germany: The British Film Institute/Road Movies Filmproduktion.
Reith (1983), Roger Milner, BBC 1 TV, 14 and 15 November.
'Rings Off Their Fingers' (1981), *Agony*, ITV/LWT, series 3, episode 7, 1 March.
Shoestring (1979), 'I'm a Believer', BBC 1 TV, series 1, episode 11, 16 December.
Shoestring (1979), 'Knock for Knock', BBC 1 TV, series 1, episode 2, 7 October.
Shoestring (1979), 'Private Ear', BBC 1 TV, series 1, episode 1, 30 September.
Shoestring (1979), 'The Link-Up', BBC 1 TV, series 1, episode 7, 11 November.

Music and live comedy

'Local Radio' (1975), Jasper Carrott [LP: *Rabbitts on and on and on...*] (DJM DJLPS 462).
'Local Radio Presenters' (1979), Jasper Carrott [LP: *The Unrecorded Jasper Carrott*] (DJM DJF 20560).
'London Calling' (1979), The Clash, composers: J. Strummer and M. Jones (CBS CBS 8087).
'Oh Yeah (On the Radio)' (1980), Roxy Music, composer: B. Ferry (Polydor 2001 972).
'On Your Radio' (1979), Joe Jackson, composer: J. Jackson [LP: *I'm the Man*] (A&M AMLH 64794).
'Pilot of the Airwaves' (1979), Charlie Dore, composer: C. Dore (Island Records WIP 6526).
'Radio' (1982), The Members, composer: N. Bennett (Genetic WIP 6773).
'Radio Free Europe' (1981), R.E.M. composers: B. Berry, M. Stipe, M. Mills and P. Buck (I.R.S. PFP 1017).
'This Is Radio Clash' (1981), The Clash, composer: The Clash (CBS A 1797).
'Turn on the Radio' (1979), The Rollers, composers: E. Faulkner, D. Faure, S. Wood and A. Longmuir (Arista ARIST 259).
'Video Killed the Radio Star' (1979), The Buggles, composers: B. Woolley, G. Downes and T. Horn (Island WIP 6524).

Radio

Burkiss Way, The (1979), 'Rise from the Grave the Burkiss Way', BBC Radio 4, series 5, episode 2, 9 April.
Burkiss Way, The (1980), 'Love Big Brother the Burkiss Way', BBC Radio 4, series 6, episode 3, 25 October.

Burkiss Way, The (1980), 'Sack the Burkiss Way', BBC Radio 4, series 6, episode 2, 18 October.
Burkiss Way, The (1980), 'The Man from the Burkiss Way', BBC Radio 4, series 6, episodes 1, 11 October.
'International Christmas Pudding, The' (1955), *The Goon Show*, BBC Home Service, series 6, episode 9, 15 November.
'Pick of the Week' (1982), *Radio Active*, BBC Radio 4, series 2, episode 6, 20 September.

Chapter 8

Novels

Byatt, A. S. (1985), *Still Life*, London: Penguin.
Keillor, Garrison (1991), *Radio Romance*, London: Viking Penguin/Faber and Faber (published in the United States as *WLT: A Radio Romance*).
Long, James (1992), *Hard News*, Ringwood, Victoria, Australia: Claremont.
Tavener, Mark (1990), *In the Red*, London: Hutchinson.

Film and TV

'Affair at the Victory Ball, The' (1991), *Agatha Christie's Poirot*, ITV/ITV Studios, series 3, episode 10, 3 March.
'Final Chapter, The' (1998), *Drop the Dead Donkey*, Channel 4/Hat Trick Productions, series 6, episode 7, 9 December.
Fisher King, The (1991), Dir. Terry Gilliam, USA: TriStar Pictures.
Good Morning, Vietnam (1987), Dir. Barry Levinson, USA: Touchstone Pictures.
Harry Enfield & Chums (1994–1998) BBC 1 TV/Tiger Aspect Productions.
Harry Enfield's Television Programme (1990–1992), BBC 2 TV/Hat Trick Productions.
In the Red (1998), adapted by Malcolm Bradbury, BBC 2, 26 May–9 June.
Kit Curran Radio Show, The (1984), ITV/Thames TV (series 2 (1986) was known as *Kit Curran*).
Living Daylights, The (1987), Dir. John Glen, UK: MGM/United Artists.
Prairie Home Companion, A (2006), Dir. Robert Altman, USA: Greenestreet Films/River Road Entertainment.
Radio Days (1987), Dir. Woody Allen, USA: Orion Pictures.
Straight Talk (1992), Dir. Barnet Kellman, USA: Hollywood Pictures.
Talk Radio (1988), Dir. Oliver Stone, USA: Alliance Atlantis.
'Tangled Web, The' (1988), *Yes, Prime Minister*, BBC 2 TV, series 2 episode 8, 28 January.

Music

'Devil's Radio' (1987), George Harrison, composer: G. Harrison [LP: *Cloud Nine*] (Dark Horse WX 123).
'Hello (Turn Your Radio On)' (1992), Shakespears Sister, composers: M. Guiot, M. Detroit and S. Fahey (London LON 330).
'I Can't Live Without My Radio' (1985), LL Cool J, composers: J. Smith and R. Rubin [LP: *Radio*] (Def Jam Recordings DEF 26745).
'I Watched It All (On My Radio)' (1990), Lionel Cartwright, composers: D. Schlitz and L. Cartwright (USA: MCA MCA-53779).
'In the Days Before Rock "n" Roll' (1990), Van Morrison with Paul Durcan, composers: P. Durcan and V. Morrison [LP: *Enlightenment*] (Polydor 847 100-1).
'Panic' (1986), The Smiths, composers: Morrissey and J. Marr (Rough Trade RT 193).
'Radio Ga Ga' (1984), Queen, composer: R. Taylor (EMI QUEEN 1).
'Radio Song' (1991), R.E.M. composers: B. Berry, M. Stipe, M. Mills and P. Buck (Warner Bros. W0072).
'Radio Station' (1988), Run DMC, composers: D. McDaniels, D. Reeves, J. Mizell, J. Simmons [LP: *Tougher Than Leather*] (London LONLP 38).
'Turn off the Radio' (1989), Ice Cube, composers: Chuck D, E. Sadler and P. Shabazz [LP: *AmeriKKKa's Most Wanted*] (4th & Broadway BRCD 551).

Radio

'Bitter Harvest' (1987), *Delve Special*, BBC Radio 4, series 4, episode 2, 4 September.
In the Balance (1997), Mark Tavener, BBC Radio 4, 6 February–13 March.
In the Chair (1998), Mark Tavener, BBC Radio 4, 5 June–10 July.
In the End (1999), Mark Tavener, BBC Radio 4, 18 November–23 December.
In the Red (1995), Mark Tavener and Peter Baynham, BBC Radio 4, 5 January–16 February.
Knowing Me Knowing You with Alan Partridge (1992–1993), BBC Radio 4.
On the Hour (1991–1992), BBC Radio 4.
Prairie Home Companion, A (1974–2016), US: Minnesota Public Radio. Selected episodes were rebroadcast in Britain on BBC 7 (later BBC Radio 4 Extra) from 2003 to 2016 as *Garrison Keillor's Radio Show*.
'Wimbledon Special' (1985), *Radio Active*, BBC Radio 4, series 5, episode, 1, 5 July.

Chapter 9

Novels

Paling, Chris (1999), *The Silent Sentry*, London: Vintage.

Film, TV and video games

2001: A Space Odyssey (1968), Dir. Stanley Kubrick, UK/USA: MGM.
'Bart Gets an Elephant' (1994), *The Simpsons*, USA: Gracie Films/20th Television, series 5, episode 17, USA: 31 March; (UK: 1994, Sky1, 1 May); (UK: 1998, BBC 2, 23 December).
Chicken Run (2000), Dirs. Peter Lord and Nick Park, UK: Pathé Distribution.
Frasier (1993), 'Dinner at Eight', USA: NBC, Grub Street Productions/Paramount Network Television, series 1, episode 3, 30 September.
Frasier (1993), 'Here's Looking at You', USA: NBC, Grub Street Productions/Paramount Network Television, series 1, episode 5, 14 October.
Frasier (1994), 'Guess Who's Coming to Breakfast?', USA: NBC, Grub Street Productions/Paramount Network Television, series 1, episode 13, 6 January.
Frasier (1999), 'Dr. Nora', USA: NBC, Grub Street Productions/Paramount Network Television, series 6, episode 20, 29 April.
Grand Theft Auto (2001–2013), [video game] series III to V, UK/USA: Rockstar Games.
Hotel Rwanda (2004), Dir. Terry George, USA/UK/South Africa/Italy: United Artists/Lions Gate Films.
Maybe Baby (2000), Dir. Ben Elton, UK: Pandora/BBC Films.
'On the Autofront' (1994), *Minder*, ITV/Central/Euston Films, series 10, episode 8, 24 February.
Psycho (1960), Dir. Alfred Hitchcock, USA: Paramount Pictures.
Shooting Dogs (2005), Dir. Michael Caton-Jones, UK/Germany: BBC Films/Adirondack Pictures (released in the United States as *Beyond the Gates*).
Sleepless in Seattle (1993), Dir. Nora Ephron, USA: TriStar Pictures.
Sometimes in April (2005), [TV movie] Dir. Raoul Peck, Rwanda/France/USA: HBO Films.
'Wavelength' (2000), *Taggart*, ITV/STV Studios, series 16, episode 3, 21 September.

Theatre

Hate Radio (2011), Milo Rau, [multimedia theatre presentation] produced by IIPM Berlin/Zürich.

Music

'Cluster One' (1994), Pink Floyd, composers: D. Gilmour and R. Wright [LP: *The Division Bell*] (EMI UK 8289842).
'Last DJ, The' (2002), Tom Petty and the Heartbreakers, composer: T. Petty [LP: *The Last DJ*] (Warner Bros. 9362-47955-2).

'Radio' (2004), Robbie Williams, composers: R. Williams and S. Duffy (Chrysalis CDCHS 5156).
'Radio Unfriendly' (2011), UK Subs, composers: C. Harper and J. Oliver [LP: *Work in Progress*] (Captain Oi! AHOY LP 310).
'Rebel Radio' (1997), UK Subs, composers: C. Harper and N. Garratt [LP: *Riot*] (Anagram Records CDMGRAM 113).
'Rock DJ' (2000), Robbie Williams, composers: E. Paris, G. Chambers, K. Andrews, N. Pigford and R. Williams (Chrysalis CDCHS5118).
'Sorted for Es and Wizz' (1995), Pulp, composers: J. Cocker, S. Mackey, R. Senior, N. Banks, C. Doyle and M. Webber (Island Records CID 620).
'Turn the Radio Up' (2001), Barry Manilow, composer: B. Manilow (Concord CCD-2165-2).

Radio

Ed Reardon's Week (2005), 'Pulp Non-Fiction', BBC Radio 4, series 1, episode 2, 14 January.
Ed Reardon's Week (2006), 'The Name-Check', BBC Radio 4, series 3, episode 1, 15 December.
Ed Reardon's Week (2013), 'The Bride of Auntie', BBC Radio 4, series 9, episode 6, 16 December.
In the Psychiatrist's Chair (1982–2001), Dr Anthony Clare, BBC Radio 4.
Radio Shuttleworth (2000), BBC Radio 4, series 2, episode 2, 2 March.

Chapter 10

Novels and graphic novels

Hanington, Peter (2016), *A Dying Breed*, London: Two Roads.
Hanington, Peter (2019), *A Single Source*, London: Two Roads.
Herron, Mick (2010), *Slow Horses*, London: John Murray.
Mitchell, David (1999), *Ghostwritten*, London: Hodder and Stoughton.
Mitchell, David (2020), *Utopia Avenue*, London: Sceptre/Hodder and Stoughton.
O'Connell, Christian (2018), *Radio Boy*, London: HarperCollins Children's Books.
O'Connell, Christian (2018), *Radio Boy and the Revenge of Grandad*, London: HarperCollins Children's Books.
Oseman, Alice (2016), *Radio Silence*, London: Harper Collins.
Paraskos, Michael (2016), *In Search of Sixpence*, Mitcham, Surrey: Friction Fiction.
Sirangelo, André and Gabriel Iumazark (2015), [graphic novel] *The Last Broadcast: An Urban Exploration Adventure*, Los Angeles, CA: Archaia.

Stratford, Sarah-Jane (2016), *Radio Girls*, London: Allison & Busby.
Sudjic, Olivia (2021), *Asylum Road*, London: Bloomsbury Publishing.
Upson, Nicola (2015), *London Rain*, London: Faber & Faber.

Film and TV

Alan Partridge: Alpha Papa (2013), Dir. Declan Lowney, UK: StudioCanal/BBC Films/BFI.
Boat That Rocked, The (2009), Dir. Richard Curtis, UK: Universal Pictures (released in the United States as *Pirate Radio*).
Bob the Builder, Project: Build It (2008), 'Radio Bob', CBeebies/HiT Entertainment, series 16, episode 2, 6 August.
Bob the Builder, Project: Build It (2008), 'Silent Scoop', CBeebies/HiT Entertainment, series 16, episode 5, 12 August.
Bob the Builder, Project: Build It (2008), 'Spud the DJ', CBeebies/HiT Entertainment, series 16, episode 4, 11 August.
Downton Abbey (2014), ITV/ITV Studios, series 5, episode 2, 28 September.
'Face for Radio, A' (2008), *New Tricks*, BBC 1/Wall to Wall, series 5, episode 3, 21 July.
'First Stone, The' (2007), *Rebus*, STV, series 4, episode 2, 12 October.
FM (2009), [television series] ITV 2/ITV Studios, 25 February–1 April.
Hospital People (2017), 'The Hospital Awards', BBC 1/Roughcut TV, series 1, episode 1, 21 April.
Hospital People (2017), 'The Local Millionaire', BBC 1/Roughcut TV, series 1, episode 3, 5 May.
Hospital People (2017), 'The New Ward', BBC 1/Roughcut TV, series 1, episode 5, 26 May.
'It's Good to Talk' (2015), *Doc Martin*, ITV/ITV Studios, series 7, episode 3, 21 September.
King's Speech, The (2010), Dir. Tom Hooper, UK: Momentum Pictures.
'Pale Horse, The' (2010), *Agatha Christie's Marple*, ITV/Agatha Christie Ltd, series 5, episode 1, 3 August.
People Just Do Nothing (2014), 'Secret Location', BBC 3/Roughcut TV, series 1, episode 1, 20 July.
People Just Do Nothing (2018), 'Car Boot', BBC 3/Roughcut TV, series 5, episode 1, 12 November.
'Radio Badge, The' (2020), *Hey Duggee*, CBeebies/Studio AKA, series 3, episode 11, 2 June.
'Theatre of the Invisible, The' (2017), *Father Brown*, BBC 1/BBC Studios, series 5, episode 12, 16 January.
'Till Death Do Us Part' (2020), *Midsomer Murders*, ITV/Bentley Productions, series 20, episode 5, 6 January.
Trouble with Maggie Cole, The (2020), ITV/Genial Productions, 4 March–8 April.
W1A (2014), BBC 2, series 1, episode 2, 26 March.

Music

'Jesus on the Radio' (2019), Jamie Kimmett, composer: J. Kimmett [EP: *Prize Worth Fighting For*] (Reunion Records [no code]).
'Radio Nowhere' (2007), Bruce Springsteen, composer: B. Springsteen [LP: *Magic*] (Columbia 88697170602).
'Radio Silence' (2016), James Blake, composer: J. Blake [LP: *The Colour in Anything*] (Polydor 00602547932983).
'Turn on the Radio' (2010), Reba McEntire, composers: M. Oakley, C. Oakley and J. P. Twang [LP: *All the Women I Am*] (Hump Head HUMP 122).
'Turn Your Radio On' (1937), Albert E. Brumley, [sheet music] Bridge Building Music/Hal Leonard (251618-DAM251618).

Radio

'Fourth Sausage, The' (2016), *Ed Reardon's Week*, BBC Radio 4/BBC Studios, series 11, episode 6, 8 November.

Sculpture

Babel (2001–2006), Cildo Meireles, [metallic structure, radio sets; (h) 450 cm (w) 260 cm], London: Tate Modern.

Primary sources (2): Contemporary non-fiction: Journals, memoirs, essays, articles and others

Bailey, Nick (2019), *Across the Waves: From Radio Caroline to Classic FM*, Otherwise.
'BBC – The Voice of Britain (1935)' *The Monthly Film Bulletin*, London: British Film Institute, September 1935, 2 (20): 117.
BBC Year-book 1932, The (1932), London: The British Broadcasting Corporation.
Bennett, Alan (1990), 'Louis MacNeice', in *Poetry in Motion*, London: Channel 4 Television, pp. 71–84.
Birt, John (2002), *The Harder Path: The Autobiography*, London: Time Warner.
Blackburn, Tony (2007), *Poptastic: My Life in Radio*, London: Cassell Illustrated.
Brennan, Maeve (2002), *The Philip Larkin I Knew*, Manchester: Manchester University Press.
Brett, Guy, ed. (2008), *Cildo Meireles* (exhibition catalogue), London: Tate Publishing.
Burgess, Anthony (1967), 'The Antis: The Weasels of Pop', *Punch*, 20 September: 430–1.
Burrows, Arthur (1924), *The Story of Broadcasting*, London: Cassell.

Buskin, Richard (2009), 'REM "Radio Free Europe": Classic Tracks', November. Available online: https://www.soundonsound.com/people/rem-radio-free-europe-classic-tracks (accessed 24 May 2021).

Collis, John Stewart ([1973] 2009), *The Worm Forgives the Plough*, London: Vintage Books.

Compton, Nic (2016), *The Shipping Forecast*, London: BBC Books.

Connelly, Charlie (2004), *Attention All Shipping: A Journey Round the Shipping Forecast*, London: Little, Brown.

Connelly, Charlie ([2019] 2020), *Last Train to Hilversum: A Journey in Search of the Magic of Radio*, London: Bloomsbury Publishing.

Conway, Steve ([2009] 2014), *Shiprocked: Life on the Waves with Radio Caroline*, Dublin: Liberties Press.

Costello, Elvis (2015), *Unfaithful Music & Disappearing Ink*, London: Penguin.

Cranson, Ros (2008), 'BBC: The Voice of Britain', in *Addressing the Nation: The GPO Film Unit Collection*, Vol. 1, DVD booklet, London: BFI, pp. 51–2.

Damazer, Mark (1980), 'Introduction', in Penelope Fitzgerald ([1980] 2014), *Human Voices*, London: Fourth Estate, pp. vii–xv.

Du Noyer, Paul (1987), 'Morrissey Interview', August. Available online: https://www.pauldunoyer.com/morrissey-interview-1987/ (accessed 24 May 2021).

Dyke, Greg (2004), *Inside Story*, London: Harper Collins.

Elmes, Simon (2007), *And Now on Radio 4: A Celebration of the World's Best Radio Station*, London: Arrow Books.

'Fergal Keane: BBC Africa Editor Leaves Role because of PTSD' (2020), BBC, 24 January. Available online: https://www.bbc.co.uk/news/entertainment-arts-51236199 (accessed 24 May 2021).

Forster E. M. (1985), *Commonplace Book*, ed. Philip Gardner, Aldershot, Hampshire: Wildwood House.

'"Freedom Radio." At the Regal: The Cinema' (1941), *The Spectator*, 31 January: 12.

Gielgud, Val (1947), *Years of the Locust, 1947*, London: Nicholson & Watson.

Goddard, F. (1934), 'Handling of the Set: Results Good and Bad', *The Times*, Broadcasting Number, 14 August: viii.

Higgins, Charlotte (2015), 'We Love W1A. But, Dear BBC, is it Wise to Lay Bare Your Foibles So Mercilessly?' *The Guardian*, 15 May. Available online: https://www.theguardian.com/commentisfree/2015/may/15/w1a-bbc-licence-fee-john-whittingdale (accessed 24 May 2021).

Hind, John (2016), 'Making Airwaves', *i* [newspaper], 17 August: 34–5.

Holmes, John (2020), *Celebrating 50 Years in Radio & Television: This Is the BBC Holmes Service*, Nottingham: self-published.

Hornby, Nick (2003), *Songbook*, New York: Riverhead Books.

'How to Listen' (1946), *Radio Times*, issue 1200, 27 September: 4. Available at https://genome.ch.bbc.co.uk/4a6f0c1eabde45478ec087c5adfaef95 (accessed 24 May 2021).

Ingrams, Richard (1983), 'Television: Meddlesome', *The Spectator*, 19 November: 46.
Jefferson, Peter (2011), *And Now the Shipping Forecast: A Tide of History Around our Shores*, Cambridge: UIT Cambridge.
Jolo [Joshua Lowe] (1935), 'Film Reviews: Radio Parade of 1935 (British Made)', *Variety*, 1 January 1935: 18.
Kelly, Danny (1987), 'Marr, interviewed by Danny Kelly, "Exile on Mainstream"', *New Musical Express*, London, 14 February: 44–5.
Lawson, Mark (2016), 'Terry Wogan: The Intriguingly Subversive National Treasure', *The Guardian*, 31 January. Available online: https://www.theguardian.com/media/2016/jan/31/terry-wogan-intriguingly-subversive-national-treasure (accessed 24 May 2021).
'Listings, BBC Radio 1' (1986), *Radio Times*, issue 3258, 5 May: 40. Available online: https://genome.ch.bbc.co.uk/schedules/radio1/england/1986-05-05 (accessed 24 May 2021).
Lloyd, David (2017), *Radio Moments: 50 Years of Radio – Life on the Inside*, London: Biteback Publishing.
Lucas, George (1998), 'The Making of *American Graffiti*' [DVD bonus material (2003), American Graffiti], Universal Studios Home Video.
Macaulay, Rose (1939), 'War and the BBC', *The Spectator*, 20 October: 10.
MacNeice, Louis ([1938] 2007), *I Crossed the Minch*, Edinburgh: Polygon.
Mair, John, ed. (2021), *What's the Point of Ofcom?* Goring, Oxfordshire: Bite-Sized Books.
Meireles, Cildo and Frederico Morais (2008), 'Material Language', trans. Stephen Berg, *Tate Etc.*, Issue 14, Autumn: 96–109.
Melly, George ([1970] 1972), *Revolt into Style: The Pop Arts in Britain*, Harmondsworth, Middlesex: Penguin.
Milne, Alasdair ([1988] 1989), *DG: The Memoirs of a British Broadcaster*, London: Coronet.
Morgan, Fergus (2019), 'Hate Radio: Review', *The Stage*, 1 March. Available online: https://www.thestage.co.uk/reviews/hate-radio-review-at-ntgent--disturbing-verbatim-play-about-rwandan-genocide (accessed 24 May 2021).
Ofcom Guidance: Offensive Language on Radio (2011), Ofcom. Available online: https://www.ofcom.org.uk/ data/assets/pdf_file/0014/40541/offensive-language.pdf (accessed 24 May 2021).
Orwell, George ([1937] 1962), *The Road to Wigan Pier*, Harmondsworth, Middlesex: Penguin.
Osborne, John (2009), *Radio Head: Up and Down the Dial of British Radio*, London: Simon & Schuster.
Patterson, John ([2004] 2008), 'A Film Without a Cinema', originally published in the *Guardian*, 2 October 2004, reprinted in *Radio On* (2008), DVD film booklet, London: BFI, pp. 15–18.
Petley, Julian (2020), 'Foxification: Just What a Divided Country Doesn't Need', in John Mair (ed.), *The BBC: A Winter of Discontent?* Goring, Oxfordshire: Bite-Sized Books, pp. 116–23.

Pile, Stephen (2004), 'The Last Laugh?', *The Daily Telegraph*, 24 January. Available online: https://www.telegraph.co.uk/culture/tvandradio/3610803/The-last-laugh.html (accessed 24 May 2021).

Priestley, J. B. (1934), *English Journey*, London: William Heinemann.

Pringle, J. M. D. (1938), 'The Ascent of F6, at the Prince's Theatre, Manchester', *The Manchester Guardian*, 5 July. Available online: https://www.theguardian.com/books/2019/jul/05/ascent-of-f6-auden-isherwood-mountaineering-play-review-1938 (accessed 24 May 2021).

Purves, Libby (2002), *Radio: A True Love Story*, London: Hodder & Stoughton.

Raeburn, Anna (1984), *Talking to Myself*, London: Elm Tree.

Rivers-Moore, H. R. (1923), 'The Wireless Transmission of Music', *Music & Letters*, 4 (2): 158–61.

Robinson, Rony (2010), *Who's Been Talking?* Sheffield: ALD Print.

Russell, Jamie (2003), 'Review: *Monsieur Hulot's Holiday* (*Les Vacances de M Hulot*) (1953)', 1 July. Available online: http://www.bbc.co.uk/films/2003/07/01/les_vacances_de_m_hulot_1953_review.shtml (accessed 24 May 2021).

Scovell, Adam (2019), 'Chris Petit on Radio On: "In a World Dedicated to Waste, the Act of Driving Becomes a Moral Choice"', 22 August. Available online: https://www.bfi.org.uk/news-opinion/news-bfi/interviews/chris-petit-radio-on-interview (accessed 24 May 2021).

'Short-Wave Radio: Tuning out' (2012), *The Economist*, 7 July: 62.

Simpson, Dave (2018), 'The Buggles: How We Made "Video Killed the Radio Star"', *The Guardian*, G2, 30 October: 11. Available online: https://www.theguardian.com/music/2018/oct/30/the-buggles-how-we-made-video-killed-the-radio-star (accessed 24 May 2021).

Simpson, John ([1998] 1999), *Strange Places, Questionable People*, London: Pan Macmillan.

Snoddy, Raymond (2020), 'Letter to the Director General', in John Mair (ed.), *The BBC: A Winter of Discontent?* Goring, Oxfordshire: Bite-Sized Books, pp. 40–6.

'"Some Artists Do Roses, But I Work Primarily with Words" – Ed Ruscha's *Hurting the Word Radio #2* (1964)' (2019), *Christies*, 4 November. Available online: https://www.christies.com/features/Ed-Ruscha-Hurting-the-Word-Radio-2-1964-10108-3.aspx (accessed 24 May 2021).

Todd, Mike (2008), 'The Greenwich Time Signal', 18 September. Available online: http://www.miketodd.net/other/gts.htm (accessed 24 May 2021).

Tusa, John (1992), *A World in Your Ear: Reflections on Changes*, London: Broadside Books.

'Visits Made in 2019 to Visitor Attractions in Membership with ALVA' (2020), Association of Leading Visitor Attractions. Available online: https://www.alva.org.uk/details.cfm?p=423 (accessed 24 May 2021).

Warner, Clive (2018), *Adventures in the Luminiferous Aether* [Kindle ed.], Citiria Publishing.

'Welcome Stranger' (1951), *Radio Times*, issue 1436, 18 May: 11. Available online: https://genome.ch.bbc.co.uk/3aa57773c78b4110bff6c43a21d33c99 (accessed 24 May 2021).

Wood, Jason (2008), '*Radio On* and the British Cinematic Landscape', DVD film booklet, London: BFI, pp. 1-3.

Woolf, Virginia ([1938] 1966), *Three Guineas*, Orlando, FL: Harcourt Brace.

Secondary sources

Abel, Jessica (2015), *Out on the Wire: The Storytelling Secrets of the New Masters of Radio*, New York: Broadway Books.

Aldgate, Anthony and Jeffrey Richards (1999), *Best of British: Cinema and Society from 1930 to the Present*, London: IB Tauris.

Allen, D. P. (2011), 'Independent Local Radio (ILR) in the West Midlands, 1972-1984: A Comparative Study of BRMB Radio and Beacon Radio', PhD diss., University of Worcester.

Andrews, Maggie (2012), *Domesticating the Airwaves: Broadcasting, Domesticity and Femininity*, London: Continuum.

Anduaga, Aitor (2009), *Wireless and Empire: Geopolitics, Radio Industry, and Ionosphere in the British Empire, 1918-1939*, Oxford: Oxford University Press.

Angé, Olivia and David Berliner (2015), 'Introduction: Anthropology of Nostalgia – Anthropology as Nostalgia', in Olivia Angé and David Berliner (eds), *Anthropology and Nostalgia*, New York: Berghahn, pp. 1-15.

Avery, Todd (2006), *Radio Modernism: Literature, Ethics, and the BBC, 1922-1938*, Aldershot, Hampshire: Ashgate.

Barnard, Stephen (1989), *On the Radio: Music Radio in Britain*, Milton Keynes, Buckinghamshire: Open University Press.

Barnes, Richard ([1982] 2000), *The Who: Maximum R&B*, London: Plexus/Eel Pie.

Baron, Mike (1975), *Independent Radio: The Story of Independent Radio in the United Kingdom*, Lavenham, Suffolk: Terence Dalton.

Barr, Charles (1986), 'Broadcasting and Cinema: 2: Screens Within Screens', in Charles Barr (ed.), *All Our Yesterdays: 90 Years of British Cinema*, London: BFI Publishing, pp. 206-24.

Barwise, Patrick and Peter York (2020), *The War Against the BBC*, London: Penguin.

Bennett, Lucy (2013), 'Discourses of Order and Rationality: Drooling R.E.M. Fans as "matter out of place"', *Continuum: Journal of Media & Cultural Studies*, 27(2): 214-27.

Berker, Thomas, Maren Hartmann, Yves Punie, Katie Ward (2006), 'Introduction', in Berker et al. (eds), *Domestication of Media and Technology*, Maidenhead, Berkshire: Open University Press, pp. 1-17.

Bevan, Alex (2019), *The Aesthetics of Nostalgia TV: Production Design and the Boomer Era*, New York: Bloomsbury Academic.
Bloom, Emily (2016), *The Wireless Past: Anglo-Irish Writers and the BBC, 1931–1968*, Oxford: Oxford University Press.
Boly, John R. (1981), 'W. H. Auden's *The Orators*: Portraits of the Artist in the Thirties.' *Twentieth Century Literature*, 27 (3): 247–61.
Bonini, Tiziano (2015), 'Introduction. The Listener as Producer: The Rise of the Networked Listener', in Tiziano Bonini and Belén Monclús (eds), *Radio Audiences and Participation in the Age of Network Society*, New York: Routledge, pp. 1–36.
Born, Georgina (2004), *Uncertain Vision: Birt, Dyke and the Reinvention of the BBC*, London: Secker & Warburg.
Breithaupt, Don (2007), *Aja*, New York: Bloomsbury Academic.
Briggs, Asa (1961), *The History of Broadcasting in the United Kingdom, Volume I, The Birth of Broadcasting*, London: Oxford University Press.
Briggs, Asa (1965), *The History of Broadcasting in the United Kingdom, Volume II, The Golden Age of Wireless*, Oxford: Oxford University Press.
Briggs, Asa (1970), *The History of Broadcasting in the United Kingdom, Volume III, The War of Words*, Oxford: Oxford University Press.
Briggs, Asa ([1979] 1995), *The History of Broadcasting in the United Kingdom, Volume IV, Sound and Vision*, revised edn, Oxford: Oxford University Press.
Briggs, Asa ([1980] 1991), 'Problems and Possibilities in the Writing of Broadcasting History', in Briggs (ed.), *The Collected Essays of Asa Briggs: Vol. III, Serious Pursuits: Communications and Education*, Urbana, IL: University of Illinois Press, pp. 114–27.
Briggs, Asa (1995), *The History of Broadcasting in the United Kingdom, Volume V, Competition*, Oxford: Oxford University Press.
Briggs, Asa and Peter Burke (2002), *A Social History of the Media: From Gutenberg to the Internet*, Cambridge: Polity.
Brown, Stephen (2018), 'Retro Galore! Is There No End to Nostalgia?', *Journal of Customer Behaviour*, 17 (1–2): 9–29.
Burns, Tom (1977), *The BBC: Public Institution and Private World*, London: Macmillan.
Campbell, W. Joseph (2010), *Getting it Wrong: Ten of the Great Misreported Stories in American Journalism*, Berkeley, CA: University of California Press.
Cardiff, David (1988), 'Mass Middlebrow Laughter: The Origins of BBC Comedy', *Media, Culture & Society*, 10 (1): 41–60.
Cardiff, David and Paddy Scannell (1981), 'Radio in World War II', in *The Historical Development of Popular Culture in Britain, U203, Block 2, Unit 8*, Milton Keynes, Buckinghamshire: Open University Press, pp. 31–78.
Carpenter, Humphrey (1996), *The Envy of the World: Fifty Years of the BBC Third Programme and Radio 3, 1946–1996*, London: Weidenfeld and Nicholson.

Caughie, John (1986), 'Broadcasting and Cinema: 1: Converging Histories', in Charles Barr (ed.), *All Our Yesterdays: 90 Years of British Cinema*, London: BFI Publishing, pp. 189–205.

Certeau, Michel de (1984), *The Practice of Everyday Life*, trans. Steven Rendall, Berkeley, CA: University of California Press.

Chapman, Robert (1992), *Selling the Sixties: The Pirates and Pop Music Radio*, London: Routledge.

Chibnall, Steve and Brian McFarlane (2009), *The British 'B' Film*, London: Palgrave Macmillan/British Film Institute.

Chignell, Hugh (2009), 'Change and Reaction in BBC Current Affairs Radio, 1928–1970', in Michael Bailey (ed.), *Narrating Media History*, London: Routledge, pp. 36–47.

Chignell, Hugh (2011), *Public Issue Radio: Talk, News and Current Affairs in the Twentieth Century*, Basingstoke, Hampshire: Palgrave Macmillan.

Chion, Michel (1999), *The Voice in Cinema*, trans. Claudia Gorbman, New York: Columbia University Press.

Cohen, Debra Rae (2009), 'Annexing the Oracular Voice: Form, Ideology, and the BBC', in Debra Rae Cohen, Michael Coyle and Jane Lewty (eds), *Broadcasting Modernism*, Gainesville, FL: University Press of Florida, pp. 142–57.

Cohen, Debra Rae, Michael Coyle and Jane Lewty (2009), 'Introduction: Signing On', in Debra Rae Cohen, Michael Coyle and Jane Lewty (eds), *Broadcasting Modernism*, Gainesville, FL: University Press of Florida, pp. 1–7.

Coleman, Josephine (2021), *Digital Innovations and the Production of Local Content in Community Radio: Changing Practices in the UK*, Abingdon, Oxfordshire: Routledge.

Connor, James A (1993), 'Radio Free Joyce: *Wake* Language and the Experience of Radio', *James Joyce Quarterly*, 30/31, pp. 825–43.

Cooper, Martin (2011), *Brazilian Railway Culture*, Newcastle upon Tyne: Cambridge Scholars Publishing.

Cooper, Martin and Kirsty Macaulay (2015), 'Contemporary Christian Radio in Britain: A New Genre on the National Dial', *Radio Journal: International Studies in Broadcast & Audio Media*, 13 (1–2): 75–87.

Cramp, Andrew ([1937] 1990), 'Introduction', in Rex Warner (ed.), *Wild Goose Chase*, London: Merlin Press, pp. vii–xvii.

Crisell, Andrew (2002), *An Introductory History of British Broadcasting*, 2nd edn, London: Routledge.

Crook, Tim (1999), *Radio Drama: Theory and Practice*, London: Routledge.

Damousi, Joy (2007), '"The Filthy American Twang": Elocution, the Advent of American "Talkies", and Australian Cultural Identity', *American Historical Review*, 112 (2): 394–416.

Davis, Fred (1979), *Yearning for Yesterday: A Sociology of Nostalgia*, New York: Free Press.

References

Dawes, Simon (2017), *British Broadcasting and the Public-Private Dichotomy: Neoliberalism, Citizenship and the Public Sphere*, Cham, Switzerland: Palgrave Macmillan.

Dika, Vera (2003), *Recycled Culture in Contemporary Art and Film: The Uses of Nostalgia*, Cambridge: Cambridge University Press.

Douglas, Susan J. ([1999] 2004), *Listening in: Radio and the American Imagination*, Minneapolis, MN: University of Minnesota Press.

Dubber, Andrew (2013), *Radio in the Digital Age*, Cambridge: Polity.

Dupéré, Mélanie (2021), 'BBC Independence and Impartiality: The Case of the 1956 Suez Crisis', *Revue Française de Civilisation Britannique [Online]*, XXVI-I 2021. Available online: http://journals.openedition.org/rfcb/6992 (accessed 24 May 2021).

Dwyer, Michael D. (2015), *Back to the Fifties: Nostalgia, Hollywood Film, and Popular Music of the Seventies and Eighties*, New York: Oxford University Press.

Dyer, Geoff (2018), *'Broadsword Calling Danny Boy': On Where Eagles Dare*, London: Penguin.

Edgerton, David (2006), *The Shock of the Old: Technology and Global History Since 1900*, London: Profile.

Ehrlich, Matthew C. and Joe Saltzman (2015), *Heroes and Scoundrels: The Image of the Journalist in Popular Culture*, Chicago: University of Illinois Press.

Ellis, John (2000), 'British Cinema as Performance Art: *Brief Encounter*, *Radio Parade of 1935* and the Circumstances of Film Exhibition', in Justine Ashby and Andrew Higson (eds), *British Cinema, Past and Present*, London: Routledge, pp. 95–109.

Elmes, Simon ([2012] 2013), *Hello Again... Nine Decades of Radio Voices*, London: Arrow.

Fildes, Gill (2010), 'Winifred Holtby and "The Voice of God": A Writer's View of Radio and Cinema between the Wars', in Lisa Regan (ed.), *Winifred Holtby, 'A Woman in Her Time': Critical Essays*, Newcastle upon Tyne: Cambridge Scholars Publishing, pp. 89–112.

Fordham, Finn (2011), 'Finnegans Wake: Novel and Anti-novel', in Richard Brown (ed.), *A Companion to James Joyce*, Oxford: Blackwell, pp. 71–89.

Fowler, Gene and Bill Crawford (2002), *Border Radio: Quacks, Yodelers, Pitchmen, Psychics, and other Amazing Broadcasters of the American Airwaves*, Austin, TX: University of Texas Press.

Fox, Jo (2005), '"The Mediator": Images of Radio in Wartime Feature Film in Britain and Germany', in Mark Connelly and David Welch (eds), *War and the Media: Reportage and Propaganda, 1900-2003*, London: I.B. Tauris, pp. 92–111.

Frith, Simon (1983), 'The Pleasures of the Hearth: The Making of BBC Light Entertainment', in Formations Editorial Collective (eds), *Formations of Pleasure*, London: Routledge & Kegan Paul, pp. 101–23.

Gazi, Angeliki and Tiziano Bonini (2018), '"Haptically Mediated" Radio Listening and its Commodification: The Remediation of Radio through Digital Mobile Devices', *Journal of Radio & Audio Media*, 25 (1): 109–25.

Gilbert, Pat (2004), *Passion Is a Fashion: The Real Story of The Clash*, London: Aurum Press.

Golubov, Nattie Liliana (2002), 'British Women Writers and the Public Sphere between the Wars: Winifred Holtby, Storm Jameson, Naomi Mitchison, and Rebecca West', PhD diss., Queen Mary College, University of London.

Hajkowski, Thomas (2010), *The BBC and National Identity in Britain, 1922–1953*, Manchester: Manchester University Press.

Hall, Stuart (1996), 'On Postmodernism and Articulation: An Interview with Stuart Hall, edited by Lawrence Grossberg', in David Morley and Kuan-Hsing Chen (eds), *Stuart Hall: Critical Dialogues in Cultural Studies*, London: Routledge. pp. 131–50.

Hall, Stuart and Paddy Whannel ([1964] 2009), 'The Young Audience', in John Storey (ed.), *Cultural Theory and Popular Culture: A Reader*, 4th edn, Harlow, Essex: Pearson Longman, pp. 45–51.

Harper, Sue and Justin Smith (2012), 'Cross-over', in Sue Harper and Justin Smith, eds. (2012), *British Film Culture in the 1970s: The Boundaries of Pleasure*, Edinburgh: Edinburgh University Press, pp. 193–207.

Harrison, Phil (2020), *The Age of Static: How TV Explains Modern Britain*, London: Melville House.

Havers, Richard (2007), *Here is the News: The BBC and the Second World War*, Stroud, Gloucestershire: Sutton Publishing.

Healey, Jo (2020), *Trauma Reporting: A Journalist's Guide to Covering Sensitive Stories*, Abingdon, Oxon: Routledge.

Hebdige, Dick (1982), 'Towards a Cartography of Taste 1935–1962', in Bernard Waites, Tony Bennett and Graham Martin (eds), *Popular Culture: Past and Present – A Reader*, Beckenham, Kent: Croom Helm, pp. 194–218.

Hendy, David (2000), *Radio in the Global Age*, Cambridge: Polity.

Hendy, David (2007), *Life on Air: A History of Radio Four*, Oxford: Oxford University Press. Hendy, David (2010), 'Listening in the Dark', *Media History*, 16 (2): 215–32.

Hendy, David (2014), 'The Great War and British Broadcasting: Emotional Life in the Creation of the BBC', *New Formations*, 82: 82–99.

Higgins, Charlotte (2015), *This New Noise: The Extraordinary Birth and Troubled Life of the BBC*, London: Guardian Books.

Higson, Andrew (1994), 'A Diversity of Film Practices: Renewing British Cinema in the 1970s', in Bart Moore-Gilbert (ed.), *The Arts in the 1970s: Cultural Closure?* London: Routledge, pp. 216–39.

Higson, Andrew (2000), 'The Instability of the National', in Justine Ashby and Andrew Higson (eds), *British Cinema, Past and Present*, London: Routledge, pp. 35–47.

Hill, John (1986), *Sex, Class and Realism: British Cinema 1956–1963*, London: BFI Publishing.
Hind, John and Stephen Mosco (1985), *Rebel Radio: The Full Story of British Pirate Radio*, London: Pluto.
Hinton, Brian (2000), *Celtic Crossroads: The Art of Van Morrison*, 2nd edn, London: Sanctuary Publishing.
Hobsbawm, Eric (1994), *Age of Extremes: The Short Twentieth Century 1914–1991*, London: Michael Joseph.
Hogg, James & Robert Sellers (2013), *Hello, Darlings! The Authorized Biography of Kenny Everett*, London: Bantam.
Hoggart, Richard (1957), *The Uses of Literacy*, London: Chatto & Windus.
Hutchby, Ian (1991), 'The Organization of Talk on Talk Radio', in Paddy Scannell (ed.), *Broadcast Talk*, London: Sage, pp. 119–37.
Jacobs, Richard (1998), 'Appendix', in Evelyn Waugh (ed.), *The Ordeal of Gilbert Pinfold: A Conversation Piece*, London: Penguin, pp. 133–66.
Jacobs, Richard (1998), 'Introduction' in Evelyn Waugh (ed.), *The Ordeal of Gilbert Pinfold: A Conversation Piece*, London: Penguin, pp. vii–xliii.
Jameson, Fredric (1984), 'Postmodernism, or the Cultural Logic of Late Capitalism', *New Left Review*, no. 146, July-August: 53–92. Available online: https://newleftrevie w.org/issues/i146/articles/fredric-jameson-postmodernism-or-the-cultural-logic-of -late-capitalism (accessed 24 May 2021).
Jenkins, Henry (1992), *Textual Poachers: Television Fans and Participatory Culture*, London: Routledge.
Kassel, Michael B. (1993), *America's Favourite Radio Station: WKRP in Cincinnati*, Madison, WI: The University of Wisconsin Press.
Kellow, Christine L. and H. Leslie Steeves (1998), 'The Role of Radio in the Rwandan Genocide', *Journal of Communication*, 48 (3): 107–28.
Korczynski, Marek, Michael Pickering and Emma Robertson (2013), *Rhythms of Labour: Music at Work in Britain*, Cambridge: Cambridge University Press.
Korte, Barbara (2009), *Represented Reporters: Images of War Correspondents in Memoirs and Fiction*, Bielefeld: transcript-Verlag.
Lacey, Alex de (2019), '"Let us know you're locked": Pirate Radio Broadcasts as Historical and Musical Artefact', *Popular Music History*, 12 (2): 194–214.
Lacey, Kate (2013), *Listening Publics: The Politics and Experience of Listening in the Media Age*, Cambridge: Polity.
Lago, Mary (1990), 'E. M. Forster and the BBC', *The Yearbook of English Studies*, 20: 132–51.
LeMahieu, D. L. (1988), *A Culture for Democracy: Mass Communication and the Cultivated Mind in Britain Between the Wars*, Oxford: Oxford University Press.
Lewty, Jane (2002), 'Broadcasting Modernity: Eloquent Listening in the Early Twentieth Century', PhD diss., University of Glasgow.

Lewty, Jane (2008), 'Joyce and Radio', in Richard Brown (ed.), *A Companion to James Joyce*, Oxford: Blackwell, pp. 390–406.

Lewty, Jane (2009), '"What They Had Heard Said Written"', Joyce, Pound, and the Cross-Correspondence of Radio', in Debra Rae Cohen, Michael Coyle and Jane Lewty (eds), *Broadcasting Modernism*, Gainesville, FL: University Press of Florida, pp. 199–220.

Light, Alison (1991), *Forever England: Femininity, Literature and Conservatism Between the Wars*, London: Routledge.

Linfoot, Matthew (2011), 'A History of BBC Local Radio in England c1960 –1980', PhD diss., University of Westminster, London.

Lloyd, Justine (2020), *Gender and Media in the Broadcast Age: Women's Radio Programming at the BBC, CBC, and ABC*, New York: Bloomsbury Academic.

Lommers, Suzanne (2012), *Europe – On Air: Interwar Projects for Radio Broadcasting*, Amsterdam: Amsterdam University Press.

Long, Paul and Nicholas Gebhardt (2019), 'Listening Again to Popular Music as History', *Popular Music History*, 12 (2): 147–51.

Lonsdale, Sarah (2016), *The Journalist in British Fiction & Film: Guarding the Guardians from 1900 to the Present*, London: Bloomsbury.

Lowenthal, David (2015), *The Past Is a Foreign Country – Revisited*, Cambridge: Cambridge University Press.

Maasø, Arnt (2008), 'The Proxemics of the Mediated Voice', in Jay Beck and Tony Grajeda (eds), *Lowering the Boom: Critical Studies in Film Sound*, Urbana, IL: University of Illinois Press, pp. 36–50.

Maconie, Stuart ([2013] 2014), *The People's Songs: The Story of Modern Britain in 50 Songs*, London: Ebury Press.

Maloney, Sean L. (2017), *The Modern Lovers*, London: Bloomsbury Academic.

Manlove, C. N. (1991), 'Everything Slipping Away: John Wyndham's *The Day of the Triffids*', *Journal of the Fantastic in the Arts*, 4 (1): 29–53.

McCann, Bryan (2004), *Hello, Hello Brazil: Popular Music in the Making of Modern Brazil*, Durham, NC: Duke University Press.

McCarthy, Liam (2019), 'Connecting with New Asian Communities: BBC Local Radio 1967–1990', PhD diss., University of Leicester.

McCoy, Jason (2009), 'Making Violence Ordinary: Radio, Music and the Rwandan Genocide', *African Music: Journal of the International Library of African Music*, 8 (3): 85–96.

McDonald, Oonagh (1995), 'Producer Choice in the BBC', *Public Money & Management*, 15 (1): 47–51.

McFarlane, Brian (2009), 'The More Things Change… British Cinema in the 90s', in Robert Murphy (ed), *The British Cinema Book*, 3rd edn, London: British Film Institute, pp. 366–74.

McIntyre, Ian (1993), *The Expense of Glory: A Life of John Reith*, London: HarperCollins.

McKibbin, Ross (1998), *Classes and Cultures: England 1918-1951*, Oxford: Oxford University Press.

McLuhan, Eric (1997), *The Role of Thunder in Finnegans Wake*, Toronto: University of Toronto Press.

McNair, Brian (2010), *Journalists in Film: Heroes and Villains*, Edinburgh: Edinburgh University Press.

Mead, Henry (2014), '"Keeping our little corner clean": George Orwell's Cultural Broadcasts at the BBC', in Matthew Feldman, Erik Tonning and Henry Mead (eds), *Broadcasting in the Modernist Era*, London: Bloomsbury Academic, pp. 169-94.

Medhurst, Andy (1986), 'Music Hall and British Cinema', in Charles Barr (ed.), *All Our Yesterdays: 90 Years of British Cinema*, London: BFI Publishing, pp. 168-88.

Mills, Tom ([2016] 2020), *The BBC: Myth of a Public Service*, London: Verso.

Mollgaard, Matt (2012), 'Pirate Stories: Rethinking the Radio Rebels', in Matt Mollgaard (ed.), *Radio and Society: New Thinking for an Old Medium*, Newcastle upon Tyne: Cambridge Scholars Publishing, pp. 51-64.

Moores, Shaun (2000), *Media and Everyday Life in Modern Society*, Edinburgh: Edinburgh University Press.

Moran, Joe (2005), *Reading the Everyday*, Abingdon, Oxfordshire: Routledge.

Moriconi, Italo (2000), '*The Hour of the Star* or Clarice Lispector's Trash Hour', *Portuguese Literary & Cultural Studies*, 4/5, Dartmouth, MA: University of Massachusetts, pp. 213-21.

Morris, Adalaide, ed (1997), *Sound States: Innovative Poetics and Acoustical Technologies*, Chapel Hill, NC: University of North Carolina Press.

Morse, Daniel (2011), 'Only Connecting? E. M. Forster, Empire Broadcasting and the Ethics of Distance', *Journal of Modern Literature*, Indiana University Press, 34 (3): 87-105.

Mugglestone, Lynda (2008), 'Spoken English and the BBC: In the Beginning', *Arbeiten aus Anglistik und Amerikanistik*, 33 (2): 197-215.

Murphy, Kate (2016), *Behind the Wireless: A History of Early Women at the BBC*, London: Palgrave Macmillan.

Nelson, Sean (2007), *Court and Spark*, New York: Bloomsbury Academic.

Nichols, Phil (2006), 'A Sympathy with Sounds: Ray Bradbury and BBC Radio, 1951-1970', *Radio Journal: International Studies in Broadcast & Audio Media*, 4 (1-3): 111-23.

Nobbs, George (1972), *The Wireless Stars*, Norwich, Norfolk: Wensum Books.

Oldham, Joseph (2017), *Paranoid Visions: Spies, Conspiracies and the Secret State in British Television Drama*, Manchester: Manchester University Press.

Parkinson, David (1995), *History of Film*, London: Thames and Hudson.

Pegg, Mark (1983), *Broadcasting and Society: 1918-1939*, Beckenham, Kent: Croom Helm.

Pinkerton, Alasdair (2019), *Radio: Making Waves in Sound*, London: Reaktion Books.

Potter, Garry (2001), 'Truth in Fiction, Science and Criticism', in José Lopez and Garry Potter (eds), *After Postmodernism: An Introduction to Critical Realism*, London: The Athlone Press, pp. 183–95.

Potter, Julian (2004), *Stephen Potter at the BBC: 'Features' in War and Peace*, Orford, Suffolk: Orford Books.

Prigozhin, Aleksandr (2018), 'Listening in: D.H. Lawrence and the Wireless', *MFS Modern Fiction Studies*, 64 (2): 264–85.

Ramsden, John (1978), *A History of the Conservative Party. Vol. 3: The Age of Balfour and Baldwin 1902–1940*, London: Longman.

Rancière, Jacques ([2017] 2020), *The Edges of Fiction*, trans. Steve Corcoran, Cambridge: Polity.

Regan, Lisa (2010), 'Introduction', in Lisa Regan (ed.), *Winifred Holtby, 'A Woman in Her Time': Critical Essays*, Newcastle upon Tyne: Cambridge Scholars Publishing, pp. 1–22.

Reynolds, Simon (2011), *Retromania: Pop Culture's Addiction to Its Own Past*, London: Faber and Faber.

Richards, Jeffrey (2010), *Cinema and Radio in Britain and America, 1920–1960*, Manchester: Manchester University Press.

Rixon, Paul (2015), 'Radio and Popular Journalism in Britain: Early Radio Critics and Radio Criticism', *Radio Journal: International Studies in Broadcast & Audio Media*, 13 (1&2): 23–36.

Roskis, Edgar (2007), 'A Genocide Without Images: White Film Noirs', in Allan Thompson (ed.), *The Media and the Rwanda Genocide*, London: Pluto Press, pp. 238–41.

Ross, Kristin (1995), *Fast Cars, Clean Bodies: Decolonization and the Reordering of French Culture*, Cambridge MA: MIT Press.

Rudin, Richard (2007), 'Revisiting the Pirates', *Media History*, 13 (2–3): 235–55.

Rudin, Richard (2011), *Broadcasting in the 21st Century*, Basingstoke, Hampshire: Palgrave Macmillan.

Ryan, Michael P. (2010), 'Radio Fimmel: German Radio in Popular Fiction, Film, and the Urban Novel, 1923–1932', PhD diss., University of Pennsylvania.

Sargeant, Amy (2005), *British Cinema: A Critical History*, London: British Film Institute.

Scannell, Paddy (1981), 'Music for the Multitude? The Dilemmas of the BBC's Music Policy, 1923–1946', *Media, Culture & Society*, 3(3): 243–60.

Scannell, Paddy (1996), *Radio, Television and Modern Life: A Phenomenological Approach*, Oxford: Blackwell.

Scannell, Paddy (2003), 'The *Brains Trust*: A Historical Study of the Management of Liveness on Radio', in Simon Cottle (ed.), *Media Organisation and Production*, London: Sage, pp. 99–112.

Scannell, Paddy and David Cardiff (1982), 'Serving the Nation: Public Service Broadcasting Before the War', in Bernard Waites, Tony Bennett and Graham Martin (eds), *Popular Culture: Past and Present – A Reader*, Beckenham, Kent: Croom Helm, pp. 161–88.
Scannell, Paddy and David Cardiff (1991), *A Social History of British Broadcasting, Volume One: 1922–1939, Serving the Nation*, Oxford: Basil Blackwell.
Schiffer, Michael Brian (1993), 'Cultural Imperatives and Product Development: The Case of the Shirt-Pocket Radio', *Technology and Culture*, 34 (1): 98–113.
Schivelbusch, Wolfgang ([1979] 1986), *The Railway Journey: The Industrialization of Time and Space in the 19th Century*, Berkeley, CA: The University of California Press.
Schlesinger, Henry (2010), *The Battery: How Portable Power Sparked a Technological Revolution*, New York: HarperCollins.
Schwartz, A. Brad (2015), *Broadcast Hysteria: Orson Welles's 'War of the Worlds' and the Art of Fake News*, New York: Hill and Wang.
Seaton, Jean ([2015] 2017), *'Pinkoes and Traitors': The BBC and the Nation, 1974–1987*, 2nd edn, London: Profile.
Sidnell, Michael (1984), *Dances of Death: The Group Theatre of London in the Thirties*, London: Faber and Faber.
Stannard, Martin (1992), *Evelyn Waugh: No Abiding City, 1939–1966*, London: J. M. Dent.
Starkey, Guy (2007), *Balance and Bias in Journalism: Representation, Regulation and Democracy*, Basingstoke, Hampshire: Palgrave Macmillan.
Starkey, Guy (2011), *Local Radio, Going Global*, Basingstoke, Hampshire: Palgrave Macmillan.
St Clair, Justin (2013), *Sound and Aural Media in Postmodern Literature*, New York: Routledge.
Stevenson, John (1984), *British Society 1914–1945*, London: Penguin.
Stokes, Jane (2000), 'Arthur Askey and the Construction of Popular Entertainment in *Band Waggon* and *Make Mine a Million*', in Justine Ashby and Andrew Higson (eds), *British Cinema, Past and Present*, London: Routledge, pp. 124–34.
Stoller, Tony (2010), *Sounds of Your Life: The History of Independent Radio in the UK*, New Barnet, Hertfordshire: John Libbey.
Storey, John (2006), *Cultural Theory and Popular Culture: An Introduction*, 4th edn, Harlow, Essex: Pearson Education.
Street, Sarah (2009), *British National Cinema*, 2nd edn, London: Routledge.
Street, Seán (2005), *A Concise History of British Radio 1922–2002*, 2nd edn, Tiverton, Devon: Kelly Publications.
Street, Seán (2006), *Crossing the Ether: Pre-War Public Service Radio and Commercial Competition in the UK*, Eastleigh, Hampshire: John Libbey.
Street, Seán (2009), *The A to Z of British Radio*, Lanham, MD: The Scarecrow Press.

Sullivan, Melissa (2012), 'A Middlebrow Dame Commander: Rose Macaulay, the "Intellectual Aristocracy", and *The Towers of Trebizond*', *The Yearbook of English Studies*, 42: 168–85.

Tolson, Andrew (2006), *Media Talk: Spoken Discourse on TV and Radio*, Edinburgh: Edinburgh University Press.

Trotter, David (2013), *Literature in the First Media Age: Britain Between the Wars*, Cambridge, MA: Harvard University Press.

Vambe, Maurice Taonezvi and Urther Rwafa (2011), 'Exploring the Communicative Function of Light, Sound and Colour in Hotel Rwanda', *Journal of African Cinemas*, 3 (1): 43–9.

Walter, Roland (2001), 'Clarice Lispector's *A Hora da Estrela*: Remapping Culture and the Nation-Space', *Tinta*, Santa Barbara, CA: University of California, Santa Barbara, 5 (Fall): 115–24.

Wegg-Prosser, Victoria (1998), 'BBC Producer Choice and the Management of Organisational Change', PhD diss., Brunel University.

Whannel, Garry (1994), 'Boxed in: Television in the 1970s', in Bart Moore-Gilbert (ed.), *The Arts In the 1970s: Cultural Closure?* London: Routledge, pp. 176–97.

Whitehead, Kate (1990), 'Broadcasting Bloomsbury', *The Yearbook of English Studies*, 20: 121–31.

Whittington, Ian (2018), *Writing the Radio War: Literature, Politics and the BBC, 1939–1945*, Edinburgh: Edinburgh University Press.

Williams, Keith (1996), *British Writers and the Media, 1930–1945*, Basingstoke, Hampshire: Macmillan.

Williams, Raymond (1961), *The Long Revolution*, London: Chatto & Windus.

Xiaotian, Jin (2014), 'Undoing Shame: Lower-Middle-Class Young Women and Class Dynamics in the Interwar Novels by Rose Macaulay and Elizabeth Bowen', *Women's Studies*, 43 (6): 693–711.

Young, Paul (2006), *The Cinema Dreams its Rivals: Media Fantasy Films from Radio to the Internet*, Minneapolis, MI: University of Minnesota Press.

Index

(For other named sources, discussed in each chapter, see the Primary Sources (1) section of the References)

acousmêtre 115 n.15, 157, 173–8, 180, 184–5, *see also* film studies, Chion, Michel
American Armed Forces Network (AFN Radio) 110, 163, 194, *see also* United States influence on British radio industry
Art Deco 9, 25, 52, 53, 92, 192, *see also* Broadcasting House, London; radio studios; receivers, nostalgic images
Auden, W. H. 7, 10, 28–9, 43, 55–6, 66–7, *see also* radio in theatre

BBC buildings, *see also* Broadcasting House, London
   Savoy Hill, London 18
   2LO, Marconi House, The Strand, London 15
BBC directors general
   Birt, John (Lord) 154, 170 (*see also* BBC management, Producer Choice)
   Dyke, Greg 131–2, 171
   fictional 50–1, 52, 71, 133
   Milne, Alasdair 85–6
   Reith, John (Lord) 16, 19, 49–50, 61, 134–5, 161–2 (*see also* Reithian values)
BBC editorial crises 144, 156, 200–1, *see also* BBC journalism
   self-censorship 23, 75
BBC Empire Service (1932–39) 7, 25, 31, 61, *see also* international radio
BBC Forces Programme (1940–45/6) 74, 78, 80, 93, *see also* BBC Light Programme
BBC Home Service (1939–67) 45, 80, 94, 133, 193
   Brains Trust, The 80

Goon Show, The 81, 83, 88, 103, 133
   Post-Second World War 61, 78–9
BBC journalism, *see also* BBC editorial crises; investigative journalism
   BH News Traffic 202
   critiques of 40, 86, 94, 145, 152, 202
   during the Second World War 66, 71–3, 74–5 (*see also* war and radio)
   fictional accounts in film 71–2, 89, 96–7, 128, 142–5
   fictional accounts in novels 33, 94, 153–5, 201–3
   foreign correspondents 40, 143, 178, 201–3
   GNS (General News Service) 154
   male-dominated 41, 142–5, 153–5, 201–3
BBC Light Programme (1945–67) 61, 78–81, 88, 90, *see also* BBC Radio 2
   Festival of Britain 87–9
   music shows 103, 127
   quiz shows 193
   soap operas 23
BBC Local Radio (1967–) 107, 121, 135–6, 181, 198, *see also* radio phone-ins
   fictional representation 125, 134, 145
   growth of 128, 133, 158, 167
   journalism 145
   management style 141–2
BBC management
   bureaucracy 11, 51–2, 104, 130–2, 135, 196
   employment practices 19, 41, 150, 169–70
   growth of professionalism 85–6, 99, 110

Producer Choice   153–4, 170–1
  (*see also* BBC directors general,
  Birt, John)
 styles of management   23, 29–30, 50,
  131–2, 161–2, 196
BBC Overseas Service (1939–65)   61, 76,
  94, *see also* international radio
BBC programmes
 Archers, The   100
 Children's Hour   23–4, 49
 cinema organ recitals   69–70
 classical music concerts   20, 41, 99, 112
 Hall, Henry and the BBC Dance
  Orchestra   27, 37, 45–6
 Sunday broadcasting   19, 40, 70, 74
BBC Radio 1 (1967–)   10, 103, 106–7,
  112, 121, 196, *see also* DJs, actual
 Breakfast Show   72, 128
 criticism of   148–9, 151, 156
 employment opportunities   150
BBC Radio 2 (1967–)   24, 71, 112, 159,
  see also BBC Light Programme;
  DJs, actual
 station launch   82, 107
BBC Radio 3 (1967–)   112, 118, 119, 205,
  see also BBC Third Programme
BBC Radio 4 (1967–)   72, 82, 125–6,
  131, 142, 152, *see also* BBC
  Home Service; satires of radio
  broadcasting; weather, BBC
  Shipping Forecast
 Down the Line   156 n.32
 People Like Us   156 n.31
 Woman's Hour   196
BBC staff and broadcasters, *see also* BBC
  directors general; DJs, actual
 Andrews, Eamonn   88
 Bannister, Matthew   149
 Burrows, Arthur   15–16, 19
 Cook, Roger   97, 155–6
 Dimbleby, Richard   90
 Freeman, John   95
 Frostrup, Mariella   197
 Gielgud, Val   8, 24–6, 192, 206
 Hanington, Peter   142, 155, 201–3
 Jameson, Derek   159
 Kennedy, Ludovic   155
 King-Hall, Stephen   41, 59

 Long, James   142, 153–4, 170
 Maschwitz, Eric (Holt Marvell)   24
 Murray, Jenni (Dame)   196
 Purves, Libby   131 n.15, 142
 Simpson, John   143
 Tusa, John   181
BBC Third Programme (1946–67)   10,
  61, 78–80, *see also* BBC Radio 3;
  radio reception, difficulties
 Evelyn Waugh's dislike of   92–3, 95, 96
BBC 2LO (1922–30)   15
BBC World Service (1965–)   61,
  136–8, 175, 176, 178, 181, *see also*
  international radio
Boots the Chemist   23, 44
Branestawn, Professor   23–5, 36, 37, 206
Brazil   3, 9
 Babel (Cildo Meireles)   57, 187–9 (*see
  also* radio in art)
 Hour of the Star, The (Clarice
  Lispector)   121–2
 Last Broadcast, The (Sirangelo and
  Iumazark)   205
 Rádio Relógio, Rio de Janeiro   122
  (*see also* radio timekeeping)
British Broadcasting Corporation (BBC),
  see also BBC management
 'Auntie' epithet   82–3, 85, 92, 109, 169
 'Beeb' epithet   83
 metro-centricity   28, 43–4, 48, 68, 88,
  145 (*see also* royal broadcasting)
 on-air accents   47–8, 89, 95, 128, 162
 transition from Company to
  Corporation   19
Broadcasting House, London   9, 11,
  70–2, 170, *see also* BBC buildings
 featured in movies   24–7, 36–7, 71–2,
  91–2, 99, 143–5
 featured in novels   42, 94, 162, 192,
  197, 202
 featured in TV programmes   162, 196

Certeau, Michel de, *see* literary theory
Chion, Michel, *see* film studies
Clapham and Dwyer   23, 30, 52
community radio, *see* voluntary radio
Covid-19 pandemic (2020–1)
  76, 130

Index

Daily Express 2, 75, 149
Daily Mail 14 n.40, 15–16, 135
DJs, actual, *see also* BBC staff and broadcasters; Savile, Jimmy; Wolfman Jack
  Alexander, Louis 123
  Bacon, Richard 196
  Blackburn, Tony 128, 156 n.33
  Butler, Tony 135
  Day, Aiden 124
  Edmonds, Noel 72, 103, 128
  Everett, Kenny 83, 103, 105, 158
  Ferrari, Nick 159
  Hayes, Brian 158
  Read, Mike 128
  Stannage, James 135
  Stone, Christopher 30
  Theakston, Jamie 196
  Travis, Dave Lee 128
  Westwood, Tim 196
  Whale, James 158
  Wogan, Terry 71
DJs, fictional
  Brackenbury, Ivan 198
  Champlain, Barry 157
  Channel, Mike 134
  The Count 194
  Curran, Kit 30, 149–51
  Daptor, Anna 134
  Farrell, Pat 199
  Flex, Mike 134
  Lucas, Jack 157
  Meredith, Dale 105
  Partridge, Alan 133, 153, 156, 169, 199
  Segundo, Bat 194
  Smashie and Nicey 30, 156
domestication of radio 17, 32, 39–40, 42, 54, 85

fan writing 6, 195, *see also* literary theory
film studies 7, 8
  Cahiers do Cinéma 174
  Chion, Michel 87 n.7, 115 n.15, 173–8 (*see also acousmêtre*)

France 9, 28, 68, 138, 161, *see also* Radio Normandy; Radio Paris
  Les Vacances de Monsieur Hulot 86–7
  Radio France Internationale 178

Germany 9, 137, 139, 145, 160, 179, *see also* war and radio, Second World War
  radio in films 8, 14
  Steppenwolf (Herman Hesse) 20–2
Grand Theft Auto 172

Hancock, Tony 95, 99–100
headphones
  used by listeners 15, 20, 33
  used in films 90, 112, 157, 163
  used in novels 202
  used in TV 121, 141, 182
histories of radio 2–3, 7–8
Hitchhiker's Guide to the Galaxy (Douglas Adams) 2, 125–6, 133–4
hospital radio, *see* voluntary radio

Independent Local Radio (ILR) 109, 120, 132, 158, 159, *see also* DJs, actual; radio phone-ins
  BRMB 135
  Capital Radio 123–5, 128, 132, 135, 147–8
  consolidation of ownership 167
  growth of 8, 10, 111, 121, 128
  journalism 139–42, 149
  LBC (London Broadcasting Company) 128, 132, 158, 159
  Piccadilly Radio 135
  Radio Aire 158
  relaxation of public service obligations 147–8
  satires and critiques of 124–5, 132–3, 135, 149–51, 195–6
  Talkradio/Talksport 132, 158
international radio 26, 31, 61, 100, 138, 181, *see also* BBC Empire Service; BBC World Service
  Christian broadcasters 208
  Cold War (*see* war and radio, Cold War)

reception problems   63–6, 137, 160, 168
Rwandan genocide   174–8 (see also war and radio, Rwandan Civil War)
Second World War   76, 107 (see also war and radio, Second World War)
short wave   61, 63, 66, 98, 122, 208
investigative journalism   96–7, 155–6, see also BBC journalism
Ireland   9, 13, 15, 68, see also Radio Athlone
  Belfast   1, 43, 117, 159
  Dublin   72
  Durcan, Paul   11, 118, 159–61
  Joyce, James (*Finnegans Wake*)   62–6, 69, 79, 80, 137, 160, 168
  MacNeice, Louis   7, 43, 55, 67, 162 (*see also* radio in theatre)
  Morrison, Van   1–2, 11, 101, 117–18, 159–61, 165
  Northern Ireland   139, 140

Listener, The   43, 99
literary theory   4–8, see also film studies
  Certeau, Michel de   5–6, 127
  Derrida, Jacques   4
  Jenkins, Henry   6 (*see also* fan writing)
  Potter, Garry   4
  Rancière, Jacques   4
  Saussure, Ferdinand de   4

McEwan, Ian   64, 143
Morse code, *see* radio telegraphy

News of the World   18
nostalgia, radio in film
  American Graffiti   10, 113–15, 117, 119, 189
  Boat that Rocked, The   11, 107, 170, 193–4, 196
  Chicken Run   168–9
  Good Morning, Vietnam   11, 163–5, 174
  King's Speech, The   11, 191–2
  Last Waltz, The   1–2, 116–17
  Radio Days   164, 165

nostalgia, radio in literature
  Byatt, A. S. (*Still Life*)   161–2
  Fitzgerald, Penelope (*Human Voices*)   130–2, 162, 171
  Keillor, Garrison (*Radio Romance*)   164–5
  McEwan, Ian (*On Chesil Beach*)   64
  Mitchell, David (*Utopia Avenue*)   194
  Stratford, Sarah-Jane (*Radio Girls*)   192 n.15
  Upson, Nicola (*London Rain*)   192
nostalgia, radio in pop music
  Buggles, The   129
  Carpenters   115–16
  Cartwright, Lionel   165
  Golden Earring   116
  Morrison, Van   1–2, 11, 101, 117–18, 159–60, 165
  Pink Floyd   168, 175
  Queen   11, 160–1
  Richman, Jonathan and the Modern Lovers   116
  Roxy Music   11, 130
  Velvet Underground   116
nostalgia, radio on TV
  Downton Abbey   11, 190–1, 196
  Father Brown   11, 193
  For the Love of Ada   89 n.12, 118–19
  'Pale Horse, The' (Agatha Christie)   192
nostalgia, theoretical approaches   113–14, 117, 189–90

Orwell, George   7, 75
  Nineteen Eighty-Four   56, 83
  social class   34, 48–9

pirate radio (land-based), fictional representations of
  Big Ben Calling [film]   25–7
  Minder [TV]   173
  People Just Do Nothing [TV]   196, 198–9
  Radio Kit [*Kit Curran*, TV]   151
  'Rebel Radio', UK Subs [music]   173
  'Sorted for Es and Wizz', Pulp [music]   172
  Special Branch [TV]   106, 123–4, 173
  Young Ones, The [film]   103–4

pirate radio (offshore), actual
    Radio Caroline   11, 85, 103, 106, 110, 128–9, 194
    Radio London   105, 106, 110, 198 n.39
    Radio 390 [Red Sands Fort]   106
pirate radio (offshore), fictional representations of
    Boat that Rocked, The [film]   11, 107, 170, 193–4, 196
    Danger Man [TV]   106
    Dateline Diamonds [film]   46, 105
    Hey Duggee [TV]   206
    Utopia Avenue [novel]   194
    'We Love the Pirates' [music]   106
    Who Sell Out, The [LP]   106, 116, 198 n.39
pop music critiques of British radio   109, 111
    Long, Norman   23
    1970s onwards   124–8, 148–9, 151–2, 172
    Roberts, Paddy   102
    Western Brothers, The   47–8
propaganda, before the Second World War   22, 55–7, 66–9, *see also* war and radio
propaganda, during the Second World War   61, 69–70, 74–8, *see also* war and radio
public service broadcasting   19, 48, 57, 92, 120, 158, *see also* Reithian values
    ILR   111, 147–8 (*see also* ILR, relaxation of public service obligations)

radio and crime in American films   13, 111–12, 157–8
radio and crime in British fiction
    Films   24–6, 89–92, 96–7, 105, 140
    Novels   14–15, 24–5, 28, 36, 153–5, 192, 201
    TV   106, 123–4, 140–2, 162, 181, 192–3, 199–201
Radio Athlone   63, 68, 160
radio in art
    Meireles, Cildo   57, 187–9
    Ruscha, Ed   118, 164

radio in British children's fiction   23–4, 25, 36, 37, 80–1, 206, *see also* BBC programmes, *Children's Hour*
    Radio Fun [comic magazine]   85
    teenage fiction   203–5, 206–7
radio in silent film   7, 13, 20
radio in theatre
    Auden, W. H. and Christopher Isherwood   10, 55–6, 66–7
    MacNeice, Louis   55–6, 162 (*see also* Ireland)
    Rau, Milo   179
radio listening, *see also* domestication of radio; radio reception, difficulties
    communal listening   39, 54–8, 169 (*see also* royal broadcasting)
    conversation topic   39, 44–6, 94
    gendered   14, 32–6
    inattention   58, 79–80, 82, 187–9
    social class   32–7, 39, 44–50, 55, 79–80, 183
    solitary listening   28, 33–5, 41–4, 99–100, 122–3, 130, 165
Radio Luxembourg   20, 27, 30, 45, 102, 137
    closure during Second World War   68
    fictionalised in film and literature   17, 52–3, 55, 74, 92
    final closure of English service   160
    nostalgia   1, 110, 128, 129
    reopening after Second World War   80
Radio Normandy   20, 55, 68, 74, 92, 110
Radio Paris   27
    closure of English service in Second World War   68
    fictionalised in film and literature   17, 28, 31, 52, 53, 92
radio phone-ins
    American radio phone-ins, fictional   115, 157–8, 165, 179–85, 194
    British radio phone-ins, fictional   132–3, 149 n.10, 150, 156 n.32, 181, 200–1
    ILR and BBC Local Radio   128, 135–6, 158–9, 181
    taste and decency   157–9

radio programme listing magazines
   Radio Pictorial 42
   Radio Times 18, 42 n.15, 79–80, 88, 92
radio reception, difficulties 50–1, 58, 62–6, 160, 168, *see also* radio listening; receiving equipment
   BBC Third Programme 80
   early difficulties of listening to music 20–2
   short-wave listening 97–8, 137–8
radio stations, fictional (to 1945)
   BVD (British Visionary Distributing Broadcasting Company) 52
   Central Radio Station 68
   General Broadcasting Company 73
   Liberty Broadcasting Company 73
   NBG (National Broadcasting Group) 50–1
   PBQ 26
   Radio France 68
   Radio Seine 53
   Radio Sopenberg 52–3
radio stations, fictional (1945–1979)
   Happening Radio 132
   Polestar – the Free Radio Network 123
   Radio Cosmopolis 96
   Radio Jolly Roger 106
   WKRP in Cincinnati [TV series] 112, 121
   W.O.L.D. 112
radio stations, fictional (1980–99)
   KACL-780 AM 182
   Radio Active [radio series] 132, 134, 160, 168, 169
   Radio Newtown 149–50
   Radio West 141–2
radio stations, fictional (2000–2007)
   Caledonia FM 181
   Hemel Sound 169
   Radio Shuttleworth [radio series] 133, 169
   SAGA Radio Digital 169
   Waverley FM 200
radio stations, fictional (2008–2017)
   Bob FM 206
   Kurupt FM 199
   North Norfolk Digital 199
   Radio Portwenn 197
   Radio Rock 194
   Roxy Radio 200
   Skin 86.5 FM 196
radio stations, fictional (2018–2020)
   Cheese Radio 206
   Coastland FM 197
   Kool FM 207
   Locomotive 97.8FM 194
   Radio Bluebeard 194
   Radio Midsomer/Midsomer FM 201
radio studios, *see also* BBC buildings; headphones
   Art Deco film representations of 9, 25, 52, 92
   studio glamour versus functionality 17, 22, 25, 53, 177, 179
radio telegraphy 13, 14, 93
   Marconi, Guglielmo 62
   Marconi Company 14, 15
   Marconigram/telegram 18
   military use of 14, 18, 29, 178
   Morse code 12, 13, 18, 72, 160
   radio telephony 12, 29
radio timekeeping 23–4, 37, 110
   Askey, Arthur, *Back-Room Boy* 71–2
   Collis, John Stewart 72–3
   Edmonds, Noel 72
   'pips, the' [automated time signal] 71–2, 80, 96, 122
receivers, nostalgic images
   transistor radio 101, 110, 118, 160, 165, 193
   valve radio 118, 142, 160, 192, 205
receiving equipment, *see also* social media
   battery-powered 44, 101, 136, 151–2
   crystal set 20
   DAB radio 119, 132, 152, 167, 194, 208
   ghetto blaster 151–2
   Internet radio 11, 119, 167, 203–5
   transistor radio 1, 105, 140, 148, 151, 173, 176 (*see also* receivers, nostalgic images)
   valve radio 20, 33, 63–4, 86, 92, 99–100 (*see also* receivers, nostalgic images)

Reithian values   19, 45, 48, 68, 81,
    see also BBC directors general;
    public service broadcasting
    satire of   50, 96, 133, 162,
    194
Richard, Cliff   46, 103–4, 144
royal broadcasting   10, 58–9, 190–2,
    see also BBC, metro-centricity
    communal listening   58–9
    King-Hall, (Commander)
    Stephen   41, 59
RTLM (Rwanda)   174–9, see also war
    and radio, Rwandan Civil War and
    genocide

satires of radio broadcasting in
    film   22, 26–7, 50–3, 71–2, 96
    radio programmes   51, 79, 133–5,
    152–3, 155–6, 169
    TV programmes   136,
    195–9
Savile, Jimmy   144, 156, 200
Simpsons, The   171–2
social media   197, 203–5

United States influence on British radio
    industry   73–4, 102, 109–11

voluntary Radio
    community radio   167–8, 189,
    197, 209
    hospital radio   194, 196, 198, 209
    professionalism, lack of   197–8

war and radio, see also propaganda
    Cold War   136–9, 208
    First World War   12, 14, 29, 48, 50
    Rwandan Civil War and genocide   11,
    67, 167, 168, 173–9
    Second World War   1, 9, 29, 66–78,
    110, 119
    Vietnam War   163–4
Waters, Elsie and Doris   30, 41, 42, 45
Waugh, Evelyn   10, 40, 92–6, see also
    BBC Third Programme
weather   19, 54
    BBC *Shipping Forecast*   5–6, 65
    topic of conversation   33, 46
Welles, Orson, 'The War of the
    Worlds'   57–8, 161, 187
wireless, change of name to 'radio'   82
Wolfman Jack   113–15, 208

24 Hours news radio & TV
    channels   152–3